THE MARINES

Other National Historical Society Publications:

THE IMAGE OF WAR: 1861-1865

TOUCHED BY FIRE: A PHOTOGRAPHIC PORTRAIT OF THE CIVIL WAR

WAR OF THE REBELLION: OFFICIAL RECORDS
  OF THE UNION AND CONFEDERATE ARMIES

OFFICIAL RECORDS OF THE UNION AND CONFEDERATE NAVIES
  IN THE WAR OF THE REBELLION

HISTORICAL TIMES ILLUSTRATED ENCYCLOPEDIA OF THE CIVIL WAR

CONFEDERATE VETERAN

THE WEST POINT MILITARY HISTORY SERIES

IMPACT: THE ARMY AIR FORCES' CONFIDENTIAL HISTORY
  OF WORLD WAR II

HISTORY OF UNITED STATES NAVAL OPERATIONS IN WORLD WAR II
  by Samuel Eliot Morison

HISTORY OF THE ARMED FORCES IN WORLD WAR II
  by Janusz Piekalkiewicz

A TRAVELLER'S GUIDE TO GREAT BRITAIN SERIES

MAKING OF BRITAIN SERIES

THE ARCHITECTURAL TREASURES OF EARLY AMERICA

For information about National Historical Society Publications, write:

The National Historical Society, 2245 Kohn Road, Box 8200,
Harrisburg, Pa 17105

THE ELITE
The World's Crack Fighting Men

THE MARINES

Ashley Brown, Editor
Jonathan Reed, Editor

Editorial Board

Brigadier-General James L. Collins, Jr. (Retd.)
Former Chief of Military History, US Department of the Army

Ian V. Hogg
Authority on smallarms and modern weapons systems

Dr. John Pimlott
Senior Lecturer in the Department of War Studies,
Royal Military Academy, Sandhurst, England

Brigadier-General Edwin H. Simmons (Retd.)
US Marine Corps

Lisa Mullins, Managing Editor, NHS edition

A Publication of
THE NATIONAL HISTORICAL SOCIETY

Published in Great Britain in 1986 by Orbis Publishing

Library of Congress Cataloging-in-Publication Data
The Marines / Ashley Brown, editor, Jonathan Reed, editor.
    p.   cm.   —(The Elite: the world's crack fighting men ; v. 3)
    ISBN 0-918678-41-2
    1. Marines. 2. United States. Marine Corps. 3. Great Britain.
Royal Marines. 4. Military history. Modern —20th century.
I. Brown, Ashley. II. Reed, Jonathan. III. Series: Elite
(Harrisburg, Pa.) ; v. 3
VE146.M37   1989
359.9'6—dc20   89-3314
                                     CIP

CONTENTS

INTRODUCTION

For generations, when someone has had to go into action first . . . take a beachhead, make a night landing behind enemy lines, carry out a daring raid against great odds . . . the nations of the world have called on their marines. Born out of a distant past in which their role was that of marksmen aboard wooden frigates, or as boarders in close naval actions, the marines have evolved around the globe as an initial strike force. On land, sea, and in the air, they pave the way for those who follow.

Come ashore with the 1st Marine Division at Inchon in 1950, making virtually a new war of the Korean conflict. Join the 4th Battalion of Royal Marines in 1918 as they carry out a daring raid against the Kaiser's principal U-boat base at Zeebrugge. Fight with their spiritual descendants twenty-seven years later when Royal Marine Commandos moved to seize German positions on Lake Commachio, near the Adriatic. Endure the fire of the Japanese as the 28th U.S. Marines battle for control of Iwo Jima in 1945, capping their triumph with the memorable raising of the Stars and Stripes over Mount Suribachi. Sit with the Marines besieged at Khe Sanh by the North Vietnamese, where for 77 days they sustained the heaviest concentrated barrage in history. Wherever the marines have had to do their dangerous, bloody task, they have done it well.

They did it on the beaches of Tarawa in the Pacific, paying a terrible price. They stood their ground at Hue in Vietnam. They followed their leader Colonel Carlson in World War II, becoming storied in words and films as Carlson's Raiders. British marines won enduring fame as "cockleshell heroes" in their nighttime exploits along the seacoasts of Nazi-held Europe. The marines have shown their daring under a host of flags, all around the world— at Suez, in the Mediterranean, all across the Pacific, Southeast Asia . . . wherever they have been called upon for that extra something that separates good soldiers and fighting men from the truly exceptional. When the demand for daring is made of marines, the answer is not long in coming . . . from THE ELITE.

US MARINES

In the 19th century, the US Marines were a small force, mainly deployed as guards aboard ship or at the gates of naval stations. There were no standing combat forces, and the Corps formed provisional units from guard detachments whenever necessary.

The role of the Marine Corps changed, however, during the Spanish-American War of 1898. Suddenly, the US Navy found itself having to provide the defence forces for overseas bases and to provide the ground troops necessary to attack and secure the bases of enemy powers. These roles naturally fell to the Navy's own ground forces, the Marine Corps.

By 1914, the Marine Corps' combat-ready element centred on the Advance Base Force, a brigade-size combined-arms force, whose prime task was to assault and defend bases for the US Navy. Prior to the creation of the Advance Base Force, each Marine barracks had had its own 'rookie squad' that had given rudimentary training to new recruits. The Advance Base Force, however, needed men with a standard level of training, and the solution was to create small Marine recruit depots at the larger naval stations. Cost considerations and the search for greater efficiency soon led the Corps to consolidate all its recruit training at two bases, one on each coast.

The Marine Barracks, Parris Island, South Carolina, established its attached recruit depot in 1915, while a similar depot was set up at Mare Island, California; the latter moved to San Diego in 1923.

WELCOME TO THE MARINES!

At the US Marine Corps Recruit Depots, tough training and iron discipline turn raw civilian trainees into closely-welded platoons of combat-ready fighting men

ASK ANY United States Marine what makes his Corps so special and he will probably answer, 'boot camp'. For the demanding, rugged, searing experience of Marine recruit training is the price of entry into that elite fraternity.

I started my Marine Corps service after I graduated from high school. The 'recruit experience' began for me and about 60 others on the bus ride from the recruiting station at Macon, Georgia. We were driving to the Marine Corps Recruit Depot at Parris Island, South Carolina. Our initially boisterous mood gradually died away as we approached the base. And once through the depot's gates, we recruits retreated into our own fears of the unknown.

Parris Island's geographical isolation contributed to our apprehension. En route, the bus had passed through many miles of flat, sandy, coastal Carolina, where huge oaks brooded over an occasional decaying shanty. Every large stream had wide desolate-looking salt marshes along its banks.

Parris Island lies between Charleston, South Carolina, and Savannah, Georgia. It is actually only a piece of slightly higher ground amid the salt marshes

lining Port Royal Sound. Channels meandering through the marshes separate it from other spots of high ground. In the not too-distant past, recruits like ourselves had reached the recruit depot by boat from Port Royal. Even now, one felt far from civilisation. Only a few distant lights across the marshes hinted to us that other people inhabited the region.

In summer, Parris Island is as hot and heavily humid as any tropical rain forest; only the frequent thunderstorms break the mugginess. Winters are also damp, but seldom cold enough to interfere with training. For us during that long, hot summer, however, the coolness of winter was only a dream.

At the receiving barracks, a khaki-clad sergeant entered the bus and brusquely ordered us inside the building. It was already after dark, but there were forms for us to complete before going to bed. The next morning we had breakfast and then sat quietly – at a sergeant's orders – until our drill instructors (always known as 'DIs') arrived. Then, the shock treatment began.

We new recruits did not realise it, but DIs take command of a brand new platoon by staging a ritual as repetitive as the nightly performances of a play in the theatre. And just as in the theatre, each performance and the individual interpretations of a role can vary. DIs judge each others' performance at platoon 'pick up' as critically as do actors, and praise from his peers establishes a DI's reputation more solidly than any other evaluation.

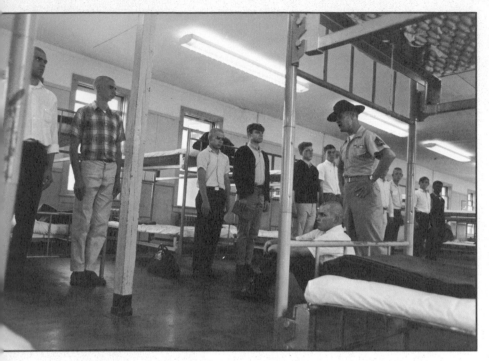

The senior DI plays the leading role in every new performance while his junior DIs comprise the supporting cast. Their costumes are the normal service uniforms with the significant addition of the peaked hat that serves as their badge of office. The script carries a new platoon through the first few hectic days of recruit training. The purpose of all this play-acting is ruthlessly simple: to strip away the recruits' civilian attitudes and reduce all platoon members to the same level as quickly as possible.

The drill instructors ceaselessly stalk about the platoon, their anger ready to boil over as they scream and shout at the young privates

Scene one opens at the receiving barracks: shouting DIs make the recruits (now known as 'boots') run outside and stand to attention in rough semblance of a military formation. The DIs ceaselessly stalk about the platoon, their anger ready to boil over at any moment. They shout or scream in ways and words most of the young privates have never heard before – and certainly not at such close quarters. For the DIs even invade the several square feet of 'personal space' that surround most people. We get uncomfortable when strangers or mere acquaintances move into that space. The DIs, however, deliberately establish their domination by entering the recruits' personal space to engage literally in face-to-face, even nose-to-nose, confrontations. Startled young men who cannot maintain the 'eyes front' positions of 'attention' and glance at a DI, suddenly find their very manhood called into question as the DI sneeringly demands if the recruit is a homosexual with a passion for the DI. By this time, the recruits have become frightened and confused; they do not comprehend the questions nor know the answers.

Soon the whole civilian frame of reference of the recruits begins to shatter under a concerted onslaught. The outward signs of status among civilian American males appear in their hair styles and clothing; so the Marines first shave off the hair. The recruits hardly recognise themselves, much less

Above: A long way from the comforts of home. A batch of new recruits, still in civilian dress, looks on with some trepidation as the DI spells out the routine for barrack-room cleanliness. In the early days of training the denial of personal privacy and the suppression of the recruits' outward signs of status reduce all men to the same level. No-one is privileged. Ruthless attention is paid to the minutest details of dress and kit maintenance and the trainee marine soon learns the unique brand of discipline that, although seemingly petty at the time, might well save his life in a combat situation later in his career. A visit to the depot barber (right) is early on the agenda and little attention is paid to particular preferences in style. There is only one. Far right, above: Before and after. Recruit Private R.A. Keller as he appeared at the Receiving Barracks, and again, three months later, on graduation from recruit training. Far right, below: A drill instructor mutters a word of encouragement to a high-school potential recruit on a military acclimatisation course on the parade ground. Close personal contact is one of the instructors' favourite ploys to disorientate the erring 'boot' and reduce him to a quivering jelly. But automatic response and obedience to orders is an essential quality that must be learnt quickly.

each other. Then, still enduring the DI's constant harangues, they pack their civilian clothes for shipment home. Disoriented, shaven-headed, and dressed in wrinkled new field uniforms, the recruits have no idea of how to act properly, speak or think in their strange new environment. For a day or so, the system isolates them from practically every influence except that of the screaming drill instructors.

The DIs do not let up with their eyeball-to-eyeball harangues as they begin their elementary instruction. The repetition of basic military movements continues until the recruits get them right. To the new recruits the DIs continue to sound like insane, violent sadists totally devoid of humanity. Nevertheless, the DIs are imparting new knowledge, and making it become second nature to the former civilians. The lessons continue until lights out, and even in sleep some of the recruits will be unable to escape their new environment: a few will wake during the night with muscle cramps from sleeping at rigid attention.

This introduction to the Marine Corps sends many young men into a terrified, bewildered state, close to shock. But human beings are adaptable creatures, and new recruits quickly learn the rules of the new society. They begin emulating the DIs, as much as their limited knowledge permits. The training system has begun to shape them.

The training system usually identifies problem 'boots' within the first day of training. For example, each platoon takes an initial physical fitness test, to measure the trainees' ability at pushups, situps, squat thrusts, and running. A few men fail this test due to lack of strength or stamina, or because of obesity. Those who fail go to the special training unit's strength platoon, which uses diet and exercises to improve fitness. A weight-control platoon uses a similar approach, but gears it to the special needs of overweight recruits. When men assigned to either platoon finally pass the initial strength test, they join a platoon just entering training.

In my year, not all recruits responded to the DIs'

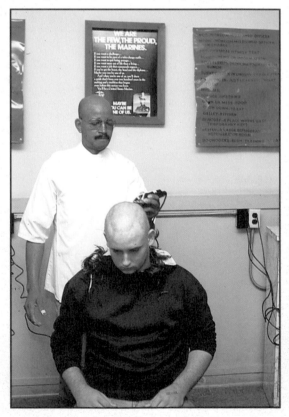

well-polished methods. Some, who simply would not give a maximum effort in training, were assigned to the motivation platoon. This platoon had two separate programmes for straightening out young men's attitudes. A one-day motivation programme worked for those who needed encouragement to give just a little more effort. Those recruits not amenable to the one-day programme became full-time members of the motivation platoon. There they received professional psychiatric evaluation and counselling, training in normal military subjects, and a good dose of physical exercise. Some had to sit in front of a large mirror for several hours of self-examination in which, hopefully, they would sort out their attitudes toward the training and the Marine Corps. They even viewed inspirational movies such as John Wayne's *Sands of Iwo Jima* as a means of increasing their self-identification with the Marine Corps.

Relatively few recruits spent time in the special training unit, which also included a hospital platoon for those found medically unfit or who needed conditioning after being in the hospital. Recruits who did join the unit remained only until ready to return to normal training or until discharged from the service.

The 'shock treatment' marked the beginning of the first of the three phases that have always characterised Marine Corps recruit training. This first phase is an intense introduction to the basic fundamentals of military life. Emphasis has always been on discipline, with close order drill under arms serving as the primary teaching tool. My platoon, like all others, learned to march smartly with and without our M1 rifles, to salute, to take care of our weapons, and to master a variety of similar military skills. Long hours marching on the huge asphalt parade ground (the 'grinder') and rigorous, daily exercise quickly improved our physical fitness.

The second phase, marksmanship training, took place at the rifle range. It was, in many ways, the most relaxed period of recruit training. The DIs, of course, never stopped demanding excellence. They did, however, ease up on the personal pressure that kept us recruits off-balance. They did so because marksmanship requires a calm approach.

We spent the first week at the range learning to coax our bodies into the proper firing positions. During this time, trained marksmanship coaches taught us the techniques of using and adjusting the rifle's sights and the proper trigger squeeze. Repetition, the key to so much Marine recruit training, gave us mastery of the subject. The platoon's members spent hours in the various firing positions, practising lining up their sights on a target and then squeezing the triggers of their empty M1 rifles. The marksmanship coaches emphasised the importance of accurate shooting. They reminded us that noise on the battlefield kills no enemy. Hitting the enemy with properly aimed fire is all that counts.

The second week of marksmanship training gave us the chance to fire live ammunition for the first time. We began on the pistol range with .22in target rifles and pistols. Later in the week we fired the .45in M1911A1 pistol, to get us familiar with this standard weapon. Each afternoon, however, we fired our M1 rifles on the regular ranges. The first few afternoons

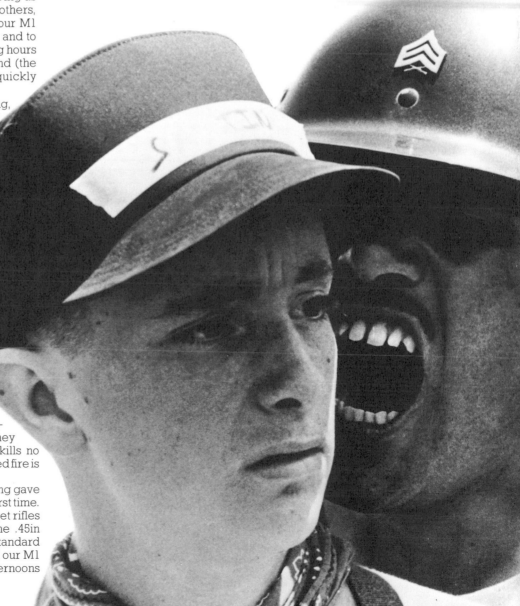

SERVICE RIFLE AND MARKSMANSHIP

A crucial aspect of Marine training is marksmanship and maintenance of personal smallarms. Many hours are spent on the ranges to familiarise the men with the service rifle and the various firing positions and techniques before the recruit becomes qualified, and earns the right to wear the Rifle Expert decoration (shown above) on the left breast-pocket of his uniform. But while accuracy of shooting is heavily emphasised, recruits must also become totally at home with the weapon and its working. Step-by-step drills for field stripping the M14 and M16 rifles are clearly laid out in the Marine service manuals and must become second nature to the new soldier. Proper care of the weapon will prevent most stoppages and mechanical malfunctions, and considerable time is spent on cleaning and lubricating procedures. When a weapon does jam the recruit must be able to identify immediately which of the main categories of stoppage has occurred and apply the standard corrective measures. All procedures must be executed in the correct order and are drilled into the men until they know them by heart; for in combat, precious seconds wasted in fumbling with the mechanism of a jammed rifle can mean the difference between life and death.
(From the Marine Training Manual)

enabled us to determine the elevation and windage required on our sights to hit the target at ranges of 200, 300, and 500yds. We also grew familiar with the qualification course and with the noise and recoil of our rifles. By the end of the week the coaches and DIs knew how well each recruit was firing, and those with low scores began receiving extra instruction.

The goal of the third week at the range was to qualify the recruits with their rifles on the Friday morning. There were three categories of qualified riflemen. Out of a possible 250 points (five points for

each of the 50 rounds fired), a man needed 190 to be a 'marksman', 210 for 'sharpshooter', and 220 for 'expert'. Failure to post a qualifying score with the rifle could bring a recruit trouble from his fellow recruits as well as the DIs. After a platoon finished its firing on Friday morning, some DIs made the non-qualifiers wear their shooting jackets backwards. These forlorn recruits marched at the rear of their platoons with their rifles carried upside down. Successful recruits felt that non-qualifiers had let down the team.

Condemnation from the DIs was to be expected, but that from the rest of the platoon reflected one of the major changes the 'boots' underwent at the range. We began looking outside the narrow confines of our own platoon and realised there were three other platoons with whom we were competing. Our platoon of about 75 men was part of a series of four such consecutively numbered units under the command of a first lieutenant. The DIs had told us before qualification day that one platoon would be the honor platoon on graduation day. Our qualification percentage on the rifle range, they said, would play a major role in determining which platoon received that recognition. Unit loyalty and pride

fuelled a new-found competitive spirit among us.

Following the marksmanship phase, a platoon normally spent a week assigned to either mess or maintenance duty. The latter included projects such as cutting grass, trimming hedges, raking leaves, or painting rocks to keep the depot a show place for the Corps. Mess duty meant working long hours in the mess halls assisting the cooks, washing pots and pans, sweeping and mopping floors, and serving food on the mess line. In my year, the recruit population – normally larger each summer after high school graduation – was so heavy that it strained the depot's billeting and training facilities. The command wanted our series to finish training, graduate, and depart as rapidly as possible. We thus escaped the drudgery of mess and maintenance duty.

The third, and final phase of basic training involved putting some polish on the recruit platoons. During this phase, the DIs coaxed maximum effort from the 'boots' by encouraging intense competition among us. The recruits responded readily – each wanted his unit to be the series honor platoon.

The increasing tempo of training reinforced our growing pride and spirit. We had our day on the Confidence Course, a special obstacle course requiring strength, agility and a degree of physical courage. On another day, tailors fitted the platoon's newly-issued summer and winter service uniforms. Even the receipt of our metal identification tags ('dog tags') added to our perception of our growing seniority and experience.

My luck ran out at this point. During physical training one day, I did not do enough satisfactory push-ups. The PT instructor put me to lifting weights to increase my upper-body strength. Unfortunately, in lowering the weights, I brought them down behind my head and

Main picture: Trainee marines let off steam as they practise their 'war faces'. Above right and below: The serious business of combat training – hand-to-hand fighting and proficiency with the M16.

dislocated my left shoulder. One of my DIs drove me to the nearby sick-bay and an ambulance took me on to the Navy hospital. The doctors there put my shoulder back in place. They also correctly diagnosed the problem as a condition existing prior to my enlistment. I quickly received a medical discharge from the Marine Corps.

The medical discharge put me in the '4-F' draft category and thus exempt from further military service. However, I didn't want to be a civilian. I wanted to be a marine – and the Marine Corps gave me a second chance. After surgery at my own expense, the Corps waived my discharge the following year and again enlisted me as a private.

The Marines sent me back to Parris Island to repeat the whole recruit experience from beginning to end. Of course, I had advantages over my fellow recruits. Not the least of these was that my DIs took care of me despite some remaining weaknesses in my shoulder. They believed that anyone who wanted to be a marine strongly enough to go through Parris Island twice deserved to graduate, despite mediocre performance at pushups and chinups. My new training was exactly as it had been the year before. Not until my new platoon entered the last phase of training did I encounter anything new.

The final days of recruit training were long and hectic as we prepared for and passed a series of tests. These included written examinations on academic knowledge, a final physical fitness test, and the series drill competition. The judges in the latter were very senior NCOs, all of whom wore the DI's peaked field hat. A platoon's close order drill had to be exceptional to win the competition.

The last major hurdle for every platoon was the 'Final Field Inspection', conducted by a team of officers and senior NCOs from the recruit training battalion. In preparation, the DIs had us recruits strip down our rifles and meticulously remove any speck of old grease, dirt and carbon. On the night before the inspection the DIs wore white gloves to check every weapon. The platoon then stacked the rifles carefully and covered them with clean white bed sheets. We completed our preparations by spit-shining our dress shoes, polishing brass belt buckles, and carefully clipping any remaining loose threads from our service uniforms.

I felt a surge of pride as the depot band played the Marines' hymn. I had made it; I was a marine

The next morning, the platoon dressed with great care to avoid wrinkling its service uniforms. When we formed up outside we stepped cautiously to avoid scuffing or kicking sand or dust on our gleaming shoes. One recruit stood by the barracks door going over the rifles with a vacuum cleaner brought from home by a DI. The inspection itself went quickly for the inspecting officers had performed this ritual many times. This was the final test. After it, only graduation remained.

At one time recruits simply completed their training, packed their gear in a seabag, and joined an operating unit. Since the 1950s, however, recruit graduations have been major events. Elaborate ceremonies, to which recruits invite family and friends, deliberately add significance to the formal bestowing of the title 'Marine'.

On graduation day, I received, probably because of my greater experience as a recruit, a promotion to private first class. That made me happy, but nothing compared to the surge of pride that came while standing in ranks on the parade ground while the depot band played the Marines' hymn. I had made it;

I was a marine!

In 1967, after commanding an infantry company in Vietnam as a captain, I joined the Recruit Training Regiment at San Diego, California. Other than being compressed into eight weeks rather than the 11 or 12 of the pre-war years, the training at boot camp had changed little. The DIs remained the key players in the process of transforming young men into marines. Of course, more men were in training and some of them had to live in tents. The corps had shortened marksmanship training from three to two weeks. Recruits began firing their service rifles during the first week and qualified on the Friday of the second week. The rifle in use had changed, from the old M1 to the M14 (marines in Vietnam recently had received the M16A1 rifle). Additionally, marines now measured the distance to the targets in metres rather than yards.

Some recruits had grown taller, others had developed muscles. All had changed, all had become marines

During the Vietnam War, the two recruit depots ran their recruit graduation ceremonies differently, yet both sought to provide a show-piece for the recruits' guests. San Diego's graduations began in the depot theatre and resembled a traditional school graduation. Afterwards, a truncated version of a military parade concluded the ceremony outside. Parris Island, on the other hand, conducted a full-scale military parade. Both depots' ceremonies included congratulatory speeches from the battalion commander and the promotion of outstanding recruits to private first class. The top man in each platoon received the Marines' blue dress uniform. Each ceremony concluded with the graduates being addressed as 'marines' for the very first time. The DIs then dismissed their platoons, which invariably let out a loud cheer, and the new marines went looking for their families and friends in the audience. This was a moment that always brought grins to the faces of veteran marines. Parents and friends often barely recognised the young man they had come to see; some of the young marines had grown taller, others had developed new muscles or deep tans. All had changed, all had become marines.

The next day, the graduates left the depot for further training. Boot camp had made them basic marines but they were not yet ready for combat. Prior to the Vietnam War, all marines received four

Left: Mud and guts. Marines get the feel for life in a monsoon-soaked trench while a close combat instructor shows a 'boot' how it's done – with a bayonet. Top: formal dress night in the mess, a social occasion that further enhances the Marine *esprit de corps*.

Corporal, US Marine Corps, 1985

This NCO wears the Marines' Dress Blue 'B' uniform, worn on ceremonial and official guard duty occasions. On the blue jacket are a number of awards, decorations and rank insignia. A Marine Corps service stripe is awarded for four years of service and one is worn here on the lower left sleeve; above that are the two stripes denoting a corporal's rank. The two ribbons on his left breast indicate a meritorious unit citation (green and yellow stripes – with star for second award) and the Marine good conduct award (red-blue-red bands). Below them – on the left – is the Marine rifle expert badge (with two bars for further awards) and – on the right – the Marine pistol sharpshooter badge. The 'blood' stripe is worn on the trouser seams and distinguishes NCOs, WOs and officers from other ranks.

weeks of infantry training at either Camp Lejeune, North Carolina, or Camp Pendleton, California. During the war, only those with infantry-related specialities took the full course. The rest received their requisite combat training during their basic specialist training courses or at the replacement battalion before going to Vietnam. Today, the course at boot camp includes a block of combat training adequate for all but infantrymen.

The development of an esprit de corps through a demanding initiation rite is the fundamental reason why the marines keep their recruit training so intense. Boot camp serves the Marine Corps as the academies serve the other armed services. It is the fountainhead of the Corps' eliteness. The training itself is on a very basic level and could be taught in a far more benign environment, while all recruit graduates require further training before joining the operating forces. Boot camp, however, gives all marines – whether infantrymen, truck drivers, aircraft mechanics, or computer operators – a common background with which they all identify. No matter what a marine's job assignment, he can claim that he is a combat-ready marine.

Back at the recruit depots, after the graduation ceremonies, the new marines who disperse to celebrate with families and friends will never be the same again; boot camp transforms them. For the rest of their lives they will know they are members of that elite fraternity, the US Marine Corps.

THE AUTHOR Dr V. Keith Fleming passed through the Marine training camp at Parris Island in 1960. He was commissioned after three years' service, and served in Vietnam from 1966-67 as a captain and company commander. He has been appointed to edit the official history of Parris Island.

2ND MARINES

The 2nd Marines, vanguard of the 2nd Marine Division in the assault on Tarawa, traces its lineage to the 1st Advance Base Regiment, which was formed at Philadelphia in 1913 and saw action in Mexico, Haiti and the Dominican Republic. The regiment was disbanded in 1934. On 1 February 1941 it reformed as the 2nd Marines and trained at San Diego until the outbreak of war with Japan the following December. After a period of coastal defence duty and further training, the regiment was deployed to the southwest Pacific in July 1942 in preparation for the Guadalcanal campaign. B Company, the first Marine unit to land during the operation, went ashore on Florida Island to protect the left flank of the forces landing at Tulagi. Soon afterwards the remainder of the regiment was landed to participate in mopping up Japanese forces on Tulagi and its neighbouring islands. The 2nd Marines then moved to Guadalcanal itself to join the 1st Marine Division's offensive along the north coast. At the end of January 1943, the regiment was withdrawn to New Zealand and trained with its parent division for several months.

The 2nd Marine Division, whose shoulder sleeve insignia is shown above, provided the bulk of the forces used in taking Tarawa and the rest of the Gilbert Islands, and also saw action in the Mariana Islands in 1944. After the surrender of Japan, the division became part of the occupying forces before returning to the United States. Since 1945 the division has had special responsibility for amphibious operations in the Caribbean and Mediterranean areas.

Lashed by Japanese machine-gun, mortar and artillery fire, the US 2nd Marines fought to the death on the beaches of Tarawa

JUST BEFORE dawn on 20 November 1943, a Japanese coastal battery on Betio Island, at the southwestern end of Tarawa Atoll, part of the Gilbert Islands in the central Pacific, opened fire at a range of about six miles. Its target was an American naval force consisting of three battleships, four cruisers, and several transports supported by minesweepers and destroyers. Shortly afterwards, two battlewagons, the task force's flagship, the *Maryland*, and the *Colorado*, deployed for counter-battery work, bombarding the shore batteries with 16in shells. The battle for Tarawa was on, and the men of Major-General Julian Smith's 2nd Marine Division, hardened veterans of the gruelling Guadalcanal campaign, were back in the war against Japan.

Elsewhere in the Gilberts, other American forces were going into action. The attempted seizure of the islands, Operation Galvanic, was the vital first step in a new offensive in the central Pacific aimed, eventually, at establishing bases in the Marianas from where strikes against the Japanese homeland could be launched. But Tarawa, a bracelet of tiny coral islands that was to become a part of US Marine Corps history, was the toughest objective in the campaign for the Gilberts, and was the most important strategically. On Betio Island itself, there was a heavily-defended airstrip suitable for fighters and light bombers. No thrust northwestwards to the Marshalls and Marianas could be considered until Tarawa had been taken.

The Japanese had established a formidable array

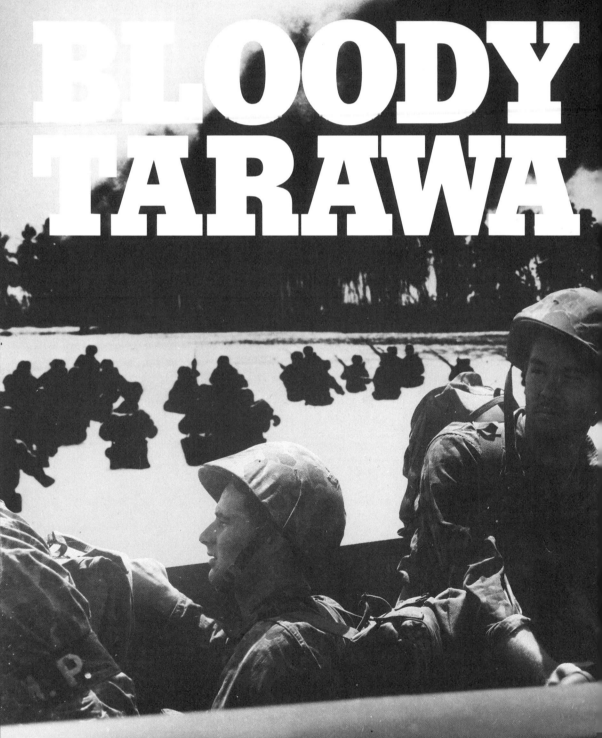

BLOODY TARAWA

of defences: mines, concrete obstacles and barbed wire were disposed offshore to channel attackers into pre-arranged killing grounds, and a four-foot-high sea wall – sufficient to halt even tracked landing vehicles – was defended by enfilading machine-gun posts able to spray a murderous hail of bullets on any assault force attempting to claw its way off the beaches. The coastal defences included four eight-inch guns and several smaller pieces, and a network of bunkers, built with reinforced concrete roofs up to six-and-a-half feet thick, served to protect the defenders. Nor was the quality of the Japanese garrison in doubt: over half of the 4800 men under Rear Admiral Meichi Shibasaki were elite Special Naval Landing Force troops.

However, the greatest obstacle that the marine assault force had to overcome was Tarawa itself. In the words of the American Central Pacific Commander-in-Chief, Admiral Chester Nimitz, 'The ideal defensive barrier has always been the one that could not be demolished, which held up assaulting forces under the unobstructed fire of the defenders and past which it was impossible to run, crawl, dig, climb or sail.' The barrier reef at Tarawa fulfilled these conditions to the letter.

The assaulting forces consisted of the 2nd Marine Division under Major-General Julian Smith. The attack would be spearheaded by Colonel David Shoup's 2nd Marines and the 2nd Battalion, 8th Marine Regiment, while the remaining two battalions of the 8th Marines were held as a divisional reserve. Additionally, a corps reserve of three battalion landing teams of the 6th Marines was held to cover the entire operation in the Gilberts and would be released to the division if needed.

As the US naval force closed on Tarawa, more of the warships joined in the bombardment, raining down ton after ton of high-explosive and high-trajectory armour-piercing shells on the Japanese defences. Some three-and-a-half miles off Betio, the assault teams transferred to their landing craft. While the larger warships stayed on station to the

Below right: Hitting the beaches. On 20 November 1943, troops of the 2nd Marine Division, under Major-General Julian Smith, pounced on the Japanese-held island of Tarawa in the Pacific. The assault was preceded by a ferocious naval bombardment, yet the marines coming in (below) were under no illusion as to the task they faced. Main picture: The shallow lagoon around Tarawa could not be navigated by the US landing craft and the men had to wade ashore, sitting targets for heavy enemy fire. Above: Battlefield conference. Colonel David Shoup (centre, holding map), commander of the 2nd Marines, confers with Lieutenant-Colonel Evans Carlson (seated), and Colonel Merritt Edson (centre, standing with hands on hips).

CLEARING THE GILBERTS

Early in 1943, the Allied forces under General Douglas MacArthur in the southwest Pacific had taken Guadalcanal and were poised to advance on Japan through the Solomons, New Guinea and the Philippines. During the months that followed, US Naval and Marine Corps forces in the central Pacific, under Admiral Chester Nimitz, prepared for a new island-hopping offensive. The offensive was designed to step up pressure on the Japanese, secure MacArthur's right flank, and eventually provide forward bases from which bombing operations, and ultimately a decisive amphibious landing in Japan itself, could be mounted.

On 20 November 1943, the central Pacific campaign opened with the launching of Operation Galvanic – the retaking of the Gilberts at the outer edge of Japan's new Pacific island empire. The forces for Operation Galvanic comprised the US Fifth Fleet, under Vice-Admiral Raymond Spruance, and V Amphibious Corps under Major-General Holland Smith. As the 2nd Marine Division moved on Tarawa, an army landing force consisting of the 165th Infantry (reinforced) went ashore on Makin Island further north, securing it by 23 November. The day after the Tarawa and Makin assaults, the Corps Reconnaissance Company landed and captured Apanama Atoll. With the end of mopping up operations on Tarawa, on 28 November, it only remained for the 2nd Division's Reconnaissance Company to sweep the neighbouring atolls for Japanese outposts. None were found. The Gilberts were safely in American hands – and within two months V Amphibious Corps was back in action, pushing forward into the next objective, the Marshall Islands.

west, giving support fire and ready to meet any Japanese naval intervention, the marines began the long, tense journey to the assault beaches on the lagoon side of the island. Only the first three waves had LVTs (landing vehicle tracked); the remainder travelled in LCVPs (landing craft vehicle, personnel) and LCMs (landing craft mechanised) – assault craft that risked going aground on the edge of the reef lying several hundred yards offshore.

Two minesweepers were already at work in the lagoon clearing a channel, with two destroyers in close support. By 0823 hours on 20 November, when the first wave of LVTs arrived, one of the minesweepers was marking the line-of-departure and would function as a control vessel from then on. H-hour was timed for 0830, but it was already obvious that the vehicles were making slower progress than had been hoped.

As the first wave of LVTs crossed the reef, the fire support lifted. The effect of the naval bombardment seemed devastating: a cloud of smoke and coral dust hung in the air and many of the enemy's gun emplacements had been disabled. In the words of the naval gunfire support commander, Admiral Kingman, 'It seemed almost impossible for any human being to be alive on Betio Island.' But Kingman had underestimated the strength of the Japanese defensive works.

Only the destroyers in the lagoon were close enough to give accurate suppressive fire during the final run-in. Taking advantage of the lull, the defenders of Tarawa returned to their posts and opened up with 75mm airburst shells and machine-gun fire.

At 0855, just as the supporting bombardment lifted, the first team of marines went into action. The scout and sniper platoon of the 2nd Marine Regiment

under Lieutenant William Hawkins reached the end of Betio's long pier by LCVP and took it by storm. Clambering up a ramp to the pier deck, Hawkins' men fought a fierce action against some 10 or 12 Japanese, destroying two wooden huts with flame-throwers and securing a flanking position that might have proved troublesome to the landing forces.

The first marines hit the beaches at 0910. Those LVTs of the first three waves that got across the reef were in most cases unable to cross the barriers sited along the shore. Their occupants reached the beaches, rolled out of the landing craft and raced for what cover they could find in front of the coastal wall. Then, pinned down by cross-fire from enemy machine guns, they began taking heavier losses. Moving forward from the beach would be an inch-by-inch, yard-by-yard, bunker-by-bunker struggle. And the struggle was going to be bloody.

The situation in the water was even worse. Some of the LVTs were destroyed by enemy fire before reaching the shore, and the non-tracked craft were unable to cross from the lagoon to the beaches. The following waves of marines had to walk ashore across several hundred yards of treacherous reef, their landing craft grounded by a tide that was lower than predicted. Lashed by withering machine-gun, mortar and artillery fire, the marines had no cover and no choice but to wade on, undaunted, through the blood-darkened water, past the bodies of their comrades. Robert Sherrod was a journalist with the Marines who faced the full fury of the Japanese fire on the approach to the beaches:

'No sooner had we hit the water than the Japanese machine guns really opened up. There must have been five or six of them concentrating their fire on us – there was no nearer target in the water at the

Below: The grisly aftermath of 'Bloody Tarawa'. Lifeless bodies, abandoned equipment and smashed amphibians litter the shoreline of Red 2 beach, the objective of the 2nd Battalion, 2nd Marines under Colonel Herbert Amey. Amey and many of his men were cut down by withering machine-gun fire from carefully hidden enemy bunkers.

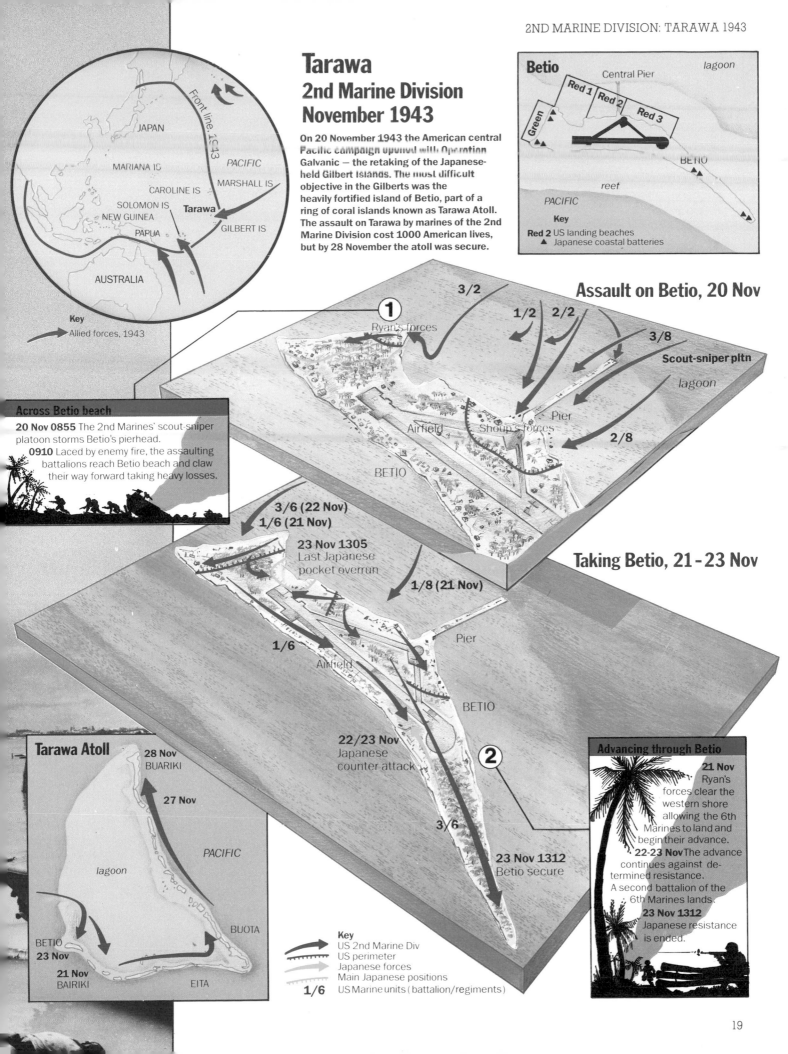

Tarawa
2nd Marine Division
November 1943

On 20 November 1943 the American central Pacific campaign opened with Operation Galvanic — the retaking of the Japanese-held Gilbert Islands. The most difficult objective in the Gilberts was the heavily fortified island of Betio, part of a ring of coral islands known as Tarawa Atoll. The assault on Tarawa by marines of the 2nd Marine Division cost 1000 American lives, but by 28 November the atoll was secure.

Betio

Central Pier · Red 1 · Red 2 · Red 3 · Green · lagoon · BETIO · PACIFIC · reef

Key
Red 2 US landing beaches
▲ Japanese coastal batteries

JAPAN · MARIANA IS · PACIFIC · MARSHALL IS · CAROLINE IS · SOLOMON IS · NEW GUINEA · **Tarawa** · GILBERT IS · PAPUA · AUSTRALIA · Front line 1943

Key
→ Allied forces, 1943

Assault on Betio, 20 Nov

3/2 · 1/2 · 2/2 · 3/8 · Scout-sniper pltn · lagoon · ① Ryan's forces · Airfield · Shoup's forces · Pier · 2/8 · BETIO

Across Betio beach
20 Nov 0855 The 2nd Marines' scout-sniper platoon storms Betio's pierhead.
0910 Laced by enemy fire, the assaulting battalions reach Betio beach and claw their way forward taking heavy losses.

Taking Betio, 21–23 Nov

3/6 (22 Nov)
1/6 (21 Nov)
23 Nov 1305 Last Japanese pocket overrun
1/8 (21 Nov)
1/6 · Airfield · Pier · BETIO
22/23 Nov Japanese counter-attack
②
3/6
23 Nov 1312 Betio secure

Tarawa Atoll
28 Nov BUARIKI
27 Nov
lagoon · PACIFIC
BETIO · **23 Nov** · BUOTA
21 Nov BAIRIKI · EITA

Advancing through Betio
21 Nov Ryan's forces clear the western shore allowing the 6th Marines to land and begin their advance.
22-23 Nov The advance continues against determined resistance. A second battalion of the 6th Marines lands.
23 Nov 1312 Japanese resistance is ended.

Key
→ US 2nd Marine Div
US perimeter
Japanese forces
Main Japanese positions
1/6 US Marine units (battalion/regiments)

time. I don't believe that there was one of the 15 men who wouldn't have sold his chances for an additional 25 dollars added to his life-insurance policy. It was painfully slow, wading in such deep water. We had 700yds to walk slowly into this machine-gun fire, looming into larger targets as we rose onto higher ground.'

Each of the three assault beaches was the objective of one battalion landing team. East of the pier, Red 3 beach was the target of Major Henry Crowe's 2nd Battalion, 8th Marines. Red 2, the centre beach immediately west of the pier, was the objective of Colonel Herbert Amey's 2nd Battalion, 2nd Marines. Amey was an early casualty and his command was taken over by Lieutenant-Colonel Walter Jordan. The westernmost objective, Red 1, was assigned to Major John Schoettel's 3rd Battalion, 2nd Marines.

Not one of the battalions arrived intact. Each suffered heavy casualties during the landing, and only one arrived on the correct beach with its commander.

Crowe's battalion

Far left: Reinforcements from the 1st Battalion, 2nd Marines wade ashore on 21 November to help their comrades pinned down on Red 2 beach. Left: Under a sky blackened by smoke from a blazing fuel dump, marines radio for further orders. Main picture: A lone marine lines up on a Japanese bunker. Below left: Forsaking the reassuring protection of Tarawa's sea wall, marines move inland to flush the enemy from their positions near the airstrip.

US Marine, Tarawa 1943
This weary marine wears the two-piece herringbone-twill fatigue suit, brown boots and M1 helmet with 'beach' camouflage cover. He is armed with the M1 Garand semi-automatic rifle.

got ashore on Red 3 under the excellent covering fire provided by the destroyer *Ringgold*. Only in the fourth and fifth waves did his casualties mount to 10 per cent. By noon Crowe had a platoon of medium tanks available and he fought aggressively, deploying 37mm guns in defence, and pushing inland with infantry, tanks and demolition teams in close mutual support.

On the other two beaches the position was less favourable. On the centre beach, Jordan took command of the 2nd Battalion, 2nd Marines, establishing a command post in a shell crater on the shore at about 1000 hours. Few of his officers had gained the beach. Many of his men were still in the water; he received a report that they could not advance due to machine-gun positions to their front and flanks, and sniper fire from trees in their immediate vicinity. Jordan was acutely aware of his precarious position, 'At this time there was no contact between elements on my right or left and I could not find out how many men of each company had landed.'

The Japanese strongpoints that were wreaking such havoc on Jordan's men were part of a chain that extended along the right half of the centre beach and covered the cove that formed most of Red 1 on the right flank. These positions ensured that neither of the two battalions on the right could establish themselves intact on their respective beaches. At least 100 of Jordan's men had been driven way over to the far right, reaching the shore on the extreme western edge of the island, where they linked up with the remnants of the 3rd Battalion, 2nd Marines.

Under deadly fire from the Japanese strongpoints along the Red 1 cove, Kyle's men crossed the reef

Major Schoettel, the 3rd Battalion's commander, had withdrawn from Red 1 under heavy fire. There were no friendly troops in position ashore and he believed that the first three waves of his landing force had been wiped out. Schoettel reported to Colonel Shoup, now embarked in a landing craft at the line-of-departure and watching the assault anxiously, that his battalion was taking heavy losses. Shoup radioed that he was to come in on the centre beach. Schoettel's last message to his commander was, 'We have nothing left to land.'

Shoup decided to reinforce the centre beach, Red 2, where Jordan's men were dangerously under-strength. He deployed the remaining battalion of the 2nd Marines, the 1st Battalion under Major Wood Kyle, with orders to land on Red 2 and push to the right. Under deadly fire from the Japanese strongpoints along the Red 1 cove, Kyle's men crossed the reef, reaching Red 2 between 1130 and 1200 hours. The battalion lost some 200 men on the way and a further 100 were forced off course by enemy fire, joining elements of the other battalions that were cut off at the western edge of Red 1.

By noon, Shoup himself had waded ashore and had established his command post on Red 2 next to a Japanese bunker. As he recalled later, 'I was never off my feet for 50 hours, standing for the most time by an enemy pillbox with 26 live Japs therein.' The situation was perilous.

Matters gradually improved, however. Shoup was soon in contact with Crowe's forces on Red 3. An attack with medium tank support was mounted across the airstrip taxiway and a joint perimeter, some 300yds deep, was established. But there were strong Japanese forces on both flanks and the possi-

TARAWA'S BLOODY LESSONS

The capture of Tarawa in late 1943 marked the beginning of the end for Japanese military supremacy in the Pacific war, but the heavy casualties suffered by the Marines, over 3000 men, forced US planners to review their island-assault tactics in the light of harsh experience.

The Tarawa landings had been preceded by a naval barrage of considerable ferocity, yet when the Marines made their run-in to the beaches they were hit by heavy fire from machine guns and artillery that had escaped the worst of the bombardment. In future operations, the scale and duration of the softening-up process would be much greater to smash the enemy's heavily fortified bunkers and trench systems.

Once on Tarawa, the Marines found it difficult to co-ordinate their actions: radio links between the assault troops and the command ships lying offshore were poor, making it extremely difficult to call up reinforcements to help relieve a hard-pressed sector or bring down air and artillery support on an enemy position.

During the critical battles fought as the Marines pushed inland from the beaches, they faced a succession of defences that could not be silenced by the relatively inaccurate fire provided by the supporting naval units. The Marines, short on heavy weapons, had to close with the enemy, and in doing so suffered. It was soon recognised that 'go-anywhere' amphibians, some equipped with bunker-busting weapons, would provide an effective counter-measure to this problem.

The lessons of Tarawa were well learnt. In later operations, the Marines had both the back-up and equipment to tackle even the most stubborn Japanese defences.

Bottom left: Leathernecks of Major Henry Crowe's 2nd Battalion, 2nd Marines on Red 3 beach, plaster enemy positions with machine-gun fire. Centre left: Shrouded by the acrid smoke of battle, a marine throws a grenade at a Japanese pillbox while his buddies take a break.
Left: Enemy dead lie where they fell in defence of Tarawa.

bility of a counter-attack at night could not be ruled out. Accordingly, one of the divisional reserve battalions was committed to the centre beach, the 3rd Battalion, 8th Marines, commanded by Major Robert Ruud. Ruud's men came in on both sides of the pier, taking casualties from the still-murderous fire from Japanese positions on the left and right.

Meanwhile, on the extreme right flank of Red 1 at the western edge of Betio Island, Major Michael Ryan assumed command of those elements of the 1st, 2nd and 3rd Battalions of the 2nd Marines that had been forced westwards by the ferocity of the Japanese defences in the cove that comprised most of Red 1. Two medium tanks arrived on the shore within Ryan's perimeter and by 1630 he had mounted an attack southwards along Green Beach, the western coast of Betio. His men pushed some 500yds along the coast, but the tanks were soon knocked out by enemy action and, lacking the flame-throwers and heavy equipment needed to take out the Japanese bunkers they encountered, Ryan's marines could not hope to hold the ground they had gained. They withdrew to a defensive position at the north end of the western beach for the night.

As night drew on, the marines and their commanders waited apprehensively for the expected counter-attack. It failed to materialise, probably because Japanese communications had been wrecked by the naval bombardment and the various strongpoints were unable to co-ordinate their actions or assess the overall position.

Ryan had two medium tanks and flame-throwers to take out enemy artillery along the coast

The following morning, Julian Smith committed the remaining divisional reserve, the 1st Battalion, 8th Marines under Major Lawrence Hays, which had spent the night on board their LCVPs at the line-of-departure. Before dawn on 21 November, the battalion set off for the reef and then began the long walk ashore. Again, the marines suffered terrible casualties, and the remnants of a shattered battalion joined the right flank of Shoup's forces in the centre of the island. An artillery battalion of the 10th Marines had also got ashore with five 75mm pack howitzers. But the combined efforts of artillery and the survivors of two Marine battalions were unable to shift the determined enemy resistance on the right and there seemed to be no chance of linking up with Ryan's forces. Crowe and Ruud, on the left, had also made no progress.

However, the tide was about to turn. Ryan's forces were reinforced during the morning: he now had two medium tanks and flame-throwers and air strikes were organised to take out enemy artillery along the western coast. At 1100 hours, with supporting naval gunfire softening up Japanese resistance, Ryan's marines once more began a southward advance. This time, properly equipped, they were able to take out the remaining enemy positions. Green Beach, never part of the original assault plan, was secured shortly after 1200. General Smith could at last think in

terms of getting whole battalions ashore with minimal casualties and with their organisation, command and equipment intact. He had already obtained the release of the corps reserve to division, and the 6th Marines were on their way.

The 2nd Battalion, 6th Marines was deployed with artillery from the 10th Marines on the neighbouring island of Bairiki to contribute its firepower to the final assault and prevent a Japanese retreat across the narrow stretch of water separating the two islands. By the late afternoon of 21 November, the 1st Battalion, 6th Marines under Major William Jones was coming ashore on Green Beach.

In the centre, Shoup's forces had also made progress after resupply during the morning. Elements of Shoup's battalions had advanced across the airstrip and reached the south coast of the island. At the end of the day, Shoup had cause for renewed optimism. He reported the position to General Smith aboard *Maryland*, 'Casualties many; percentage dead not known; combat efficiency: we are winning.'

At 0805 on the morning of 22 November, Major Jones, commander of the first battalion landing force to arrive on Betio intact, began his advance along the island's south coast. He made rapid progress, although for lack of a sufficient number of medium tanks, he experienced difficulties in taking out some of the enemy bunkers. The 8th Marines under Crowe and Ruud made progress during the afternoon, advancing slowly along the northern shore in the teeth of fierce Japanese resistance. General Smith was now ashore to direct the final operation, and by nightfall Jones' marines had linked up with the 8th Marines to their left, forming a line across the island.

During the evening, the long-expected counter-attack came. But it was now too late. As the Japanese massed for the assault, naval gunfire and artillery from Bairiki and Betio were called down to devastating effect. The marines held off firing until the last moment, and the Japanese casualties were heavy as they surged into the attack.

During the following morning, 23 November, one more fresh battalion was deployed, the 3rd Battalion, 6th Marines. Under Lieutenant-Colonel Kenneth McLeod, the new forces pushed forward, renewing the attack to the eastern end of the island, while the exhausted remnants of the initial assault force concentrated on the remaining enemy pocket, along the cove of the original Red 1 beach. At around 1300, this pocket was finally eliminated. McLeod's forces reached the eastern end of the island at about the same time, and at 1312 General Julian Smith pronounced Betio secure.

The following day, the battered, depleted and exhausted 2nd and 8th Marines left Betio Island. With only Betio and Bairiki captured, the 6th Marines were left with the task of tracking down the few remaining enemy forces. On the northern island of Buariki some 175 Japanese made a final stand, but by 28 November the bitter struggle for Tarawa was over. Of the original Japanese garrison of over 4800 men, only 146 prisoners were taken. Taking Tarawa cost the Marine Corps over 1000 dead and 2000 wounded, but the lessons learned there had far-reaching effects on the conduct of future amphibious assaults in the Pacific war. And the bloody assault across Betio reef has passed into legend.

THE AUTHOR Barry Smith has taught politics at Exeter and Brunel Universities. He is a contributor to the journal *History of Political Thought* and has written a number of articles on military subjects.

THE 1ST MARINE DIVISION

The 1st Marine Division was formed by the redesignation and expansion of the 1st Marine Brigade on 1 February 1941. In World War II it fought at Guadalcanal, New Britain, Peleliu and Okinawa. After the war it was part of the US occupation force in North China.

In Korea, the division had three infantry regiments – the 1st, 5th and 7th Marines – and an artillery regiment, the 11th Marines. Combat support and combat service support were provided by a number of organic and attached battalions, including the 1st Amphibian Tractor, 1st Armored Amphibian, 1st Combat Service, 1st Engineer, 1st Medical, 1st Motor Transport, 7th Motor Transport, 1st Ordnance, 1st Service, 1st Shore Party, 1st Signal, 1st Tank (with M-26 Pershings) and Headquarters Battalion, and the 1st Combat Service Group. Attached to the division were two aviation units – Marine Observation Squadron 6 and Marine Helicopter Transport Squadron 161.

Following the Korean War, the 1st Marine Division fought in Vietnam. From its arrival in July 1965 until its departure in April 1971, the division operated from Chu Lai, Da Nang, Dong Ha, Qui Nhon, Hue, Phu Bai and Quang Tri. Interestingly, a Korean Marine Brigade also fought in Vietnam under the guidance (but not command) of the US Marines.

The colours of the division, which is now based at Camp Pendleton in California, fly the streamer of the Presidential Unit Citation (PUC), with one silver and two bronze stars indicating that the PUC has been awarded to the division seven times.

ENTER THE MARINES

General MacArthur's audacious landing of the 1st Marine Division at Inchon was a masterstroke that radically altered the strategic balance of the Korean War in 1950

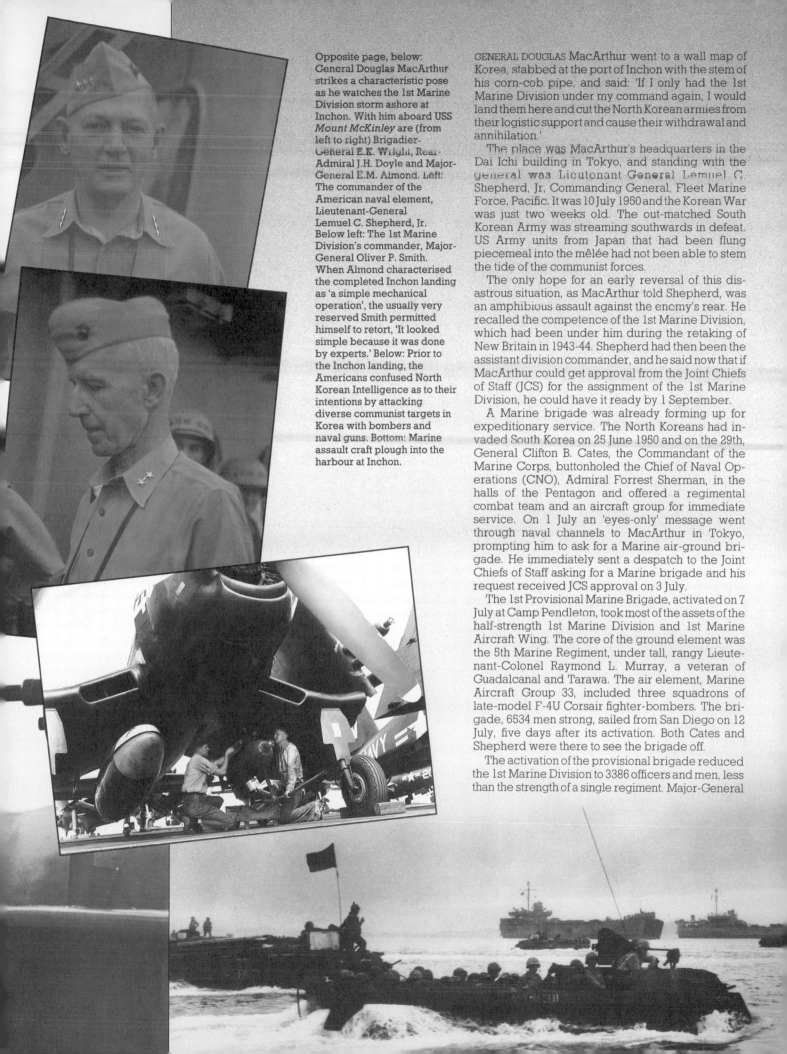

Opposite page, below: General Douglas MacArthur strikes a characteristic pose as he watches the 1st Marine Division storm ashore at Inchon. With him aboard USS *Mount McKinley* are (from left to right) Brigadier-General E.K. Wright, Rear-Admiral J.H. Doyle and Major-General E.M. Almond. Left: The commander of the American naval element, Lieutenant-General Lemuel C. Shepherd, Jr. Below left: The 1st Marine Division's commander, Major-General Oliver P. Smith. When Almond characterised the completed Inchon landing as 'a simple mechanical operation', the usually very reserved Smith permitted himself to retort, 'It looked simple because it was done by experts.' Below: Prior to the Inchon landing, the Americans confused North Korean Intelligence as to their intentions by attacking diverse communist targets in Korea with bombers and naval guns. Bottom: Marine assault craft plough into the harbour at Inchon.

GENERAL DOUGLAS MacArthur went to a wall map of Korea, stabbed at the port of Inchon with the stem of his corn-cob pipe, and said: 'If I only had the 1st Marine Division under my command again, I would land them here and cut the North Korean armies from their logistic support and cause their withdrawal and annihilation.'

The place was MacArthur's headquarters in the Dai Ichi building in Tokyo, and standing with the general was Lieutenant General Lemuel C. Shepherd, Jr, Commanding General, Fleet Marine Force, Pacific. It was 10 July 1950 and the Korean War was just two weeks old. The out-matched South Korean Army was streaming southwards in defeat. US Army units from Japan that had been flung piecemeal into the mêlée had not been able to stem the tide of the communist forces.

The only hope for an early reversal of this disastrous situation, as MacArthur told Shepherd, was an amphibious assault against the enemy's rear. He recalled the competence of the 1st Marine Division, which had been under him during the retaking of New Britain in 1943-44. Shepherd had then been the assistant division commander, and he said now that if MacArthur could get approval from the Joint Chiefs of Staff (JCS) for the assignment of the 1st Marine Division, he could have it ready by 1 September.

A Marine brigade was already forming up for expeditionary service. The North Koreans had invaded South Korea on 25 June 1950 and on the 29th, General Clifton B. Cates, the Commandant of the Marine Corps, buttonholed the Chief of Naval Operations (CNO), Admiral Forrest Sherman, in the halls of the Pentagon and offered a regimental combat team and an aircraft group for immediate service. On 1 July an 'eyes-only' message went through naval channels to MacArthur in Tokyo, prompting him to ask for a Marine air-ground brigade. He immediately sent a despatch to the Joint Chiefs of Staff asking for a Marine brigade and his request received JCS approval on 3 July.

The 1st Provisional Marine Brigade, activated on 7 July at Camp Pendleton, took most of the assets of the half-strength 1st Marine Division and 1st Marine Aircraft Wing. The core of the ground element was the 5th Marine Regiment, under tall, rangy Lieutenant-Colonel Raymond L. Murray, a veteran of Guadalcanal and Tarawa. The air element, Marine Aircraft Group 33, included three squadrons of late-model F-4U Corsair fighter-bombers. The brigade, 6534 men strong, sailed from San Diego on 12 July, five days after its activation. Both Cates and Shepherd were there to see the brigade off.

The activation of the provisional brigade reduced the 1st Marine Division to 3386 officers and men, less than the strength of a single regiment. Major-General

Encircled by China, Japan and the Soviet Union, the mountainous and largely inhospitable peninsula of Korea has long been coveted by its powerful neighbours. In 1942 Korea was made an integral part of Japan, but the fall of that nation in 1945 resulted in the Korean peninsula being divided between the victorious Allies. The Soviet Union occupied the area north of the 38th parallel of latitude and later formed the People's Democratic Republic of Korea (PDRK). The United Nations, who would have preferred independence for the entire territory, formed the Republic of Korea (ROK) to the south of the parallel. By July 1949, all Soviet and US troops had been withdrawn from the peninsula: in their place was the experienced and well-equipped North Korean People's Army (NKPA), and the understrength and outnumbered ROK Army, equipped with outmoded weapons left behind by the Americans.

On 25 June 1950 the NKPA seized the chance to control the whole of Korea. Seven infantry divisions swept south, taking the ROK Army completely by surprise. On the same day, the UN declared the move a 'breach of the peace' and requested military aid for the ROK army. Seoul was lost on 29 June, and on the 30th General MacArthur confirmed that Korea would be lost without US military intervention. This was authorised by President Truman, and by 18 July three US divisions were deployed against the NKPA. They proved no match for the highly motivated and well-equipped North Koreans, however, and by 4 August the joint UN forces were thrust back to form the Pusan Perimeter on the southeastern tip of Korea. Reinforced during the following weeks, the perimeter held against determined NKPA offensives until relieved by the landing of the 1st Marine Division at Inchon on 15 September.

Oliver P. Smith arrived from Washington on 18 July to take command of the skeletal division. The slender, white-haired Smith had led the 5th Marines at New Britain, had been the assistant division commander at Peleliu, and had been the deputy chief of staff of the US Tenth Army on Okinawa.

Not until 25 July did the JCS approve MacArthur's request for the complete 1st Marine Division. Cates was ordered to build the division to war strength and have it sail for the Far East by mid-August. The formula for the build-up was conceived in four stages. First, the 1st Provisional Brigade was to re-combine with the division when it arrived in the Far East. Second, units of the half-strength 2nd Marine Division at Camp Lejeune, North Carolina, were to be ordered to Camp Pendleton in California. Third, regulars were to be stripped out from stateside posts and stations. Finally, the gaps in the division were to be filled with those reservists judged to be combat-ready.

By the end of July, Lieutenant-General Walton Walker's mixed American and South Korean Eighth Army had been driven back into a defensive position, roughly a quarter-circle drawn at a radius of 100 miles from Pusan in the southeast corner of Korea. MacArthur reluctantly decided that the 1st Provisional Marine Brigade had to be landed to help shore up the army's so-called Pusan Perimeter. The brigade, under Brigadier-General Edward A. Craig, debarked on 3 August and four days later was in action, counter-attacking southwest of Masan.

President Truman had authorised the mobilisation of the Marine Corps Reserve on 19 July. The first reservists began arriving at Camp Pendleton on 31 July. Battalions of the 2nd Marine Division at Camp Lejeune began boarding troop trains for the West Coast on the same date. Within a week, 13,703 marines had arrived at Pendleton and the divisional strength stood at 17,162. Nearly half of the new arrivals – 7182 marines – had come from the 2nd Marine Division, 3630 were from posts and stations, and 2891 were Reserves, most of them veterans of World War II. A second infantry regiment, the 1st Marines, was pulled together in 10 days by Colonel Lewis B. 'Chesty' Puller, who had commanded the same regiment at Cape Gloucester and Peleliu.

General Smith, commanding the 1st Marine Division, did not learn that his objective was to be Inchon until 8 August. He arrived in Tokyo on 22 August, and by then MacArthur had decided to activate X Corps for the operation and to give its command to his chief of staff, Major-General Edward M. Almond, US Army. Also reporting to MacArthur was Joint Task Force 7, essentially all of Vice-Admiral Arthur D. Struble's US Seventh Fleet. The Attack Force for the landing would be Amphibious Group One, with the 1st Marine Division embarked, under the navy's amphibious expert, Rear-Admiral James H. Doyle. Smith was met at Haneda Airfield by Doyle, and together they drove to the command ship USS *Mount McKinley*. Once on board, Smith learned that D-day had been tentatively set for 15 September and that the landing had to be made at high tide late in the afternoon. There would be no time for rehearsals.

The first day of September found the 5th Marines alongside the 2nd Infantry Division in a bitter defence of the Naktong Bulge. Not until 5 September could the provisional brigade be pulled from the line to prepare for Inchon.

The 7th Marines, the division's third infantry regiment, was created by a redesignation of the 6th Marines at Camp Lejeune, North Carolina. Unfortunately, neither the parent 7th Marines nor one of its battalions, which was then in the Mediterranean, could be in the Far East in time for the landing. To provide a reserve regiment for Inchon, therefore, the newly-formed 1st Korean Marine Corps (KMC) Regiment, along with its US Marine Corps advisors, was attached to the division.

US Intelligence reported 21,500 North Korean troops, most of them second-rate, in the Inchon-Seoul area. Of these, between 1500 and 2500 were thought to be at Inchon itself. Aerial photographs and South Korean intelligence sources indicated a well developed system of caves and emplacements.

The degree of expected enemy resistance was much less frightening than the hydrographic conditions. Inchon is about 20 miles from Seoul and is separated from it by the additional barrier of the Han river. Admiral Doyle's Attack Force would have to

Below: Marines use ladders to climb out of their landing craft and over the high sea walls bordering the harbour at Inchon. Against a strongly defended objective such a landing would have been very costly, but the Koreans had not reinforced the Inchon garrison and the Marines' swift execution of the task kept casualties to a minimum.

The Invasion of South Korea
25 June-mid Sept 1950

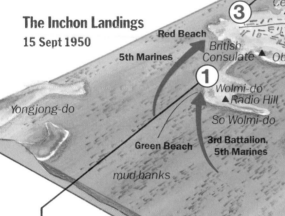

SEA OF JAPAN

NORTH KOREA

38°N

● Seoul

Inchon

SOUTH KOREA

YELLOW SEA

● Pusan

Straits of Tsushima

Key
→ NKPA thrusts
→ US landings
⊢⊢⊢ Pusan perimeter

MacArthur's Masterstroke

On 25 June 1950 seven infantry divisions of the North Korean People's Army, backed by a tank brigade, launched an all-out offensive against South Korea. Caught off balance and outnumbered, the South Koreans surrendered their capital Seoul and retreated. Within five days US units were involved in the fighting but were too few to stem the North Korean tide. By the end of July, the South Korean forces and their US allies had been forced back to Pusan in the southeast of the country, where they formed a defensive perimeter. To relieve the pressure on Pusan, General Douglas MacArthur, appointed commander of the UN forces in Korea on 7 July, planned a daring amphibious assault on Inchon, deep behind North Korean lines. With their lines of communication under threat, the North Koreans would have to scale down their attacks on the Pusan perimeter. On 15 September, after weeks of hurried preparation, the first US assault wave hit the Inchon beaches.

Key
→ US landings

Assault on Red Beach

1733 The leading elements of the 1st and 2nd Battalions, 5th Marines, land and begin to push inland to the south and east.
1755 A single amber flare signals the capture of Cemetery Hill after close-quarters fighting.
2400 Under cover of darkness two companies from the 2nd Battalion occupy the summit of Observatory Hill.

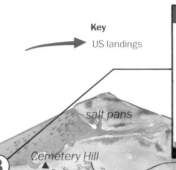

The Inchon Landings
15 Sept 1950

salt pans

Red Beach

5th Marines

Cemetery Hill

British Consulate

Observatory Hill

Hill 117

Hill 233

③

②

Blue Beach

Hill 94

Wolmi-do
▲*Radio Hill*
So Wolmi-do

①

tidal basin

mud banks

1st Marines

Yongjong-do

Green Beach

3rd Battalion, 5th Marines

mud banks

Flying Fish Channel

Assault on Blue Beach

1732 Assault troops from the 1st Marines land and strike out for the Inchon-Seoul highway.
1900 After taking casualties from a hidden machine gun, the 3rd Battalion, 1st Marines, secures Hill 233.
2400 Hill 94, the 3rd Battalion's final objective, is captured and the Marines dig in.

Assault on Green Beach

0545 US ground-attack aircraft and naval units plaster North Korean positions.
0633 Preceded by a rocket barrage, men from the 3rd Battalion, 5th Marines, hit Green Beach and begin the assault on Radio Hill.
0655 The US flag is raised over Wolmi-do, but mopping-up operations continue throughout the morning.

By dawn on 16 September, 1st Marine Division had secured Inchon and established a defensive perimeter to the east of the city. To maintain the pressure on the North Koreans, the Marines, backed by regular US and Republic of Korea forces, then struck out for Seoul and Kimpo airfield. Defended by 20,000 North Koreans, the capital proved a tough nut to crack but superior US firepower was used to blast the enemy into submission. By the 20th US troops were on the outskirts of Seoul but it took another seven days of hard fighting before the objective was captured. The North Korean forces were virtually annihilated. MacArthur had won his 'impossible victory'.

The March on Seoul 15-22 Sept 1950

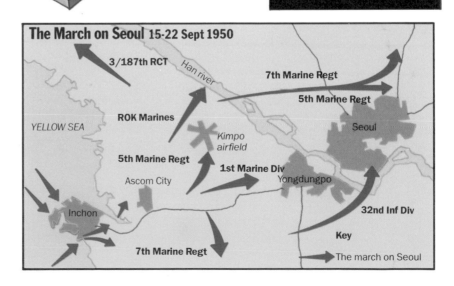

3/187th RCT

Han river

7th Marine Regt

5th Marine Regt

ROK Marines

YELLOW SEA

Kimpo airfield

Seoul

5th Marine Regt

Ascom City

1st Marine Div

Yongdungpo

Inchon

32nd Inf Div

7th Marine Regt

Key
→ The march on Seoul

thread its way from the Yellow Sea through the tortuous Flying Fish Channel. The best date would be 15 September, when morning tide (which rose to an incredible 31½ft) would be at 0659 and evening tide at 1919. When the tide fell, the currents ripped out of the channel at a rate of seven to eight knots, leaving exposed mud flats across which even amphibious tractors could not be expected to crawl.

The northern arm of this dubious harbour was formed by the island of Wolmi-do, which was connected to the Inchon dock area by a 600yd causeway. 'Wolmi-do,' wrote General Smith, was, 'the key to the whole operation.'

As part of the pell-mell demobilisation after World War II, much of the US Navy's amphibious shipping had been given away or allowed to rust. Many of the LSTs (landing ship, tank) to be used in the landing had to be reclaimed from the Japanese. Some came complete with Japanese crews, while others were crewed by US Navy reservists from America.

The plan was to take Wolmi-do on the morning tide by landing the 3rd Battalion, 5th Marines, under Lieutenant-Colonel Robert D. Taplett, across Green

Above: Once the Marines were ashore at Inchon, beachheads were rapidly organised to receive reinforcements and heavy equipment. Below: A column of Marine amphibious vehicles moves out of Inchon towards Seoul. To the left of the LVTs (landing vehicles, tracked) are DUKW 'Duck' amphibians. Right: The Inchon landings on Blue and Red beaches were preceded by the fight to secure Wolmi-do island. Top and centre: Marines scour the island, clearing out stragglers and suicide snipers. Bottom: A Marine Sherman tank neutralises bunkers on Wolmi-do.

Beach. There would then be a long wait of 12 hours until the evening tide was in and the remainder of the division could be landed. The rest of Murray's 5th Marines would come across Red Beach to the north of Wolmi-do, and Puller's 1st Marines would land across Blue Beach in the inner harbour to the south. Actually, to call the landing sites 'beaches' was misleading, for the harbour had cut granite sea walls at its edge which would have to be scaled.

The 1st Marine Aircraft Wing, under Major-General Field Harris, would provide close air support from the decks of the light carriers USS *Sicily* and *Badoeng Strait* (known as 'Bing Ding' to the marines). After the beachhead was secured, the 7th Infantry Division (its ranks filled out by 8000 Korean conscripts) was to land and occupy the area. Almond's X Corps, once ashore, was to capture Kimpo airfield, then cross the Han and take Seoul, and finally, in accordance with MacArthur's concept, act as the anvil against which the NKPA would be crushed.

Three rocket ships sent their loads, thousands of 5in rockets, screeching against the objective

---

The softening up of Wolmi-do began on 10 September with napalm strikes flown by Marine squadrons VMF-214 and VMF-323. These air attacks were followed by naval gunfire. Six destroyers steamed close in to the island on 13 September to draw out the defenders' fire. Three of the destroyers were hit but the enemy guns, now revealed, got a pasting from four supporting US and British cruisers and carrier-based aircraft.

Doyle's Attack Force eased its way up the channel towards Inchon before daylight on 15 September. General MacArthur was embarked in the *Mount McKinley*, along with General Shepherd as his amphibious advisor. Struble, Almond, Doyle, and Smith were in the same ship.

L-hour was to be 0630. At 0545, the pre-landing shore bombardment began. Taplett's battalion was aboard the boats by 0600. The air attacks lifted at 0615 and then three rocket ships sent their loads, thousands of 5in rockets, screeching against the objective. The first wave of marines grounded on Green Beach at 0633 and was met by only a few scattered shots.

Company G, under First Lieutenant Robert D. Bohn, swung to the right and moved up the slopes of Radio Hill. A sergeant fastened an American flag to a

shell-torn tree at 0655 and MacArthur, watching through binoculars from his swivel chair on the flat bridge of the *Mount McKinley*, saw the flag go up. 'That's it,' he said. 'Let's get a cup of coffee.' By noon the fight for Wolmi-do was over. Taplett had taken 136 prisoners and counted 108 enemy dead. His own losses were 17 wounded and not one of his force had been killed.

With Wolmi-do in hand, a satisfied MacArthur sent a despatch from the *Mount McKinley*, 'The Navy and Marines have never shone more brightly than this morning.' Throughout the day naval gunfire and carrier aircraft continued to hit everything that could be found in the way of targets within a 25-mile radius of Inchon. H-hour for the main landing was 1730. The smoke of the bombardment and burning buildings had mixed with the rain to create a grey-green pall that hung over the landing area.

Murray's 5th Marines were to land on the left across Red Beach and take most of the city, while Puller's 1st Marines, landing on the right across Blue Beach, swung in a right hand hook to cut off Inchon from Seoul. The 1st and 2nd Battalions, 5th Marines, were to scale the sea wall at Red Beach. Lieutenant-Colonel George R. Newton's 1st Battalion was to take Cemetery Hill and half of Observatory Hill. Lieutenant-Colonel Harold S. Roise's 2nd Battalion was to take the remaining half of Observatory Hill, the British Consulate, and the inner tidal basin.

Three miles to the southeast of Red Beach, Puller would land his 2nd Battalion across Blue Beach One and his 3rd Battalion across Blue Beach Two. He hoped that there would be enough breaks in the sea wall to allow his amphibious tractors to crawl ashore. At 1645, the 18 US Army armoured amphibious tractors that made up the first wave crossed the line of departure and headed for Blue Beach. Again the naval gunfire preparation reached a crescendo, with 6000 rockets flying forth against the beach area. From the troops' position in the amphibious tractors no landmarks could be seen. The assault waves criss-crossed during the run-in as they blindly sought their respective landing sites.

In his seat on the bridge of the *Mount McKinley*, MacArthur peered through the gathering gloom of smoke, rain and darkness, listening to the reports crackling over the loud-speaker. No-one was sure what the opposition might be. While Taplett's battalion laid down supporting fire from Wolmi-do, the landing craft carrying Newton's and Roise's battalions bore down on Red Beach. Naval gunfire lifted

and the Marine F-4U Corsairs overhead took over, strafing the North Korean positions. Company A of the 1st Battalion, on the left flank, clambered up its scaling ladders and over the sea wall, heading for Cemetery Hill.

Captain John R. Stevens' Company A was stopped by a bunker to its front and by flanking fire. There was a very hot fight at hand grenade range. Then, at 1755, an amber star cluster went up, signalling that Cemetery Hill had been taken. The cost to Stevens was eight marines killed and 28 wounded.

Captain Samuel Zaskilka's Company E, 2nd Battalion, landed on the right and pushed 100yds ahead, meeting no resistance at all. The British Consulate was seized by 1845. Meanwhile, Companies B and D, whose waves had become intermixed while coming ashore, paused to reorganise and then moved up in the darkness against Observatory Hill. By midnight, Murray's 5th Marines had secured its objectives.

To the south, Lieutenant-Colonel Alan Sutter's 2nd Battalion, 1st Marines, crawled in its tractors across Blue Beach One and after some confusion attacked northwards. In reaching its main objective, the high ground that covered the Inchon to Seoul highway, Sutter's battalion killed an estimated 50 enemy and took 15 prisoners at a cost of one marine dead and 19 wounded.

Lieutenant-Colonel Thomas L. Ridge's 3rd Battalion, faced with a sea wall at Blue Beach Two, had a more difficult task getting ashore. Most of the battalion's few casualties were caused by a single machine gun firing from a tower. The principal objectives in front of Ridge's battalion were Hill 233, taken by 1900, and, on the extreme right flank, Hill 94, which was taken before midnight.

Before morning the 1st Marine Division had secured all of the objectives that had been designated for the first day. Resistance had been scattered and of the sort that goes down in the situation report as 'light to moderate'. The enemy had been the North Korean 226th Marine Regiment, reinforced by two

US Marine, Inchon 1950

This member of the 1st Marine Division is wearing USMC M 1944 herring-bone twill fatigues with web leggings and brown World War II-pattern boots. His M1 steel helmet has a USMC camouflaged cover, and the cotton bandoliers contain 0.3in clips for his M1 (Garand) rifle. The handle of an M1 bayonet is projecting from his small shoulder pack, easily accessible for immediate use.

Below: Marines march in the bright Korean sun to recapture Seoul from the North Korean People's Army. They are passing a knocked out Soviet-built T-34 tank of the NKPA.

Left: A Marine tankman stands by his M46 at the Inchon beachhead. Below: The author, Major E.H. Simmons. Bottom left: Major-General Oliver P. Smith (centre), photographed with two of his officers in Korea. On his left is Colonel Lewis B. 'Chesty' Puller, commander of the 1st Marine Regiment. Standing on his right is Lieutenant-Colonel Raymond L. Murray, CO of the 5th Marines. Bottom right: Marines caught by the camera during the house-to-house fighting in Seoul.

companies of the 2nd Battalion, 918th Coast Artillery Regiment. Total US Marine casualties were 22 killed and 174 wounded.

The axis for the advance on Seoul was the intertwined highway and railroad. On D+1 the 1st Marine Division moved out, Puller's 1st Marines astride the road and Murray's 5th Marines to the left, with the Korean Marine regiment remaining behind in Inchon to mop up.

On 17 September MacArthur, accompanied by a swarm of correspondents, came ashore to visit the battlefield. On the Inchon-Seoul road he was shown the still-smoking hulls of a column of North Korean T-34 tanks that had counter-attacked at dawn. MacArthur presented Silver Stars to Craig, Puller, and Murray, and told General Smith that the 7th Infantry Division would begin landing the next day, coming in on the Marines' right flank.

That same day, 17 September, Murray's 5th Marines took the critically needed Kimpo airfield. Three days later, Taplett's battalion led the way across the Han in amphibious tractors. The 1st Marines followed the 5th Marines across the river. Then the 7th Marines, including the Mediterranean battalion, which had sailed through the Suez Canal, arrived in time to join the battle. There was heavy fighting in the city, but by 27 September it was secured. Two days later, President Syngman Rhee, escorted by MacArthur, made a triumphal re-entry into his capital. MacArthur's target date of 26 September had been missed by only three days.

The victory was everything that MacArthur had predicted. The resurgent Eighth Army burst out of the Pusan Perimeter and the shattered elements of the North Korean People's Army were sent reeling northward whence they came. MacArthur had every reason to regard Inchon, as he did, as his strategic masterpiece, and once again the 1st Marine Division had carried out his plan to the letter.

THE AUTHOR Edwin H. Simmons is a retired brigadier-general of the US Marine Corps and a widely published military historian. He was present at the Inchon landing as CO, Weapons Company, 3rd Battalion, 1st Marine Regiment.

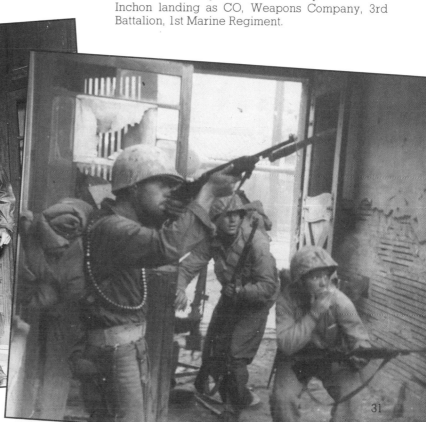

ST GEORGE FOR ENGLAND

The inland port of Brugge
became Germany's main
U-boat base on the North
Sea following the
occupation of Belgium in
1914. Brugge is connected to
the sea by two canals which
open at Zeebrugge and
Ostend, and in 1918 the
British Admiralty mounted a
daring operation to
incapacitate the port by
blocking the entrances to
the canals. Five old cruisers,
filled with cement, were to
be manoeuvred into the
entrances and sunk by the
detonation of charges in
their hulls.

The canal entrance at
Ostend was to be sealed by
the blockships *Sirius* and
Brilliant. The main
objective, however, was the
canal at Zeebrugge, and the
assault posed many
difficulties. Lying in a
northeasterly arc ahead of
the entrance was a great
mole, one and a half miles in
length and 81ft wide, with a
seaward wall 16ft high. Any
ship rounding the mole
would face point-blank fire
from a fearsome array of
naval guns, shore batteries
and machine-gun nests.

To begin the attack on
Zeebrugge, two monitors,
Erebus and *Terror*, were to
open fire on the port. A
flotilla of motor launches
and coastal motorboats
would lead in the raiding
force, laying a smoke-
screen off the mole. Landing
parties were to be inserted
onto the mole to attack the
defences from the
converted cruiser
Vindictive and two
Merseyside ferries, *Daffodil*
and *Iris*, escorted by the
battleship *Warwick* and two
smaller ships. Two
submarines would then be
towed in and exploded
under the viaduct linking
the mole with the mainland,
to cut off reinforcements.
Finally, benefiting from the
diversions that were to
precede them, the three
blockships *Thetis*,
Iphigenia and *Intrepid*
were to fight their way to the
canal entrance and blow
their charges.

In April 1918 the 4th Battalion of the Royal Marines sailed with the Dover Patrol in a daring bid to block the Brugge canal at Zeebrugge

'ST GEORGE for England.' So ran Admiral Sir Roger Keyes' signal to the Fleet, a signal that was to become as famous as Nelson's at Trafalgar over 100 years before. 'May we give the dragon's tail a damn good twist,' was HMS *Vindictive's* response. It was just after dusk on Monday, 22 April 1918. The weather report was by no means ideal, but it did promise some bright moonlight during the night as the strong northerly wind drove the scudding clouds along the line of the Belgian coast. The tides had not been right since the abortive attempt to attack Zeebrugge Mole on 11 April, when the wind had changed unexpectedly, forcing Keyes to take the crucial last-minute decision to postpone the operation.

On the mess decks of *Vindictive*, Royal Marines of the 4th Battalion, specially raised for this operation at their depot in Deal, prepared for the ordeal ahead. Intelligence sources had shown that the mole at Zeebrugge, some 1840yds long, was heavily defended with guns. It was to be the job of the Seamen Landing Parties and the Royal Marines to neutralise as many of these as possible in the short time they were to be ashore. This would enable the blockships *Intrepid*, *Iphigenia* and *Thetis* to be sunk in the entrance to the canal, in addition to a submarine to be blown up near the causeway, thus denying the use of the port to German U-boats marauding into the North Sea and the Atlantic.

Not until the Fleet had sailed from England on 6 April were the Royal Marines told where they were going, such was the secrecy maintained. They had practised on Kingsdown,

near Deal, where the shape of the mole had been marked out, attacking it from every angle by day and night. But few, if any, had guessed its true location as they had been told it was a fortified post just behind the enemy lines in France. But now, in the cramped spaces between decks, a clay model of the mole was produced along with some aerial photographs and the officers carefully explained the plan. The 4th Battalion consisted of Royal Marine Light Infantry (RMLI) companies from Chatham (A), Portsmouth (B), and Plymouth (C). There were also men of the Royal Marine Artillery (RMA) in the Trench Mortar and Machine Gun Sections. Lots had been drawn to see which company should lead the assault and C Company from Plymouth had drawn the honour. In its ranks was Sergeant Harry Wright of No. 10 Platoon. The days of waiting had seemed interminable during the three weeks at sea and it had been one of his responsibilities to keep the men occupied and their morale high.

The marines, somewhat apprehensive after being at sea for so long, were nervously joking on the mess decks, some even attempting to play cards, but their minds were not entirely on their games. Many were deep in thought, remembering the families they had left behind who knew nothing of their whereabouts nor of the terrible dangers that awaited them.

At about 2230 the order was passed to fall in on the upper deck. The marines gathered up their weapons and kit. Each of the leading platoons was equipped with two ladders, and ropes, knotted at intervals with a hook at the end, were to be used to negotiate the 20ft drop from the top of the mole wall. The marines had been ordered to remove the steel plates from the toes

Far left: Great numbers of volunteers put themselves forward for 'hazardous service' prior to the Zeebrugge raid. Here, volunteers from *King George V* await selection. Far left, inset above: Special landing gangways were constructed on *Vindictive* to get the landing parties quickly onto Zeebrugge Mole. Far left, inset below: The blockships *Iphigenia* and *Brilliant* set sail. Above: Captain Edward Bamford, commander of B Company of the 4th Battalion, who was awarded the Victoria Cross after the raid. Below: Showing the scars of her duel with the shore batteries, the battered converted cruiser *Vindictive*. Sandbags have been laid around many of the battle stations to give extra protection.

and heels of their boots so they would not slip on the concrete when landing. Other companies wore soft-soled shoes or sea service boots. Wright led his men up the darkened ladders to the starboard waist where specially prepared landing ramps had been rigged to enable the assault force to get ashore as soon as the ship berthed alongside the mole. The sea was beginning to get rough, and they were conscious that *Vindictive* was moving very slowly. Ahead of them they could just make out the silhouettes of the vessels laying a smoke-screen to cover their approach. No lights were showing and the men spoke in whispers. The marines stood in silence, shoulder to shoulder, packed tight in five ranks, scarcely daring to breathe. Only the thrumming of the propellers could be heard. Lieutenant R.G. Stanton stood in front of No. 10 Platoon, while Wright waited to the rear in the shelter of one of *Vindictive's* cutters.

Withering enemy fire swept the upper deck as the ship slowly edged her way towards the mole

Suddenly, a starshell floated over the ship, lighting everything as though it were day. No sooner had it died down than another took its place. Then another. One young marine asked if they were their own, but Wright's previous experience told him 'no'. The eerie silence was suddenly broken by a terrible crash as an enemy shell tore into the rigging above, where machine gunners of the Royal Marine Artillery had taken up station. Then all hell was let loose. Shells screamed over them, fragments cascading down on deck, killing or wounding many of the men waiting there. Just as suddenly, the wind changed direction, blowing the smoke-screen away to the south. They could see the mole clearly, barely 200yds away on the port quarter. The waiting Royal Marines felt as naked as the day they were born. Withering enemy fire swept the upper deck as the ship slowly edged her way towards the mole. Captain A.F.B. Carpenter, RN, cool and seemingly unconcerned as the shells rained down upon him, concentrated on the task of bringing his ship alongside as quickly as possible. The marines were stunned to learn that one of the first enemy shells had killed their commanding officer, Lieutenant-Colonel B.N. Elliot, who had won a DSO in Serbia, and his second-in-command, Major A.A. Cordner. The Portsmouth marines of B Company had been reasonably protected by breast-high, splinter-proof mattresses on the port side, but C Company in the starboard waist had taken a terrible toll. About 30 of them had been hit by shell fragments and many were mortally wounded. Lieutenant Stanton lay dying,

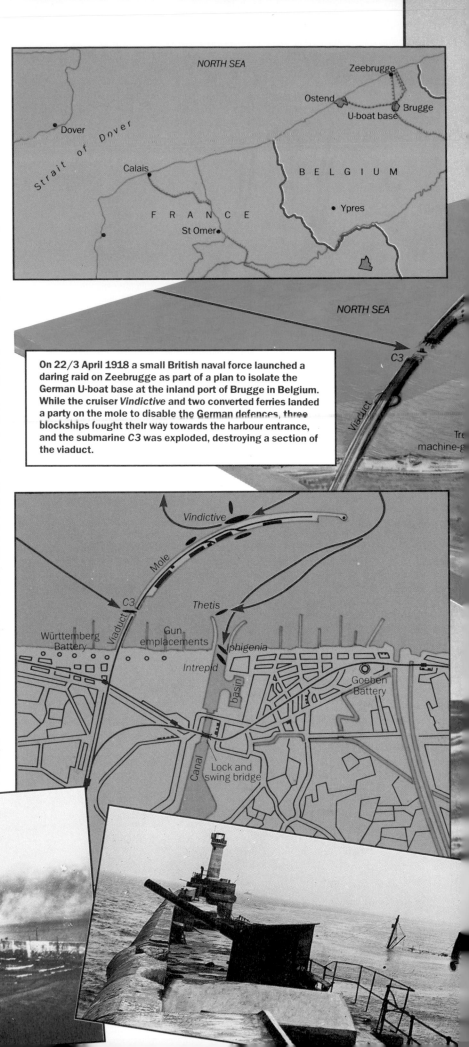

On 22/3 April 1918 a small British naval force launched a daring raid on Zeebrugge as part of a plan to isolate the German U-boat base at the inland port of Brugge in Belgium. While the cruiser *Vindictive* and two converted ferries landed a party on the mole to disable the German defences, three blockships fought their way towards the harbour entrance, and the submarine *C3* was exploded, destroying a section of the viaduct.

Zeebrugge raid
22-23 April 1918

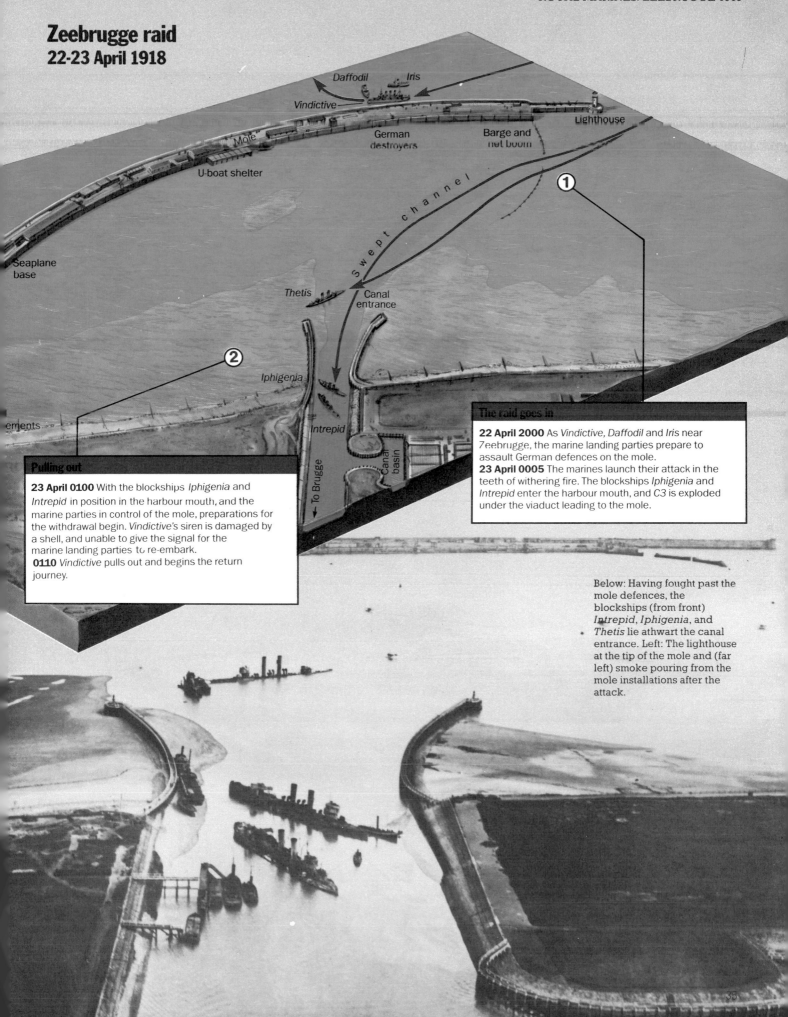

Daffodil
Iris
Vindictive
Lighthouse
Mole
German
destroyers
Barge and
net boom
U-boat shelter
Seaplane
base
S w e p t   c h a n n e l
Thetis
Canal
entrance
Iphigenia
emjents
Intrepid
Canal
basin
To Brugge

1

The raid goes in

22 April 2000 As *Vindictive*, *Daffodil* and *Iris* near Zeebrugge, the marine landing parties prepare to assault German defences on the mole.

23 April 0005 The marines launch their attack in the teeth of withering fire. The blockships *Iphigenia* and *Intrepid* enter the harbour mouth, and *C3* is exploded under the viaduct leading to the mole.

2

Pulling out

23 April 0100 With the blockships *Iphigenia* and *Intrepid* in position in the harbour mouth, and the marine parties in control of the mole, preparations for the withdrawal begin. *Vindictive*'s siren is damaged by a shell, and unable to give the signal for the marine landing parties to re-embark.

0110 *Vindictive* pulls out and begins the return journey.

Below: Having fought past the mole defences, the blockships (from front) *Intrepid*, *Iphigenia*, and *Thetis* lie athwart the canal entrance. Left: The lighthouse at the tip of the mole and (far left) smoke pouring from the mole installations after the attack.

Below: The men aboard the Mersey ferryboat *Iris* suffered heavy casualties in the assault: 77 officers and men were killed and 105 wounded as she steamed past the coastal batteries. Bottom left: Four men who participated in the raid, wounded but alive to tell the tale. Many were not so fortunate: 188 officers and men died on the raid, 384 were wounded and 16 went missing. Bottom right: A Royal Marine poses in a hole in the shell-blasted upper deck of *Vindictive*. Below right: The jubilant crew and fighting complement of *Vindictive* after the raid. With his arm in a sling is Captain A.F.B. Carpenter, who was elected by ballot to receive the VC, and on his left is Commander E. Osborne, the gunnery officer who directed *Vindictive's* guns against the shore batteries.

Sergeant Wright, at the rear, who had been protected from this devastation by the cutter, knelt beside the young officer. Stanton's final words were 'Carry on, Wright,' and he died in the sergeant's arms.

Sergeant Wright hastily took charge; and as the specially constructed ramps were lowered only moments later, he led the remnants of No.9 and 10 Platoons onto the mole. The time was a few minutes after midnight, but Wright and his men were now oblivious to the fact that this was St George's Day. Only two of the gangways had survived the enemy shells and as they struck the mole the landing parties scuttled across to its concrete walkway, which was also being swept by machine-gun fire. More marines fell in their tracks, but Wright shouted to his men to drop their ladders over the higher edge of the mole on the seaward side to get down to the lower, inner part of the mole, and they all quickly slithered down the 20ft ropes and across the road on the massive stone pier into the shelter of its No.3 shed. Wright saw four or five Germans run into the road to throw hand grenades at them, but the marines were not hit. In return they mowed down the enemy, none of whom survived. When Wright mustered his platoon, he found that only 12 of the original 45 remained. The Royal Marines, anxious to avenge their fallen comrades lying dead and wounded on the deck of *Vindictive*, charged the nearest enemy positions, their long bayonets glinting in the brightness of the starshell illumination. They were to find that their prey had retreated into one of the mole's many recently constructed concrete bunkers.

The noise and dust were overwhelming, but Wright took out his Very pistol and fired a red flare

into the sky to let those following know that he had reached and taken his first objective. The *Iris*, a converted ferry boat, which had gallantly pushed *Vindictive* into position alongside the mole, now came alongside herself. She had taken a terrible battering and all the Royal Marine officers except Lieutenant D. Broadwood had been killed or wounded, along with 50 marines of Chatham Company. Some of the Seamen Landing Party had survived. They stormed ashore and joined up with the marines of No.9 and 10 Platoons. About 75yds along the mole ahead of them was their main target, a 5in gun battery. Wing Commander F.A. Brock, RN, (of the former Royal Naval Air Service) the son of the famous fireworks inventor, was one who survived. He had been responsible for inventing and providing the expertise on illuminations, flame-throwers, fog-screens and pyrotechnics for the operation, but had no military command role. He landed with the blue-jacket (Seamen Landing Party) survivors and proceeded to lead them in a brave but futile frontal assault against an enemy blockhouse. He was last seen charging through the smoke and rubble.

Meanwhile, the Germans had failed to extinguish the lighthouse on the end of the mole, and this gave the blockships a leading mark. Ponderously, they forged ahead into the canal entrance, *Intrepid* and *Iphigenia* leading. Suddenly, a tremendous explosion rent the air, causing a shiver to go down the length of the mole. The submarine *C3*, commanded by Lieutenant Richard Sandford, RN, had rammed the viaduct which connected the mole to the mainland. Sandford, after seeing his crew safely into their motor boat, lit the fuses and jumped for it. To their horror, the boat's propeller had broken and they could do nothing but row for it, with seconds running out before the explosion. In the nick of time, Sandford's brother Francis came alongside them in a picket boat and took them off. As they shot away they had the satisfaction of seeing their target disintegrate before their very eyes.

Sergeant Wright looked anxiously at his watch, reckoning that the recall signal should have been made. It was still not 0100 hours and they had been ashore for only about 55 minutes. Unknown to him, the *Vindictive's* siren had been put out of action by a direct hit, so the expected series of short blasts did not come. There was so much noise and smoke that it was difficult to discern anything or anybody other than those marines still left alive near him. Although he heard a series of short and long blasts on another ship's siren, Wright did not realise they were the recall signal, and he hung on to his position.

Another 10 minutes or so passed with little or no action in their area, although the sound of gunfire and whistling shells was ever present. In the dark a young voice called out and he recognised it as a hoarse version of that of one of his own marines: 'Sarg, the *Vindictive* is shoving off!' He moved quickly across the mole and there, to his horror and dismay,

THE U-BOAT MENACE

The Battle of Jutland in 1916 marked the last major attempt by the German High Seas Fleet to destroy the Allied blockade of Germany using surface ships. From that time, increased emphasis was given to U-boat production, and by January 1917 111 U-boats were operating in the Atlantic.

Their successes were limited at first by the restrictions which had been in force since the controversial sinking of the *Lusitania* in May 1915, but on 9 January 1917 the Kaiser ordered that from 1 February the unrestricted U-boat campaign should be re-opened. The results were dramatic, and the early months of 1917 saw unprecedented losses of Allied merchant shipping. In February 540,000 tons were sent to the bottom; in March 590,000 tons; and in April the month's total rose to a staggering 881,000 tons of shipping sunk. Had the losses continued at such a level, it is doubtful that Britain could have persevered with the war.

The heart of the Allied problem was that the widely dispersed merchant ships, straggling across the Atlantic in small groups, could be detected and attacked by submarines without fear of reprisal from nearby warships. In May 1917 Lloyd George insisted that merchantmen should sail in convoy under armed escort, and the effect was immediate. The Allies lost 169 ships in April; July's losses were 99 ships, and in November only 65 ships were sunk.

Such losses were still unacceptable, however, and in 1918 the Admiralty began making plans to paralyse Germany's largest U-boat base, the Belgian port of Brugge.

HERO OF THE FORE TOP

The 1½-pounders and Lewis machine guns of *Vindictive's* 'fighting fore top' (right) provided valuable support for the fighting parties on Zeebrugge Mole. When a heavy shell practically destroyed the top, killing most of the guncrews, Sergeant Norman Finch (far right) continued to fire single-handed until he collapsed from wounds. He was subsequently elected by ballot to receive the VC by his fellow Royal Marines.

he saw their only means of escape slowly disappearing into the night. The ship had gone, believing that all those alive had been recalled and had embarked; there was nothing Wright could do. It seemed a cruel fate for those who had come through this terrible ordeal almost unscathed that they should now find themselves not only abandoned but also being shelled by their own withdrawing ships. Naval shells were now falling fast onto the mole as Wright peered into the gloom, hoping that someone had realised they were missing and had sent in a motor boat to take them off. In his heart he knew it was wishful thinking. He ordered his remaining marines to cross the mole, take off their life-jackets and lie still in the shadows. For more than two hours they lay there pretending to be dead. The unlucky remnants of No. 10 Platoon, together with a signals sergeant and an able seaman, had the mole to themselves. The noise of the ships and firing had now receded, although the occasional starshell still floated over them.

When one of them moved, the startled Germans jumped back as though they had seen a ghost

Sergeant Wright made his plans, first to escape down and off the mole, and then to lay up during the next day. Surely someone would realise they were missing and send a boat for them. But his plans were thwarted when a party of Germans was heard approaching. 'Let's 'ave a bash at the buggers, Sarg,' said a voice to his right, 'They'll kill us whatever happens.' But discretion and common sense prevailed when Wright saw the size of the enemy party. The marines lay still, even when the Germans shone torches on their stiffened faces. Taking them for dead, the Germans moved on, but half an hour later they returned with more men and started to search the 'dead' bodies. When one of them moved, the startled Germans jumped back as though they had

seen a ghost. They shouted at the British marines to put their hands up and, after threatening them with their bayonets, took them as prisoners of war.

But many had not been so lucky in the hour-long engagement. The 4th Battalion had lost eight officers and 96 marines killed, while a further 206 were wounded, nearly half the original battalion strength. During this raid and a simultaneous attack on Ostend, eight Victoria Crosses were won, two of them going to Royal Marines by ballot. Under the provisions of the Ninth Statute of the Royal Warrant dated 29 January 1856, it was laid down that the VC could be awarded to individuals by secretly balloting those who had taken part in the action. The results clearly showed that Captain Edward Bamford, RMLI, who had already won the DSO at Jutland in 1916, and had commanded B Company at Zeebrugge, and Sergeant Norman Finch, RMA, who had been second-in-command of the Bofors and Lewis gun crews in the foretop of the *Vindictive*, should be awarded the two Victoria Crosses allocated to the Royal Marines. Their medals are in the Royal Marines Museum at Eastney, Southsea, lying beside the Corps' eight other Victoria Crosses.

It was also decided that, in memory of their gallant exploit at Zeebrugge, no other unit of the Royal Marines should ever bear the title of 4th Battalion, Royal Marines, a name that would remain for ever as their lasting memorial. Since that time, the date of 23 April, St George's Day, has been celebrated as a Corps Memorable Date, and an annual service is still held on Merseyside. The ferry *Royal Iris*, which bears the memorial plaque from her predecessor, puts to sea and wreaths are strewn on the waters, remembering the dead of that terrible night.

THE AUTHOR Captain Derek Oakley, MBE, served with the Royal Marine Commandos in Malaya, Hong Kong, the Middle East, Northern Ireland, Brunei and Borneo. He is now the editor of *The Globe and Laurel*, the journal of the Royal Marines.

Below: Accidentally abandoned to their fate by *Vindictive*, a total of 12 Royal Marines of the 4th Battalion's C (Plymouth) Company, with a signals sergeant and an able seaman, were taken prisoner before they could make their escape from Zeebrugge Mole. Of the 86 officers and 1698 men who sailed to Zeebrugge, about 750 were drawn from the Royal Marines. Most of the other fighting elements had come forward from the Royal Naval Reserve and the Royal Naval Volunteer Reserve.

TAKING THE
PUNCHBOWL

Following the 1st Marine Division's successful landing at Inchon on 15 September 1950 and re-capture of Seoul, the marines were transported to Wonsan on the Korean east coast, from where they moved northward until ordered to the northwest by General MacArthur on 24 November. It was MacArthur's plan to trap the remnants of the North Korean People's Army (NKPA) between X Corps, of which the 1st Marine Division was a part, and the Eighth Army, which was advancing to their west. On 25 November the picture changed completely – many thousands of Chinese 'People's Volunteers' entered the war in support of the NKPA. The huge wave of infantry caught the 1st Marine Division at the Chosin Reservoir, and the vastly outnumbered marines were forced into a fighting withdrawal to the evacuation port of Hungnam, 60 miles to the south through rugged mountains. By 31 December the UN forces were back to the south of the 38th parallel. In January 1951 the United Nations had 365,000 men ranged against 500,000 communist infantry with a million reserves at their back. The UN forces were ordered to inflict high casualties and then fall back to well prepared defences, and this tactic worked well against communist attacks that began on 1 January 1951.

Following General Ridgway's Operations Killer and Ripper, the Chinese began their first spring offensive on 22 April. By the 29th the UN forces were thrown back to the No-Name Line, lying between Seoul and Taepori, where they sustained the second communist spring offensive on 15 May. After five days, the communist effort ground to a halt and General Van Fleet ordered his troops to deploy 'in hot pursuit of the enemy'.

When the 1st Marine Division struck towards North Korea in August 1951, the way was barred by the heavily defended northern rim of a volcanic crater – the Punchbowl

THE DEFEAT of the second communist spring offensive in Korea, which ended on 20 May 1951, was followed by an intense counter-attack to the north of Hong-chon as the US Marines and the 5th and 7th Republic of Korea (ROK) Divisions advanced through mountains towards 'the Punchbowl', a volcanic crater lying about 25 miles north of Inje. Colonel Wilburt S. 'Bigfoot' Brown, commanding the 1st Marine Regiment, said of his 2nd Battalion: 'In the last analysis 2/1 had to take its objective with the bayonet and hand grenades, crawling up the side of a mountain to get at the enemy. It was bloody work, the hardest fighting I have ever seen.' And this was from a marine whose own combat experience stretched back to 1918!

When a ceasefire was proposed on 23 June, the 1st Marine Division occupied hard-won positions on the Kansas Line. Negotiations were begun on 10 July between the United Nations and the communist forces, and five days later the Marines were relieved and sent into reserve for replacements and re-training. But on 22 August the communists walked out, alleging that the Americans had violated the neutrality of Kaesong, the town lying behind communist lines where the talks had been taking place, by dropping napalm in the vicinity.

Four days later, the 1st Marine Division was ordered back to the front. Major-General Gerald C. Thomas, an exceptional officer who had served with the 6th Marines at Belleau Wood in 1918 and was the 1st Marine Division's operations officer at Guadalcanal, was in command. To a large extent his was a new 1st Division, for the veterans of the Pusan Perimeter, Inchon, the Chosin Reservoir and the spring fighting had been thinned out almost to vanishing point by casualties and rotation.

The division's objectives were too complex, strongly defended ridges just north of the Punchbowl. The 7th Marine Regiment and the Korean Marine Corps (KMC) Regiment started forward in a downpour on 27 August. The 5th Marine Regiment was to follow the 7th up the narrow Soyang valley, while the 1st Marine Regiment was to remain near Hongchon in X Corps reserve. The motor march to the forward assembly areas should have taken only five hours, but summer rains had dissolved the roads and several were blocked by landslides.

Typical was the experience of the 3rd Battalion, 7th Marines. They struck their tents, ready for an early morning departure. The trucks that were to take them did not arrive. They sat in the rain, ate a hot meal at noon, then a cold C-ration supper. The trucks finally drove up at 2100 hours. The convoy crawled forward over bad roads and through the jumble of

Page 39 : A member of the 1st Marine Division ducks down as a North Korean People's Army (NKPA) bunker is obliterated by a satchel charge. Left, above: Snow melts on the hillsides as American tanks and infantry advance on Hongchong in early 1951. Left, below: Marines carrying M1 rifles and carbines on the move following Major-General Thomas' order to advance north in late August 1951. Below: Troops pass through the beginnings of an advance base towards the complex of hills around 'the Punchbowl'.

traffic until 0330 on the 28th, when the battalion arrived at a bivouac area a foot deep in water. Lieutenant-Colonel Bernard T. Kelly, the battalion commander, ordered his men to stay in the trucks. Not until the afternoon of the 29th did they get to their assembly area on the far side of the rain-swollen Soyang river. They then moved up to relieve an element of the 8th ROK Division. Getting into position on Hill 000, they were greeted by 200 rounds of mortar and artillery fire.

The zone of action assigned to the 1st Marine Division was as forbidding a piece of terrain as could be found in Korea. A new line – the Hays Line – had been drawn across the map marking the northern edge of the Punchbowl. It was dominated by Yoke Ridge, the high points of which were Hills 930, 1000, 1026 and 924. Defending the ridge, according to the Division G-2, was the 6th Regiment, 2nd Division, II North Korean People's Army (NKPA) Corps. Aerial reconnaissance indicated the southward movement of reinforcements in the form of two or three more enemy regiments, and prisoners indicated that a major communist offensive was to begin on 1 September.

The 1st Marine Division had one day to beat the North Koreans to the punch. The 7th Marines, under Colonel Herman 'Herman the German' Nickerson, and the 1st KMC Regiment, under Colonel Kim Tai Shik, were ordered to attack at 0600 on 31 August. The 5th Marines were to protect their rear and patrol the division zone along the Kansas Line.

On the morning of the 31st, the 1st and 3rd KMC Battalions jumped off in column against moderate resistance, with Hill 924 as their first objective. Mines

CLOSE AIR SUPPORT

Vital to the Marine Corps' way of fighting is its own integral close air support. In the attacks at the Punchbowl, for example, the 1st Marine Division's artillery, 54 105mm and 18 155mm howitzers, was out-gunned or at least matched by an estimated 92 enemy field pieces, mostly 76mm, 105mm and 122mm weapons. According to Marine Corps doctrinal thinking, therefore, it was Marine Corps close air support that should have given the marines the edge they needed. That this was not adequately provided was due to a long-standing conflict of tactical approach between the Marine Corps and the US Air Force.

To support the division more effectively, the 1st Marine Aircraft Wing had moved two squadrons of F-4U Corsairs to K-18, an airfield on the east coast less than 50 miles behind the division's zone of action. But the 1st Marine Aircraft Wing was under the operational control of the Fifth Air Force, and the Fifth Air Force, following US Air Force doctrine of isolating the battlefield, sent off a good measure of the marines' aircraft on deep interdiction missions. Few of the Corsairs were made available to the division. During the 18-day fight for the Punchbowl, General Thomas' forward air controllers requested air strikes 182 times. Some 127 of these requests were honoured, but in only 24 cases did the aircraft arrive in time to make a difference to the battle. Thomas bitterly reported that many of the 1621 casualties suffered by his division in September 1951 were the direct consequence of inadequate close air support. It was a doctrinal fight that would continue throughout the Korean War and on into Vietnam.

Right: South Korean 'cargadores' carry supplies up to a Marine regiment's positions in central Korea. Centre right: A wounded marine is lifted from an HTL-4. He will receive emergency surgery in the advance camp before being sent on to the rear area. Far right: Marine artillerymen pound the NKPA.

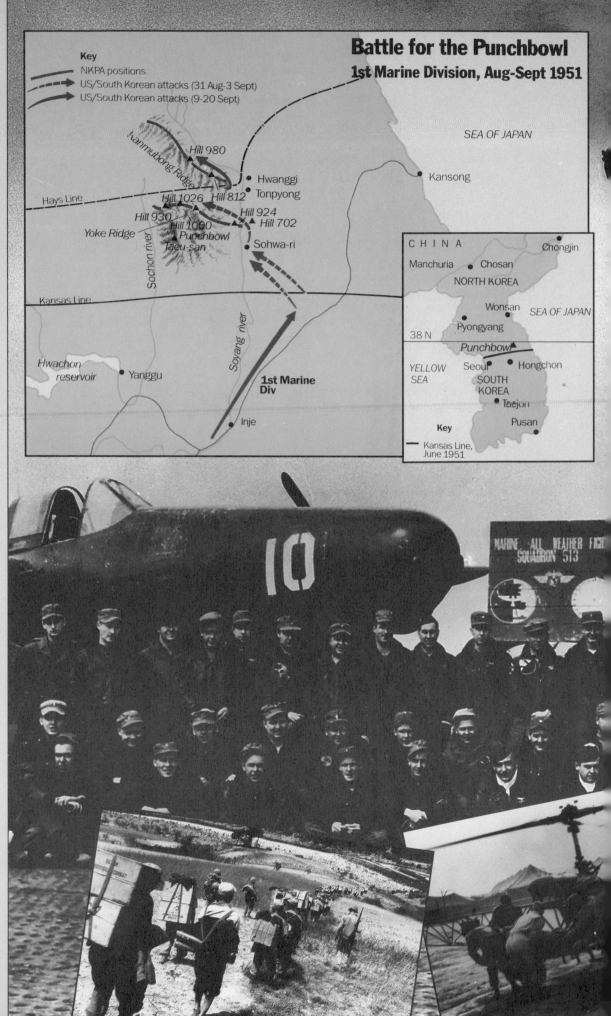

Battle for the Punchbowl
1st Marine Division, Aug-Sept 1951

Key
NKPA positions
US/South Korean attacks (31 Aug-3 Sept)
US/South Korean attacks (9-20 Sept)

Hanmubong Ridge
Hill 980
Hwanggi
Tonpyong
Hays Line
Hill 1026   Hill 812
Hill 930   Hill 924
Hill 1000   Hill 702
Yoke Ridge
Punchbowl
Taeu-san
Sohwa-ri
Sochon river
Kansas Line
Soyang river
1st Marine Div
Hwachon reservoir
Yanggu
Inje

SEA OF JAPAN
Kansong

CHINA
Manchuria   Chosan   Chongjin
NORTH KOREA
Wonsan   SEA OF JAPAN
Pyongyang
38 N
Punchbowl
YELLOW SEA   Seoul   Hongchon
SOUTH KOREA
Taejon
Pusan

Key
Kansas Line, June 1951

MARINE ALL WEATHER FIGHTER SQUADRON 513

gave them more trouble than enemy fire – both enemy mines and 'friendly' mines left behind by former occupants of the lines. Kelly's 3rd Battalion, 7th Marines, on the right of the KMC advance, moved up the slopes of Hill 702, which also turned out to be heavily mined, and received intermittent mortar and artillery fire. All three assault battalions were still 1000yds short of their initial objectives when the approach of night brought their forward movement to a halt.

They jumped off again the next morning, the 3rd KMC Battalion moving through the 3rd Battalion, 7th Marines, to take the ridgeline from the northeast, while the 1st KMC Battalion came in from the southeast. Pushing through a curtain of mortar and machine-gun fire and continuing to take casualties from mines, the South Korean Marines managed to get one company to within 200yds of the top of Hill 924 by nightfall. Their success was short-lived, for during the night the North Koreans drove them back off the hill.

On the morning of 2 September, the 2nd KMC Battalion came into the battle. It went forward behind a thunderous artillery preparation fired by five battalions of artillery, three of them US Army and two US Marine Corps. By dusk the fresh 2nd KMC Battalion was within half a mile of the crest of Hill 1026.

Throughout 1 September, Kelly's battalion had fought its own battle on Hill 702, holding out against four counter-attacks coming from Hill 602. Kelly, having brushed off a final dawn counter-attack, moved out two hours later and by noon on 2 September had taken Hill 602. The North Koreans showed their stubbornness by mounting three counter-attacks against him that afternoon.

Next day, 3 September, while Kelly dug in on Hill

Above: A Bell HTL-4 casevac helicopter. Its outriggers are adapted to carry stretcher cases. **Below:** A portrait of the aircrews and ground staff of VMF (N)-513 with two of their aircraft, a Grumman F7F-3N night-fighter (left) and an F4U Corsair.

602, Kim's Korean Marines pressed on towards the crest of Hill 1026. To narrow the KMC front, the 2nd Battalion, 7th Marines, was moved up to a sector that included Hill 924, and by mid-morning the KMC had taken Hill 1026. They fought off a counter-attack that afternoon and, as evening fell, the 1st Marine Division stood triumphant on the northern rim of the Punchbowl. The cost to the US and South Korean Marines had been 109 killed in action and 404 wounded.

The division then stayed in place for six days while it built up new reserves of ammunition. The front lines were 50 miles north of the base area at Hong-chon, creating considerable logistical difficulties. The two-lane road was good as far as Inje, but after that it petered out into a narrow trail of churned mud that twisted its way up the Soyang valley. On 1 September, 20 US Air Force transports, flying from Japan, dropped ammunition and rations to the KMC, but otherwise all supplies were carried by trains of Korean 'cargadores', 150 to 250 of them working for each battalion.

Nickerson's plan was to seize the eastern end of Kanmubong and then 'run the ridge'

The North Koreans were not idle during the six-day lull. Air recce again showed the movement of troops southwards and it was learnt from POWs that the 1st Division, III NKPA Corps, had come in to relieve the battered 2nd Division, II NKPA Corps.

At 0300 on the morning of 9 September, Nickerson's 7th Marines led off a new attack with two objectives, Hills 673 and 749. The 1st Marine Regiment, released from X Corps reserve, was to be prepared to pass through the 7th Marines and continue the attack against Hill 1052.

From their line of departure on Yoke Ridge, the 7th Marines had to descend into a narrow valley, cross a stream, and then climb Kanmubong Ridge. This ridge was dominated by Hills 812, 980, and 1052. Nickerson's plan was to seize the eastern end of Kanmubong and then 'run the ridge'. To get to that tip of Kanmubong, Lieutenant-Colonel B.T. Kelly's 3rd Battalion first had to take Hill 680, directly north of his position on Hill 602. Taking Hill 680 proved to be an all-day fight. Across the valley to the east, the 1st Battalion, 7th Marines, commanded by another Kelly, Lieutenant-Colonel James G. Kelly, found it equally heavy going against Hill 673.

Nickerson, with both of his assault battalions in trouble, ordered his reserve battalion – the 2nd Battalion under Lieutenant-Colonel Louis C. Griffin – to make a night march up the narrow valley lying between the two hills. When morning came on 12 September, Griffin hit the North Korean defences on the crest of Hill 673 from the rear while J. G. Kelly's battalion came storming up the other side of the hill. Griffin's battalion then faced around and took a section of Hill 749. B.T. Kelly's 3rd Battalion, on the other side of the valley, did equally well, getting to the crest of its objective by mid-morning.

There was still, however, a strong force of North Koreans occupying bunkers on Hill 749 and the ridgeline running from there to Hill 673, and their positions could not be bypassed. It was to take fresh troops to dig them out.

The 1st Marines, now commanded by Colonel Thomas J. Wornham, came up to relieve the 7th Marines on the night of 12/13 September. By daybreak his 3rd and 2nd Battalions had relieved

Nickerson's 3rd and 1st Battalions. The 2nd Battalion, under Lieutenant-Colonel Franklin B. 'Brooke' Nihart, had to fight its way forward to relieve the 2nd Battalion, 7th Marines, and complete the taking of Hill 749. In addition to the obstinacy of the North Koreans, there were problems with supply shortages, for the cargadores could not keep up with the drain of full-scale battle. Major David W. McFarland's VMO-6, with its handful of light Bell helicopters, was also having trouble handling the number of wounded coming off the hilltop positions. Fortunately, a Marine medium helicopter squadron, HMR-161 under Lieutenant-Colonel George W. Herring, had arrived on the last day of August with 15 Sikorsky HRS-1s. The HRS-1 could lift a 1420lb payload at sea level, and in terms of passengers this meant up to six combat-equipped marines or up to five casualties on litters.

The airlift took off late in the afternoon, Herring's helicopters twisting their way up the valley

On 10 September, HMR-161 moved up to share X-83 airstrip with VMO-6. On the 12th, after orientation flights, Herring reported his squadron ready for its first combat mission. He was ordered to lift a day's supplies to Nihart's battalion and to take out his casualties: on 13 September, Operation Windmill I got under way. The airlift took off late in the afternoon, Herring's helicopters twisting their way up the valley. Marine artillery masked the landing zone on Hill 673 with smoke and at 1610 hours the first HRS-1 released its cargo net. Herring flew a total of 28 flights in two and a half hours, delivering over seven tons of supplies, mostly ammunition, in what was the world's first helicopter re-supply mission. Seventy-four casualties were flown out.

Nihart's 2nd Battalion, 1st Marines, continued to be heavily engaged with North Koreans dug in on Hill 749. This stoppage in turn blocked the progress of Lieutenant-Colonel Foster C. 'Frosty' LaHue's 3rd Battalion, 1st Marines, on Nihart's left. Not until 2025 did Nihart's unit completely relieve the remaining two companies of Griffin's 2nd Battalion, 7th Marines, who had been holed up and waiting, not too patiently it can be assumed, on Hill 749.

Wornham's 1st Marines went forward the next morning with their 2nd and 3rd Battalions in the assault. Log bunkers had to be knocked out one by one. It was the end of the day before LaHue's battalion was on top of Hill 751, and Nihart's battalion, with heavy artillery support, was able to advance 300yds forward of Hill 749.

On the 16th, the 5th Marines, now commanded by

Colonel Richard C. Weede, was to pass through the 3rd Battalion, 1st Marines, which in turn was to relieve the 1st Battalion, 1st Marines. This last unit had not yet been in the fight and was now to pass through the 2nd Battalion to take the lateral ridge running west to Hill 812 – it was altogether a very complicated day's work. It came off as planned, but not without interruptions by the enemy.

A minute or so after midnight, 15/16 September, Nihart's 2nd Battalion was pounded by a North Korean artillery barrage of unprecedented intensity, followed by a four-hour attack by what was estimated to be an NKPA regiment. Nihart's line held and when morning came he was still on the hill.

The 1st Battalion, 1st Marines, under Lieutenant-Colonel John E. Gorman, passed through the thinned ranks of the 2nd Battalion at 0830, moved out along the lateral ridgeline, and, after a hard day's fighting, finally secured Hill 749 and its vicinity.

That ended the operation for the 1st Marines; it was now the turn of the 5th Marine Regiment. Its first objective was Hill 751. Lieutenant-Colonel Houston 'Tex' Stiff's 2nd Battalion had the main effort. The 3rd Battalion, under Lieutenant-Colonel Donald R. Kennedy, was to come around on Stiff's left, prepared to take Hill 980 on order. With delays in the reliefs, however, it was early afternoon before the attack began and not much ground was gained.

Tex Stiff (who had fought with the Edson's Raiders in World War II and had a bullet-stiffened wrist to show for it) moved out again early the next morning and caught the North Koreans at breakfast. Rapid progress was made at first along the ridgeline to Hill 812, then the battalion's leading edge ran into a heavy crossfire. An air strike was called but failed to materialise, so the lead company went on with the support of mortars and artillery. Stiff sent one company straight ahead and one on the flank and this secured him Hill 812. After barely a pause he continued on towards Hill 980. However, his regimental commander, Colonel Weede, ordered Stiff and Ken-

Background: In a terrain of blasted earth and burning scrub, Marine infantrymen press forward past a blasted communist bunker. The North Koreans and their Chinese allies rapidly built strongpoints and trench systems during the several ceasefires of the Korean War, as the UN forces learned to their cost.

Among the officers serving with the 1st Marine Division at the time of the Punchbowl assault were (bottom, from left to right): Colonel Herman 'Herman the German' Nickerson, CO of the 7th Marines; Brigadier-General William J. Whaling, assistant division commander; Major-General Gerald C. Thomas, commanding general; Colonel Victor H. Krulak, chief of staff; Colonel Thomas A. Wornham, successor of Colonel Wilbert S. 'Bigfoot' Brown as CO of the 1st Marines; and Colonel Richard G. Weede, CO of the 5th Marines.

nedy to hold where they were as it was thought that Hill 980, if taken, would be untenable while the NKPA still held Hill 1052.

For several days enemy fire from Hills 980 and 1052 continued to bother Stiff's battalion. He had too few supplies to dig in properly and this set Operation Windmill II into motion. On 18 September, 10 of Herring's HRC 1s brought in five tons of sand-bags, barbed wire and mines, but these did not prevent Stiff's battalion from taking heavy casualties on 19 September. On that day, Lieutenant-Colonel William P. Alston's 1st Battalion, 5th Marines, moved up on Stiff's right flank, giving the division a fairly solid defensive line that extended two miles eastward almost to the Soyang river. The North Koreans tried to oust Stiff from Hill 812 before dawn on the 20th, gaining some ground before losing it again to the Americans. This action marked the last episode in the Marines' battles for the Punchbowl.

After three weeks of unceasing combat, the 1st Marine Division was holding a broad front. The 1st KMC Regiment, on the left flank, was patrolling vigorously to the north. The 5th Marine Regiment was holding a wide sector in the centre of the line. The 1st Marine Regiment lay to the east, extending to the corps' boundary, while the 7th Marine Regiment was in reserve at Wontong-ni.

General Van Fleet had visited the X Corps front on 16 September to see for himself the condition of the 1st Marine Division and the 2nd Infantry Division, which had been fighting to the west on Bloody Ridge. He was satisfied with their morale and had no adverse criticism of their operations. Nevertheless, he ordered 'that the Corps Commander firm up his line by 20 September and to plan no further offensives after that date.'

All across the front the United Nations offensive had been successful. By mid-October the communists were back at the conference table, and while they worked to win there what they could not win on the battlefield, a static, stalemated war of position began, similar to the entrenched warfare of World War I. The war of manoeuvre had ended for the Marines. For the 1st Marine Division, the next major fight was not to occur until nearly a year later, when units of the division would go against Hill 122, a fortified Chinese position better known as 'Bunker Hill'.

THE AUTHOR Edwin H. Simmons is a retired brigadier-general of the US Marine Corps and a widely published military historian. He was present during the 1st Marine Division's advance to the Punchbowl as CO, Weapons Company, 3rd Battalion, 1st Marines. He was slightly wounded on 2 June 1951 and returned to the US shortly afterwards.

BATTLE FOR COMACCHIO

In April 1945, the Royal Marine Commandos were tasked with the destruction of strong enemy positions on the shores of Lake Comacchio

AS THE COMMANDOS assembled on the southern shore of Lake Comacchio at midnight, 1/2 April 1945, their sounds were drowned by multiple loudspeakers playing Wagner's *Ride of the Valkyrie* fortissimo into the cold night air. Every night for the past week the music had blared forth, masking the reconnaissance patrols operating beyond the Reno river. Now vehicles were approaching the muddy shoreline, carrying sections of commandos and the amphibious, tracked 'Fantails' which would take them to the enemy. The transports were becoming bogged down in the treacherous mud and the Fantails were being manhandled by cursing commandos through 1500yds of stinking, glutinous silt to the channels beyond, where they could be floated. It was 0430 hours before the men were aboard and ready to move. Dawn was not far off, but Brigadier Ronnie

Tod decided to go ahead.

Briefing of the men had been completed only hours before, but now the four Commandos of 2 Commando Brigade were ready at their start-lines. The Royal Marine Commandos were to attack up the length of the spit that divided Lake Comacchio from the Adriatic, No.43(RM) Commando moving up the eastern side and over the tongue of sand separating the Reno estuary from the sea, while No.40(RM) Commando held the southern end of the spit, creating diversions and acting as a reserve. Information collected on reconnaissance sorties had been organised by the Intelligence Staff and each of the strongpoints manned by the Turkoman Division on the spit had been allotted a Biblical name. No.2 and 9 Army Commandos were to mount an amphibious assault on the enemy positions named 'Ezra', 'Isaiah I', 'Isaiah II', and 'Leviticus', situated some two miles north of the Reno on the western side of the spit.

At 0430 the preliminary bombardment began; rockets and artillery opened up from the rear, smoke-bombs blossomed, and diversionary mortar and machine-gun fire ripped out. At 0500 A and B Troops of No.43 Commando moved out of cover and began their advance on 'Joshua'. Soon enemy mortar and machine-gun fire burst among them, forcing them down. Then B Troop swept in a long, triumphant rush into the strongpoint and began mopping up. It was quickly joined by D Troop, while A Troop

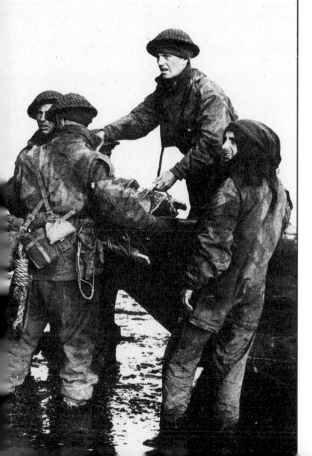

Left: Members of No.2 Commando wait for action in the chill winds blowing over Lake Comacchio. The following night they moved up to the shoreline to begin preparations for their amphibious assault over the lake. Below: The Heavy Weapons Troop of No.40 (RM) Commando unloads the storm boats that were used a week later to capture the western shore of Lake Comacchio. Below left: Lieutenant-Colonel R.W. Sankey (seated with binoculars), commanding officer of No.40 (RM) Commando, discusses the operation with his signals adviser.

raced through and over the tongue of sand to 'Numbers' at the northern end. By 0738 the enemy had been cleared from the tongue.

Now C Troop came up with inflatable dinghies, passed through 'Joshua', and began crossing the Reno just to the north. Four men were killed and one badly wounded by fire from 'Acts' before they were across. Men from B and D Troops then formed a bridgehead and E Troop joined them. The commanding officer of No.43 Commando, Lieutenant-Colonel Ian Riches, initiated a perfectly timed and positioned smoke and artillery barrage from behind their starting-point, then launched the marine commandos out of the bridgehead on a swift assault on the 'Acts' position. It contained two anti-tank guns, an 88mm and an Italian 47/32, both well sited in scrub and protected by full infantry companies. The action was brief, violent, but surprisingly free of bloodshed, as the defenders were so astonished by the marines' speed that most became prisoners before they realised it.

Piat anti-tank grenade projectors were brought up to blow in the dug-outs and eventually the positions were destroyed

Now all attention turned to the main enemy positions along the north bank of the river, where it crossed the base of the spit. Machine guns had been sited in dug-outs hollowed out of the reverse side of the river bank, and minefields were everywhere. Half a mile from the nearest of the positions designated 'Hosea', the commandos were pinned down in the open. Piat anti-tank grenade projectors were brought up to blow in the dug-outs and gradually the positions were destroyed. B, D and E Troops were now formed into a compact force under Captain Gourlay, and eventually he gave the order which sent them together in a storming rush down the northwest bank, through 'Hosea I' and into 'Hosea II'.

While the men broke out their iron rations, news arrived that No.9 Commando had been held up at 'Leviticus'. The marine commandos immediately deployed to assist them: smoke and artillery fire was called up and the men pressed westwards. The greatest hazard was a complex of anti-personnel mines, for the defences were directed south across the river and No.43 Commando was driving in from the east. By mid-afternoon of 2 April all the positions on the north bank were in the marines' hands and casualties were being evacuated by No.40 Commando. Danger was ever-present, however, as there were numerous foxholes further inland occupied by snipers from one of the German Jäger regiments, and these had to be systematically cleared. E Troop also made a wide detour to capture 'Mark', which so far had had to contend only with the diversionary efforts of No.40 Commando.

Meanwhile, the army commandos carrying out their amphibious assault were gaining their objectives. No.9 Commando finally subdued 'Leviticus' and the positions just north, and No.2 Commando cleared the south bank of the Bellocchio canal, halfway up the spit. Of the two bridges over the canal, the western one had been blown up, but the other, codenamed 'Peter', was captured intact. As the men of No.43 Commando regrouped at dusk, many were showing the strain of battle. Faces were grey, and men who had lost friends, or had been shocked by near bomb blasts, sat staring abstractedly into the distance. However, most of them managed to gain

During the winter of 1944 the Allied campaign in Italy ground to a halt along a front just south of Bologna. Ammunition was short and the waterlogged ground allowed no decisive action by either side. In the spring of 1945, however, Field Marshal Sir Harold Alexander, C-in-C Allied forces in Italy, determined to mount an offensive in April which would finally break German resistance in Italy.

Alexander's plan called for a push northwestwards by the British Eighth Army to Ferrara, using the Argenta Gap, which lay between extensive floodlands to the west and the lagoons of Lake Comacchio on the eastern coast. At the same time, the US Fifth Army was to strike northwards to the west of Bologna. To weaken resistance in the Bologna area, a small British commando force was to strike first, at Lake Comacchio, drawing reserves away to the east. Before the Eighth Army could begin its advance, it was necessary to remove the threat posed to its right flank by enemy forces positioned around Lake Comacchio. The western and northern shores were defended by German units, while a long sand spit on the lake's coastal perimeter had numerous gun emplacements manned by the Turkoman Division. The task of seizing the lake for the Allies was given to 2 Commando Brigade. While two Army Commandos, No.2 and 9, were to strike at the western shore and the western side of the spit from assault boats, two Royal Marine Commandos, No.43 and 40(RM) (whose badge is shown above), supported by the 24th Guards Brigade, were to drive northwards over the spit, wiping out the Turkoman positions.

Comacchio
April 1945

In August 1944 the British Eighth Army and the US Fifth Army crossed the Gothic Line. The British made good progress initially but German resistance stiffened and it was not until 21 September that Rimini fell. The Eighth Army pushed north along the Adriatic coast and by mid-January Ravenna was in British hands. Further advance was blocked by the marshy expanse of Lake Comacchio.

The western and northern shores of the lake were held by German troops, and the sand spit on the seaward side was manned by a Turkoman division which held a series of strong blockhouses and mined defensive positions. An operation by 2 Commando Brigade was determined upon to seize the far shores of the lake and thus secure the right flank of the planned breakthrough by the Allied armies in the Argenta Gap. On 1 April 1945 the operation was launched: while the army commandos advanced westwards, the Royal Marine Commandos were tasked to fight their way north along the sand spit. The brigade pushed forward some three miles during the next two days, and on 9 April the main offensive was launched.

From the Gothic Line to Comacchio
Aug 1944 – April 1945

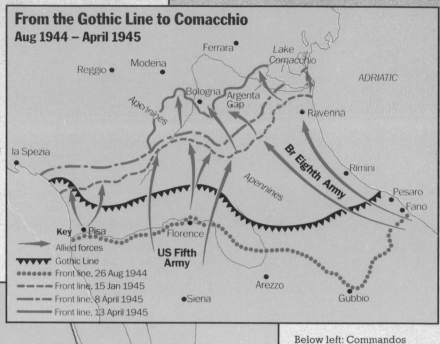

Key
- Allied forces
- Gothic Line
- Front line, 26 Aug 1944
- Front line, 15 Jan 1945
- Front line, 8 April 1945
- Front line, 13 April 1945

Securing Lake Comacchio
April 1945

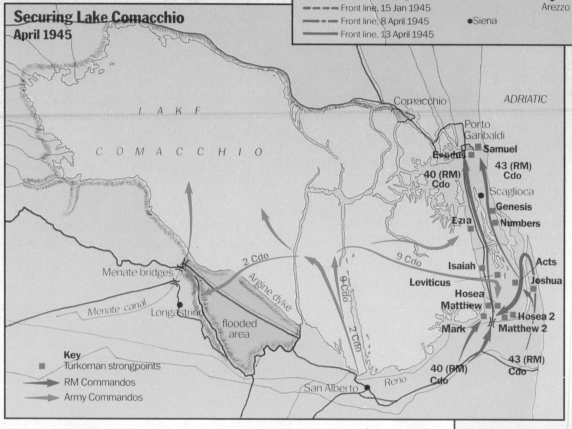

Key
- Turkoman strongpoints
- RM Commandos
- Army Commandos

Below left: Commandos clamber over the grid of dykes and waterways of the eastern spit at Lake Comacchio towards their objective. Below: Amphibious 'Fantail' personnel carriers take commandos foward. Below right: It was in such featureless landscape as this that Corporal Thomas Hunter of No.43 (RM) Commando (right) saved his troop from a waiting ambush of three machine guns in the village of Scaglioca. The citation of his posthumous VC stated, 'Throughout the operation his magnificent courage, leadership and cheerfulness had been an inspiration to his comrades.'

some sleep, the only cure for the shock of battle, in spite of the intermittent bursts of machine-gun and mortar fire that broke out during the night.

The morning of 3 April brought food, hot drinks, briefings for the day and reorganisation. The ground stretching before them, leading up to the Valetta canal, was as flat as the polderlands of Holland. There where clumps of shrubs, two of them barely concealing the enemy positions of 'James' and 'Jeremiah', while on the route to the canal and off to the right were the shabby barns and hovels of the village of Scaglioca. Some four miles of this unattractive country separated the Bellocchio and Valetta canals, criss-crossed with waterways which indicated the presence of cross-dykes and banks of rushes, features which would seriously hamper progress.

Two dreary, nerve-racking hours were spent lying amid damp grassy hummocks, prodding the ground and inserting markers

It was 1400 hours before No.43 Commando was ordered to advance. C Troop led, carrying out a copybook 'fire and move' manoeuvre, the rifles moving first under the cover of the Bren gun, then the Bren up and through, covered by the rifles. To their surprise and relief, the commandos found both 'James' and 'Jeremiah' unoccupied, but when they followed a faint track that veered towards the east, they found themselves in an extensive minefield. Since it lay directly across the path of the advancing troops, it had to be probed and marked. Two dreary, nerve-racking hours were spent lying amid damp grassy hummocks, prodding the ground and inserting markers.

It was at about this time that Corporal Tom Hunter, whose section was covering C Troop's marking operation from a position a little to the north, became aware of a new danger. If the barns and cottages of Scaglioca, now 200yds in front, should contain enemy troops, they would have a clear field of fire over the route about to be followed by the entire Commando. More specifically, C Troop would pre-

THE ROYAL MARINE COMMANDOS

In early 1942 Combined Operations HQ decided to form a Royal Marine Commando of volunteers from the Royal Marine Division. It came into being on 14 February at Deal in Kent, commanded by Lieutenant-Colonel J. Picton Phillips. Known as RM 'A' Commando, it suffered heavy casualties on the August 1942 Dieppe raid and Picton Phillips was killed.

The battalions of the Royal Marine Division underwent a reorganisation into Commandos that began in October, with the renaming of the 8th and 1st Battalions as Nos.41 and 42(RM) Commando respectively. 'A' Commando was renamed No.40(RM), and by the end of the year the 2nd, 3rd and 5th Battalions had become Nos.43, 44 and 45(RM) Commando. By March 1944, the formation of No.48(RM) Commando completed the establishment of nine Royal Marine Commandos.

In November 1943, 2 Special Service (renamed Commando) Brigade was formed in Italy, comprising Nos. 2, 9, 40(RM) and 43(RM) Commando, together with the Belgian and Polish Troops of No.10 (Inter-Allied) Commando. It was commanded by Brigadier Ronnie Tod.

Following VE-Day, No.40(RM) absorbed No.43(RM), only to be disbanded in 1946. The unit was re-formed as 40 Commando RM in 1947 from the wartime No.44(RM) Commando. Within the present Royal Marine establishment there are three Commandos, Nos.40, 42 and 45. Nos.43 and 41 Commando RM were disbanded in 1968 and 1981 respectively.

Below: Brigadier Ronnie Tod, commander of 2 Special Commando Brigade.

sent an easy target once the men stood up to continue their advance.

Whether the enemy machine guns opened fire before Corporal Hunter began his charge, or whether it was already Hunter's intention to investigate the situation, is uncertain, but suddenly fire came tearing out from three machine guns in the huddle of buildings. They were concentrating on Hunter's lone figure racing towards them, firing his Bren expertly from the hip. In addition, six more machine-gun posts along the bank of the Valetta canal, their attention attracted by the noise, began to add their fire to the concentration on Hunter. Mortar bombs began to thump down on the troops clustered behind, some of them still at work in the minefield.

To the astonishment of everybody watching, Hunter made the shelter of the buildings, kicked in the door of the first house, wrecked the gun and captured its thoroughly demoralised crew. He then changed his magazine and repeated the operation in the next house. Before he could tackle the third gun, however, its crew abandoned their post, ran to the canal, and 'scuttled across a footbridge onto the north bank'. Scaglioca was in Hunter's hands.

Hunter threw himself onto a heap of rubble and took on the six machine guns with an inspired accuracy

But not the gun positions along the canal; as C Troop raced up to cross the open ground which Hunter had just traversed, these poured out a hail of bullets. Some of the running figures stumbled and fell, but others kept going even though they were highly exposed on the open ground.

Bursting out of a back door, Hunter threw himself onto a heap of rubble and took on the six machine guns with an inspired accuracy. The nearest ones fell silent, and then his own Bren went quiet as the magazine emptied. This did not deter Hunter: yelling encouragement to everyone behind and demanding more magazines – these were promptly thrown to him – Hunter engaged yet another machine gun and knocked it out. By now, in response to his example and urgings, other marines had left the cottages and were racing for the canal bank. Hunter was still firing, still shouting, still attracting all the

enemy attention to his seemingly invulnerable figure.

It could not last, of course. As some of his friends of C Troop threw themselves down into the shelter of the southern canal bank, Hunter rose to join them, launching himself forward with a defiant cry; he was hit in the head by a machine-gun burst that killed him instantly. For his courage, leadership and self-sacrifice, he was subsequently awarded a posthumous Victoria Cross. He was just 21 years of age.

That evening the marine commandos tried to consolidate along the line of the Valetta canal, and E Troop succeeded in placing one section up on the right and in place. But despite their covering fire, nobody else reached the bank, and after dark they all withdrew to the cover of scrub and dunes with their wounded commander. During the night, reinforcements ordered to the area by the German High Command began to arrive, and with the coming of dawn the commandos found themselves under a heavy barrage of mortar and heavy artillery fire. Late that afternoon, the men of No.43 Commando were told that they were being relieved. That night a company of Coldstream Guards took over their positions.

During the Comacchio operation, 2 Commando Brigade had advanced seven and a half miles in two days. The Royal Marines had taken 450 prisoners for the loss of 53 all ranks, of which nine, including Corporal Hunter, had been killed. They had cleared the enemy from the eastern flank of the projected assault, and valuable German reserves had been drawn away from the main thrust of Field Marshal Alexander's offensive. On 9 April, the main attack was launched, and by 23 April the entire length of the Po Valley was in Allied hands. Six days later, two German officers signed the instrument of unconditional surrender of all German troops in Italy. It was the first German theatre capitulation of the war.

While No.43(RM) Commando was finally disbanded in 1968, No.40(RM) Commando is still in existence and based in the West Country. The marine commandos' achievement on that cold, bleak spit of sand on the Italian coast will never be forgotten by the Royal Marines. Indeed, one specialised unit of the modern Royal Marine establishment, which is responsible for the protection of Britain's maritime assets, is based at Arbroath in Scotland, and is named after the action and commands the respect of all servicemen who know it. That unit is the Comacchio Company.

THE AUTHOR Barrie Pitt is well known as a military historian. He was editor of Purnell's *History of the Second World War* and *History of the First World War*. Among his many books is *Special Boat Squadron*, a history of the SBS in the Mediterranean.

Breakthrough! Top left: Following the success of 2 Commando Brigade at Lake Comacchio, commando signallers take over trenches only recently occupied by the German and Turkoman defenders. Centre left: Commandos, one wearing a captured German peaked cap, mop up. Bottom left: A column of Fantails moves up alongside one of the area's many canals. Bottom right: German prisoners await their fate after the attack.

Royal Marine, No.40 (RM) Commando, Italy 1945

Over his khaki serge battledress he wears '37 pattern web equipment and anklets. A field dressing is tucked under his helmet netting and he has a Thompson M1928A1 sub-machine gun.

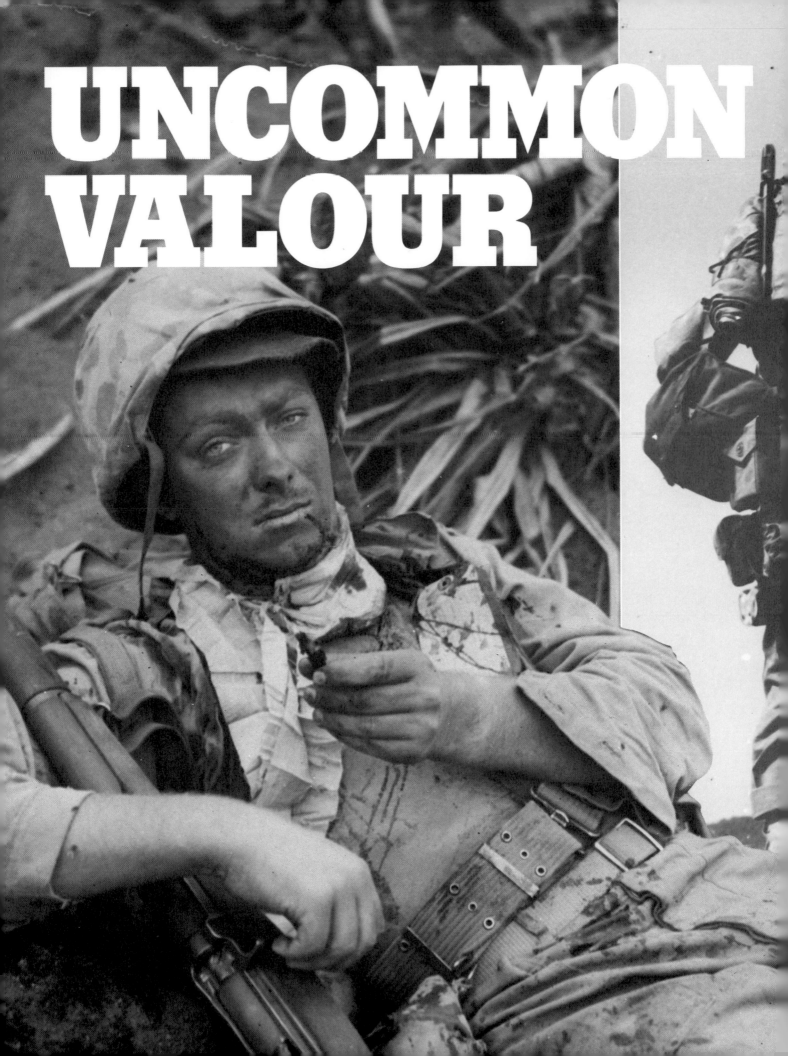

UNCOMMON VALOUR

On Iwo Jima, in the shadow of Mount Suribachi, the leathernecks of the US 28th Marines fought one of the toughest battles of the Pacific War

Bottom: Storming Iwo Jima – assault waves head for the beaches under the menacing bulk of Mount Suribachi. Far left: An early casualty, Corporal Rudolph Engstrom, lies wounded in a shell crater, examining the piece of shrapnel that did the damage. Left: A heavily laden leatherneck moves inland to take on the Japanese defenders.

IT WAS the easiest landing I ever made; I didn't even get my feet wet. It was the only thing about Iwo Jima that was easy. D-day, 19 February 1945, was bright and clear with a blue sky and moderate sea. Much too beautiful a day to be killed, I thought, although a lot of us would be.

We left the hard-packed beach, flung ourselves against the terraced, black-sand escarpment and stalled. Trying to run in that loose sand was like running on the spot or, as someone said later, like trying to climb a waterfall. I looked around to see where I was. Glowering down at me personally on my left was the 556ft Mount Suribachi. On my right, also glowering, was six-foot four-inch Colonel Harry B. 'Harry the Horse' Liversedge, commander of the 28th Marine Regiment, whose job it was to take Suribachi away from the Japanese.

According to the plan, we were to take Suribachi in 12 hours. It took us four days and cost 904 casualties, including 212 dead. But Suribachi was only the beginning: the 28th took nearly three times that many casualties after we joined the fighting for the northern half of the island. But we didn't know about all that when we landed – thank God.

Liversedge looked at me as if he expected me to do something, but I wasn't about to do anything until he did. 'We can't just sit here,' Liversedge growled to his operations officer, Major Oscar Peatross. We stood up and waded perhaps 50yds more inland through the shifting sand. H-hour, the beginning of the landings, was 0900 hours. Within the next half hour, all the assault forces were ashore. It seemed extraordinarily quiet, and I remembered something a rose-cheeked naval gunnery officer had said back aboard ship during the thunder of the pre-landing bombardment, 'There won't be a live Jap left on that island.' I said something rude because I was at Tarawa, where the admirals learnt, or should have learnt, at the expense of Marine lives that naval gunfire had certain limitations.

Except for a few mortar rounds and some sniper fire, we were getting very little resistance. 'There's something screwy,' said Cor-

ASSAULT FORCES

The build-up to the US assault on Iwo Jima began long before the first waves of assault troops hit the beaches on 19 February 1945. On 15 June 1944 carrier aircraft raided the island for the first time, and the bombing continued for the rest of the year.

Nearer D-day, a 72-hour naval bombardment from six battleships and their escorts pulverised the known enemy positions. With unremitting fury, some 1950 rounds of 16in shell, 1500 rounds of 14in, 400 of 12in, 1700 of 8in, 2000 of 6in, and 31,000 of 5in turned the island into an apparently lifeless moonscape. Overhead, flight after flight of aircraft bombed, napalmed and rocketed the Japanese as they hid in their tunnels and caves.

The invasion fleet earmarked for Iwo Jima comprised some 800 ships of all types: on board the transports were the 60,000 assault troops of Major-General H. Schmidt's V Amphibious Corps. The first wave to hit the beaches consisted of the 4th and 5th Marine Divisions under the command of Major-Generals Clifton B. Cates, a veteran of Guadalcanal, and Keller E. Rockey, a marine who had fought in World War I. Both divisions were to land a little way north of Mount Suribachi and then be transported to their objective by nearly 500 amphibious vehicles.

The 3rd Marine Division, commanded by Major-General Graves B. Erskine, was the corps reserve. At 47, Erskine was one of the youngest serving generals in the US Marine Corps. His men were expected to come ashore three days after the initial landings.

Above: The shoulder insignia of the 5th Marine Division.

Leonce 'Frenchy' Olivier, a Louisiana Cajun. He had been one of the first men ashore at Tarawa and commanded respect. Then, as if responding to a gigantic electric prod, Iwo Jima leaped into life. More than 20,000 Japanese defenders, all of them underground, came out shooting. Suribachi, far more deadly now than when it was a live volcano, spewed fire on the Marines from 1000 caves, block-houses, pillboxes, trenches and spider traps. The jagged hills and ridges to the north, where the main defence lines lay, exploded simultaneously. As if on cue, somebody was heard to say, 'Oh Christ, the honeymoon is over.'

Things were proceeding exactly as Lieutenant-General Tadamichi Kuribayashi, the Japanese commander, had planned. A good family man, a fifth generation samurai and a very smart general, he had made his key decision months before. Against the bitter opposition of dissident officers, especially members of the navy, Kuribayashi had decided that he would not fight for Iwo on the beaches. The Japanese had not been able to stop the Americans on the beaches at Tarawa, Guam, Saipan or Tinian, Kuribayashi argued. Nor had the Germans been able to stop the Allies in Normandy. Why have his forces blown away by naval gunfire on the beaches?

Instead, Kuribayashi decreed, his men would hold their fire until after the Americans had landed and started moving inland. Then, as we struggled through the loose black sand towards the narrow neck of desolate earth that linked Suribachi to the main body of the island, we would be naked and exposed. Then, he could slaughter us. And he did.

Kuribayashi knew that Iwo Jima was doomed; that, indeed, Japan was doomed. On 3 February, he wrote to his wife, 'Please stop hoping that I can return alive, that you will ever see me again.' Hence, his whole effort was geared to take as many of us with him as possible. There would, for example, be no banzai charges. 'Do not go and get them,' Kuribayashi ordered. 'Stay in your holes and make them come and get you.'

Johnson turned to his troops and yelled, 'Okay, you bastards, let's get the hell off this beach.'

Late on D-day, aboard his command ship offshore, Lieutenant-General Holland M. 'Howlin' Mad' Smith, the terrible-tempered overall commander of the Marine forces, told war correspondents, 'I don't know who he (Kuribayashi) is, but the Jap general running the show is one smart bastard.' Just how smart none of us would know until the battle ended five weeks later. Iwo Jima was the only battle of the Pacific War in which the Americans suffered more casualties, although not more dead, than the Japanese.

The 28th's plan of attack was simple: cut across the island at its 750yd-wide isthmus, then wheel to the left and drive towards Suribachi. Second Lieutenant Frank J. Wright had two of his men still with him when they reached the opposite beach 90 minutes after landing.

They blew up some pillboxes, by-passed others, knocked out a 20mm gun emplacement and shot their way through a Japanese command post because they had no choice. In retrospect, that was the easy part.

Marines on the eastern slope of Suribachi were temporarily paralysed by the intensity of the enemy fire. Somebody had to get up. One who did was

Second Lieutenant Norman D. Brueggman. 'If you want to win this war, you'd better get the hell up here,' he shouted. A moment later, he was a dead hero. A short, fat man had better luck. He was Lieutenant-Colonel Chandler W. Johnson, whose 2nd Battalion, 28th Marines, was destined to plant the flag atop Suribachi. Casually contemptuous of enemy fire, Johnson turned on his cringing troops and yelled, 'Okay, you bastards, let's get the hell off this beach.' And they did. They would follow Johnson anywhere. His luck ran out weeks later at the northern end of the island. He literally vanished after a direct hit by a high-explosive shell. Afterwards, all they found was a shoe.

An awed private, his face pressed against the sand, turned to his sergeant and asked, 'Was Tarawa anything like this?' 'No,' was the reply, 'Nothing was ever like this.' The private felt better right away, although the dead and dying lay all around him. Now, he knew how to react.

The first of the walking wounded came into the aid station by himself. The flesh of his jaw hung by a piece. A navy doctor pushed the sagging mass of flesh and bone back into place and wrapped a bandage around his head. A couple of hospital corpsmen stood up to take him down to the beach for evacuation. He waved them aside and tried to talk, but only a strange mumble came from what was left of his mouth. A big, powerful man with hair cut so close you could see his sunburned scalp, he tried to write in the loose volcanic sand. But as fast as he wrote, the sand filled in what he had written. Disgusted, he gave the sand an indignant brush and stood up. He was ready to go now.

To its immense regret, the 28th had to leave its regimental mascot, a young lion named Roscoe, in Hawaii. But on D-day we discovered that we had a four-footed companion: a feisty brown-and-white fox terrier named George. The dog gambolled through the carnage as if the whole battle was some new kind of game, often stopping to lick the hand of a nervous marine. He survived the battle; his master did not.

Captain Dwayne E. 'Bobo' Mears, who charged across the island attacking enemy positions with a pistol, was stopped by a bullet in the neck and collapsed from loss of blood. A hospital corpsman crawled to Mears' side and began covering the big man with sand to make him less of a target to Japanese marksmen. 'Get the hell out of here and get going,' Mears snapped. 'I'm all right.' He died the next morning aboard ship after being evacuated.

Then there was Tony Stein, at 24 a veteran of three campaigns in the Solomon Islands. A toolmaker back in Ohio, Stein had designed his own special weapon for Iwo. It was a hand-held machine gun made from the wing gun of a wrecked navy fighter. Stein called it his 'stinger'. Working with two other marines, one of them a demolitions man, Stein knocked out one pillbox after another. During his first hour on the island, he killed at least 20 Japanese. Then he took off his helmet and shoes and ran for the beach to get more ammunition. According to one historian, Stein made a total of eight trips to the beach that day and twice his stinger was shot from his hands. But at the end of the day, he was still going. As his Yugoslavian mother always said, 'He's a tough one, that Tony'.

By the end of D-day there were 30,000 Marines ashore, but the 28th was only interested in its private

Right: The savage beaches of Iwo Jima. Pinned down by Japanese machine-gun fire from Mount Suribachi, men of the 28th Marines await the order to advance.

Iwo Jima
3rd, 4th and 5th Marine Divisions, Feb–Mar 1945

As the American central Pacific offensive entered its final phase, three US Marine divisions launched their assault on the island of Iwo Jima. The battle for the island raged for nearly a month before the invading forces could declare it secure — and by then, nearly 6000 marines had lost their lives.

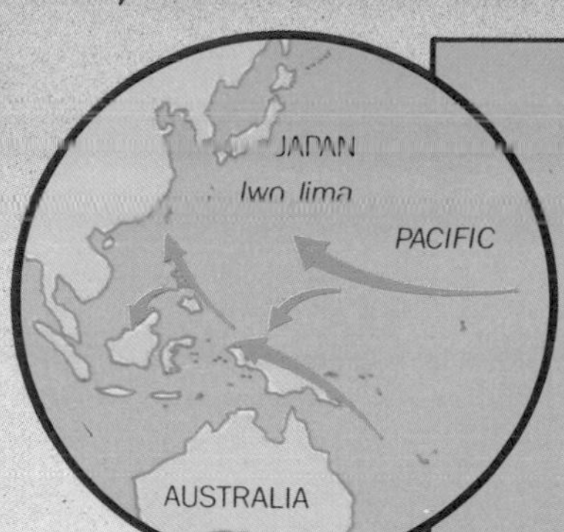

JAPAN
Iwo Jima
PACIFIC
AUSTRALIA

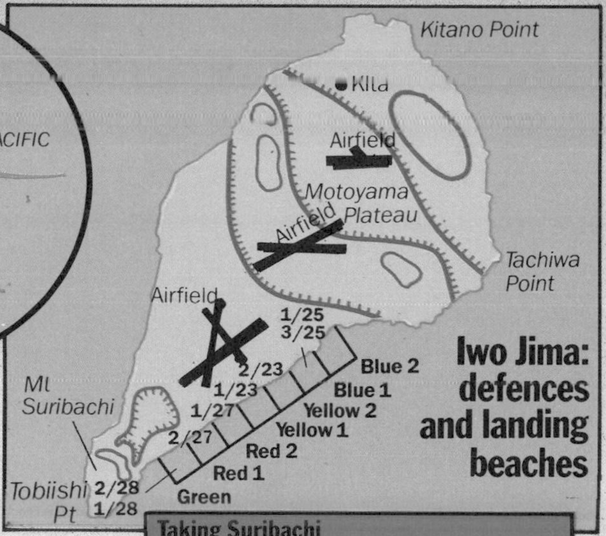

Key
- Allied Pacific offensives, Aug 1942 – Feb 1945
- Japanese defensive lines
- Japanese artillery positions
- 1/27 US Marine units (battalion/regiment)
- US landing beaches
- US Marines

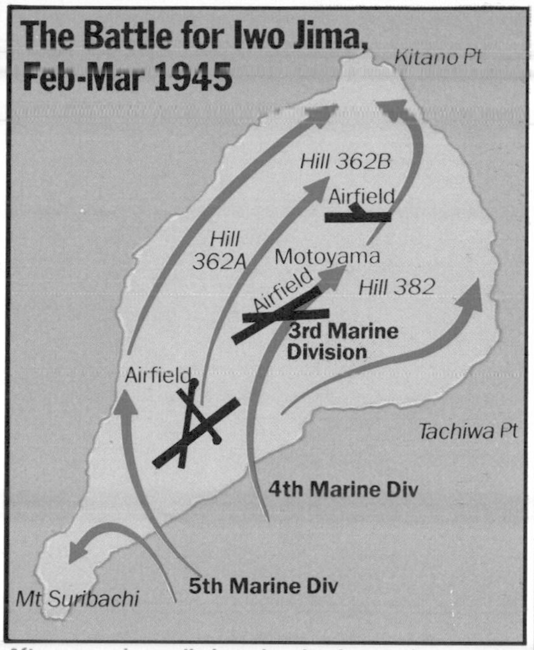

Kitano Point
Kita
Airfield
Motoyama
Plateau
Airfield
Tachiwa Point
Airfield
Mt Suribachi
Tobiishi Pt

1/25
3/25
2/23
1/23
1/27
2/27
2/28
1/28

Blue 2
Blue 1
Yellow 2
Yellow 1
Red 2
Red 1
Green

Iwo Jima: defences and landing beaches

The Battle for Iwo Jima, Feb–Mar 1945

Kitano Pt
Hill 362B
Airfield
Hill 362A
Motoyama
Hill 382
Airfield
3rd Marine Division
Airfield
Tachiwa Pt
4th Marine Div
5th Marine Div
Mt Suribachi

Taking Suribachi

22 Feb After four days of fighting, the 28th Marines completely encircle Suribachi and prepare for the final assault.

23 Feb The 2nd Battalion, 28th Marines claw their way up to the peak of Suribachi.

②

Mt Suribachi

28th Marines

27th Marines

①

Mount Suribachi
28th Marines, Feb 1945

Onto the beaches

19 Feb 0900 The first marines hit the beaches of Iwo Jima. Little resistance is encountered at the outset. Struggling through the sand, the 28th Marines cross the neck of Iwo Jima and wheel left towards Mount Suribachi.

1030 As the men of the 27th Marines push northwards, and B Coy, 28th Marines, reaches the west shore of Iwo Jima, the bulk of the 28th Marines begins the hard fight for Suribachi. By the end of the day, Japanese resistance has stiffened considerably.

After a massive preliminary bombardment, the assault on Iwo Jima went in at 0900 on 19 February 1945, with the 4th Marine Division on the right flank and the 5th Marine Division on the left. As the leading elements reached positions some 200 yards inland, the marines came under a withering crossfire from the defending Japanese forces — and from that moment onwards the fight for Iwo Jima became a grim and bloody contest.

While the 5th Division struggled to secure the southwest end of the island — with the 28th Marines assaulting Mount Suribachi — the 4th Division pushed north and east. On 24 February, with Suribachi secure, the two divisions, now reinforced in the centre by the reserve 3rd Marine Division, advanced slowly through Iwo Jima's central plateau. After five days of bitter fighting the assault on the complex of tunnels and bunkers on Hills 382 and 362A began. Hill 382 fell on 1 March and Hill 362A was taken the following day after a night attack. The pocket at Kitano Point was cleared by 16 March.

Below: As an M4 Sherman tank is consumed by fire after taking a direct hit from a hidden anti-tank gun, a carbine-armed leatherneck blazes away at Japanese positions around Nishi. This village in the northwest of the island formed part of the enemy's last line of defence and was held with fanatical determination. Below right: Exhausted by the bitter fighting, a group of marines takes shelter in an abandoned pillbox. Right: 'Devil's breath on Hell island' – two marines use their flame-throwers to clear out a Japanese bunker at the foot of Mount Suribachi.

war for Suribachi. Harry the Horse Liversedge moved his command post about 200yds closer to the front. It was, in fact, well ahead of his three battalion command posts. When Lieutenant-Colonel Robert H. Williams, the executive officer, was asked if this wasn't a bit unusual, he grinned and said, 'It isn't exactly SOP [standard operating procedure] but it's a hell of a good way to make your battalions move faster.'

The importance of Suribachi was that it was the island's dominant terrain feature. So long as the Japanese held it, they could observe every move we made. But it also had great psychological importance to the Americans. Said one report:

'Suribachi seemed to take on a life of its own, to be watching these men, looming over them, pressing down upon them... In the end it is probable that the mountain represented to these marines a thing more evil than the Japanese.'

Liversedge was under relentless pressure from higher headquarters to get the job done. But, despite heavy casualties during the first 24 hours, his request for relief forces was flatly rejected.

Suribachi itself was formidable enough. But the desolate wasteland of stone and scrub that covered the approach to the mountain was, if anything, worse. When the 28th reported a pillbox every 10ft, it was

DEFENDING IWO JIMA

The Japanese commander on Iwo Jima, Lieutenant-General Kuribayashi, was well aware of the position's importance, saying, 'this island is the gateway to Japan'. Knowing that he could not expect any help, he turned the island into a deathtrap, to be held to the last.

Kuribayashi's men had worked hard to improve Iwo Jima's natural defences. Although covering an area of less than 10 square miles, the island bristled with some 800 pillboxes, three miles of tunnels, as well as extensive minefields and trenches. Gun emplacements were sited to cover the beaches and a succession of inland defensive lines.

Kuribayashi had charge of a large, fanatical garrison. Aside from the 13,586 men of the 109th Division, he also had some 7347 Navy troops to hold Iwo Jima. Artillery support was lavish: 361 guns over 75mm calibre, 300 anti-aircraft guns, 20,000 light guns, 130 howitzers, 12 heavy mortars, 60 anti-tank guns and 70 rocket-launchers. Over 20 tanks were placed in hull-down positions.

When the 4th and 5th Marine Divisions hit Iwo Jima on 19 February, they faced the most extensive defence system seen in the Pacific theatre in World War II.

only a slight exaggeration. So many men were fighting in such a small place that as one marine observed, 'You don't dare sit down on this goddam rock for fear of getting a bayonet up your ass.' Enemy fortifications were so dense that one company inadvertently set up its command post on a bunker still full of Japanese.

Fighting was often hand-to-hand. Private First Class Leo Jez was moving towards a pillbox when a Japanese officer charged him swinging a sword. Jez caught the blow with his hands, wrenched the sword away from the officer and chopped off his head with it. Jez turned up later at the aid station with a nearly severed thumb, a gash on the back of his hand – and the sword.

The 22nd was a miserable day with a cold, hard rain and strong winds. Weapons clogged. There was no air support. Artillery support was negligible. A mortar fell on the 28th's command post, killing, among others, the regimental surgeon. But, by the end of the day, Marine patrols had encircled Suribachi. More men would die for that ugly little pile of real estate, but for all practical purposes the mountain was ours. A sergeant, who had scrambled part way up the north face of the mountain and met no resistance, paused to ask if he should continue. Liversedge decided it was too late in the day for the final ascent. That would come the next day. Thus the stage was set for the greatest picture of World War II: the flag-raising atop Mount Suribachi.

With Suribachi secured, members of the 28th were allowed a few days of rest. Many wrote letters home saying that now that they had taken Suribachi, their job was done and they would be leaving the island. What they didn't know was that the worst was

It would have been hard to find two more dissimilar men than Colonel Harry B. 'Harry the Horse' Liversedge, the commander of the 28th Marine Regiment, and his executive officer, Lieutenant-Colonel Robert H. 'English Bob' Williams.

Whereas Liversedge was tall and awkward looking, Williams was slim and elegant. Whereas Liversedge was shy and taciturn, Williams was sophisticated and articulate. Whereas Liversedge was as American as apple pie, Williams cultivated the airs of a British officer and gentleman. If Liversedge slouched, Williams was ramrod straight. If Liversedge cared little about his personal appearance, Williams was always immaculate. As an unshaven Liversedge gave orders for the assault on Mount Suribachi, Williams shaved – with an old-fashioned straight razor and a steady hand. They made a formidable fighting pair. Both had collected Navy Crosses in the Solomon Islands, where Williams also collected a bullet in his left lung.

An early 1920s Olympic track and college football star, Liversedge was six-feet four-inches tall with a long, loping stride that made his nickname inevitable. 'Hell, he even looked like a horse,' said a fellow marine. Given the task of capturing an extinct volcano, Liversedge was, in fact, born in Volcano, California.

More than anyone else, Liversedge and Williams personified the 28th Marines. 'Liversedge taught me compassion,' one officer said, recalling an incident where he had recommended stiff punishment for an erring enlisted man only to have Liversedge dismiss the man with a fatherly talk. Williams was well-versed in the military technology of his day. Liversedge was more at home leading a patrol through the jungles of Nicaragua. One day he confessed to an aide, during training, that he didn't really understand how to operate a radio. He was taken out into the boondocks for some private lessons, but he was never really comfortable with the radio.

A man who liked his drink, Liversedge was addicted to slot machines. At Camp Pendleton, California, a 50-cent machine was installed in the officers' club for the colonel's special use. When Liversedge hit a winning combination and the machine refused to pay out, he picked it up and hurled it through a window into a gulch 15ft below. It made an enormously satisfying crash, according to witnesses.

HARRY THE HORSE AND ENGLISH BOB

Below: The two masterminds of the capture of Mount Suribachi, Colonel Harry 'Harry the Horse' Liversedge (left), commander of the 28th Marines, and his executive officer, Lieutenant-Colonel Robert 'English Bob' Williams (right), confer on their next move. Independent, strong-willed characters, they nevertheless formed a formidable fighting team, and their calmness under pressure inspired the 28th Marines to battle on despite taking heavy losses. Both men had long, distinguished careers with the Marine Corps, seeing action in many of the island-hopping operations of the Pacific campaign.

The son of a Wisconsin clergyman, Williams liked gracious living. Some of his happiest days were as a member of the famed 4th Marines in pre-war Shanghai, where he was a member of the polo team. The duty hours were short, eight to noon, and the nights were long. As a dashing young lieutenant in the late 1930s, Williams served a hitch as a White House aide under President Roosevelt. He loved the social whirl. His British mannerisms alternately amused, angered or outraged his fellow officers. In addition to his nickname, 'English Bob,' he was also known as 'The Stick', for the swagger stick he carried.

Upon returning to Camp Pendleton one night in a carnival mood, he lost his stick through a hole in the floorboard of the rusty old car he was driving. Next day, according to a possibly exaggerated account, he had a whole battalion out looking for it.

Williams became famous for his carefully laid out officers' mess, with crisp white linen, and special mess nights in the British style. In Hawaii, he insisted on being served pheasant under glass. One officer thought this was going too far and said so. 'Look at it this way, Fred,' Williams said, 'Think of all the time we've spent in chow lines. We've earned it.'

In 1947 Williams got himself assigned to The Staff College in England. He couldn't have been more pleased. He had a batman to shine his leather and press his uniforms. He managed to stretch his six-month tour to two more years.

Williams divided his later years between Washington DC and Wisconsin. When he learned that he had terminal cancer, he returned to the family home in Wisconsin. He died there in 1983 at the age of 75.

Right: Two marines bring up extra machine-gun ammunition during the fight for Hill 362. The position was finally taken by the 28th Marines. Centre right: Two gunners turn a captured Hotchkiss machine gun on the enemy. Bottom right: Jubilant marines display the trophies of their victory; some 23,000 of their comrades were killed or wounded.

yet to come. Having fought and won their own private war against Suribachi, the 28th Marines now joined the main battle in the north.

After taking Suribachi, the 28th Marines and the rest of the 5th Division began moving up the west coast of the island, heading for the enemy's main defensive line along the Motoyama plateau. In a cruel sea of jumbled rock and stinking sulphur pits, the regiment took 240 casualties daily for three straight days. Advances were measured in tens rather than hundreds of yards. On 28 February, five days after the fall of Suribachi, the division faced the Japanese defenders holding Hill 362A. The first attack by the 27th Marines was thrown back after bitter hand-to-hand fighting.

It took three days of savage fighting to neutralise the enemy defences on Nishi ridge

On the following day, the 28th Marines took over. A Company went round the right side of the position in a flanking attack. Corporal Tony Stein, back in action after receiving a shrapnel wound in his shoulder on the 21st, led 20 men into the fray. Only seven returned; Stein was one of the dead. Three of the men who raised the two flags on Suribachi, Sergeant Hanson, Sergeant Strank and Corporal Block, were also killed. By nightfall, however, the hill was in American hands. Harry the Horse Liversedge won his second Navy Cross.

Pushing north along the coast, the regiment hit Nishi ridge, a jagged volcanic outcrop running from the plateau to the sea. It took three days of savage fighting to neutralise the defences. On the day of the ridge's capture, 3 March, Sergeant William G. Harrell, a tough Texan, won the Medal of Honor. Losing his left hand to a grenade during a night attack, he fought on. Undaunted, he continued to battle until his other hand was torn off by a second grenade.

By 9 March, the division was in sight of the sea on the northern coast of the island. The remnants of the Japanese defenders were holed up along a ridge overlooking Kitano gorge. It took over a week of hard fighting, using flame-throwers and satchel charges, to clear out the warren of caves and pillboxes that covered the area. Iwo Jima was declared secure on 16 March, but the mopping-up operations continued until the end of April.

The capture of the island had cost the lives of 5931 marines and a further 17,372 were wounded. Fewer than 250 of the garrison were taken alive. The 28th Marines had suffered appalling losses: of the 3900 men who had landed on 19 February, only 600 remained fit for action by the end. Commenting on their outstanding contribution to victory, Admiral Chester W. Nimitz paid them the ultimate tribute, 'Among the Americans who served on Iwo Jima, uncommon valour was a common virtue.'

THE AUTHOR Keyes Beech served with the 28th Marines as a sergeant combat correspondent during the landings on Iwo Jima. After the war, he was a correspondent for the *Chicago Daily News* and won the Pulitzer Prize for his coverage of the Korean War.

It was probably the hottest flag raising in history. Without doubt it produced the most famous photograph of World War II or, perhaps of any war. This was Joe Rosenthal's picture of the raising of the American flag on Mount Suribachi taken on 23 February 1945. Forty years after the event, that picture is still the subject of controversy.

Some people say there were two, not just one, flag ceremonies. That is correct. Some people say that because Rosenthal was too late for the first flag raising and 'shot' the second, that his picture was posed, a fake, a re-enactment. Not true. As Rosenthal himself has often said, 'If I had posed that picture I would be a great photographer. As it happened, all I did was click the shutter at the right time.'

Here's what happened that day. Lieutenant-Colonel Chandler W.

STARS AND STRIPES OVER SURIBACHI

The true story behind the raising of the American flag over Iwo Jima by Keyes Beech.

Below: Signal victory. Triumphant leathernecks raise the Stars and Stripes over Mount Suribachi after days of hard fighting. Taken by Joe Rosenthal, this picture remains one of the 'classic' war shots of all time.

Johnson, the rough, tough commander of the 2nd Battalion, 28th Marines, told First Lieutenant Harold G. Schrier to take a patrol to the top of Suribachi, now subdued and strangely silent after four days of bitter fighting. 'And put this up on the hill,' Johnson told him, handing him a flag. As Schrier, a lean-lipped ex-raider, and his 40 man patrol climbed the north face of Suribachi, they were easy targets for Japanese marksmen. But nothing happened. When they reached the top at about 1015 hours, somebody found a length of pipe and the marines proceeded to plant the flag. Sergeant Louis R. Lowery, a *Leatherneck* magazine photographer, started clicking away.

A short, sharp firefight followed as a few Japanese defenders came out of their holes. One Japanese threw a grenade and ran towards the flag, waving his sword. A marine shot him dead. Another Japanese threw a grenade in Lowery's direction. Lowery threw himself over the rim of the crater, rolling down the mountain side 50ft or more before coming to a stop. His camera was smashed. But the film was safe inside. As Richard F. Newcomb wrote later; 'This was the flag raising on Iwo Jima that thrilled the troops. The one that thrilled the world was still to come, nearly two hours later.'

Joe Rosenthal, who wore thick glasses and was so myopic that he had been rejected by all the services, reached the summit just as the marines were preparing to raise the second flag. It was much bigger and could be better seen elsewhere on the island and offshore. Rosenthal looked around for a good shooting spot.

Rosenthal shot 18 pictures that day, some of which were posed. The film pack was sent back to the photo pool on Guam for processing. When he received a query from his photo editor asking if 'the' picture was posed, Rosenthal, who had seen neither the negative nor the prints, said yes. He thought the editor was talking about the last pictures he had taken, which were posed.

In 1962 Captain Jeremy Moore led the men of L Company, 42 Commando in an up-river operation from Brunei to free hostages held at Limbang in Sarawak.

IT WAS A beautifully clear, tropical day. At 0600 hours, 11 December 1962, as the early morning sun rose over Brunei airport, Brigadier 'Pat' Patterson greeted Captain Jeremy Moore, the newly arrived commander of L Company, 42 Commando, Royal Marines. Moore was a veteran of the campaigns in the Malayan jungle 10 years before, and had been awarded the Military Cross. Perched on the bonnet of his Land Rover, Brigadier Patterson, commander of 99 Gurkha Infantry Brigade and now head of operations against the North Kalimantan National

Below left: By a stroke of extraordinary good fortune, the Royal Marines located two Z Craft on the harbourside at Brunei Town. These front-loading lighters were to make excellent amphibious assault craft for the raid on Limbang. Below right: Brigadier 'Pat' Patterson (seated on left at rear) travels up the Limbang river on the afternoon of the raid. Bottom: The harbour at Brunei, with a lighter alongside the outer jetty.

Army (TNKU) in Brunei, made his directive quite plain: 'Your company will rescue the hostages in Limbang.'

Situated just across the border in the 5th Division of Sarawak, Limbang was a small community 12 miles up river from Brunei Town. On 8 December, pursuing a well co-ordinated plan, the TNKU had moved into Limbang, Seria, Miri, and other towns to seize pro-British hostages. The terrorists held about a dozen of them in Limbang, including the British Resident of the 5th Division, Dick Morris, and his wife Dorothy, another woman, and Fritz Klattenhof, a US Peace Corps officer.

As Captain Moore, his second-in-command Lieutenant Paddy Davis, and his company sergeant-major, QMS Scoins, took stock of the situation, the marines prepared themselves for the task ahead. Only 56 men of L Company had reached Brunei, together with a section of medium machine guns. Three hours after Moore's landing in Brunei, the commanding officer of 42 Commando, Lieutenant-Colonel Robin Bridges, and his intelligence officer,

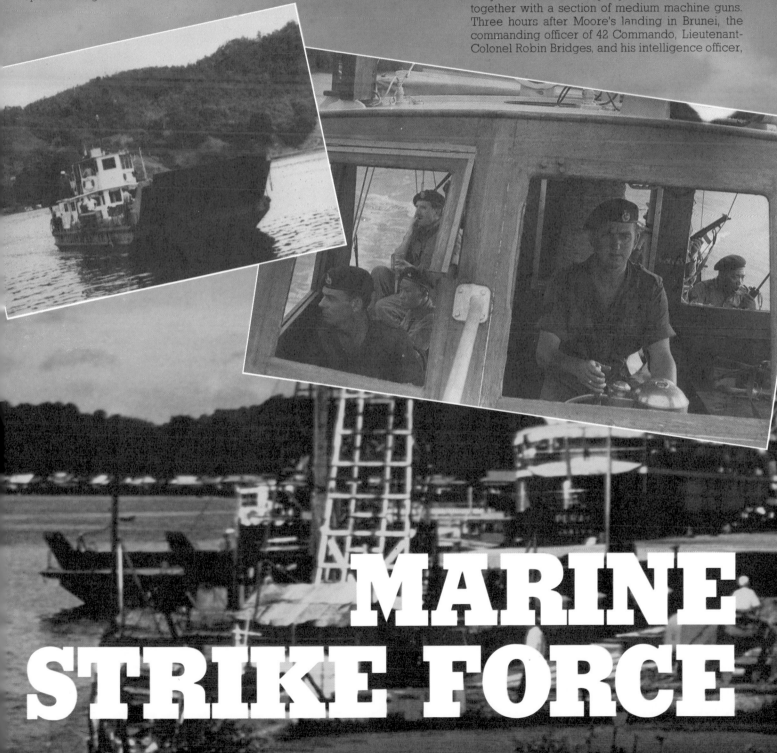

MARINE STRIKE FORCE

REBELLION IN BRUNEI

On 8 December 1962, the 4000-strong North Kalimantan National Army (TNKU) rose up to wrest power from the Sultan of Brunei. There was no immediate reaction from the British, other than placing units on full alert, as it appeared that the Brunei police had the situation in hand. However, it soon became clear that the revolt was far more widespread than previously thought, and two companies of the 2nd Gurkhas were ordered from Singapore to Brunei Town. They deployed in support of the police and attempted to relieve the oil complex at Seria, but were beaten back. Meanwhile the security forces in Brunei Town were coming under heavy fire and further reinforcements were requested. They included another company of the 2nd Gurkhas and elements of the Queen's Own Highlanders. On 11 December Seria was taken and the hostages held there were released. The TNKU were holding hostages all over Brunei, and additional units were summoned to confront their captors. At the time, 42 Commando was awaiting Christmas in Singapore after an extremely busy year of exercises, and on 8 December the commandos were put on short notice to move to Brunei. Two days later they were on their way, with Commando Headquarters and L Company flying via Labuan to Brunei Town, where the Gurkhas had restored order. They were given the task of ousting the rebels from the town of Limbang, situated on a river in the area of Sarawak which separates the two enclaves of Brunei protectorate.

Royal Marine, 42 Commando, Brunei 1962

This marine has the standard jungle-green uniform issued to men serving in the Far East. He is wearing the green Royal Marine beret and 1958-pattern web equipment. Woollen puttees are worn over leather boots with rubber soles. His armament is the British 7.62mm L1A1 rifle with a curved 30-round magazine, and the bayonet is worn on his left side.

Lieutenant Bengie Walden, arrived to take over the difficult task of obtaining information and intelligence for the coming operation. It was clear in everyone's mind that speed and surprise were essential, and the decision was soon made that the raid would have to take place at dawn the following morning.

Of prime importance was the need to find some river craft in which to mount the operation. Paddy Davis and I set about this task by inspecting the myriad of small boats along the Brunei waterfront. There were hundreds of them, but none particularly suitable for transporting the men up river for 12 miles and then carrying out a frontal assault. Just as we reached the north end of the extensive waterfront, we came across two old lighters, known as Z Craft, which belonged to the Brunei government and appeared to be in working order.

Just after midday, two coastal minesweepers HMS *Fiskerton* and HMS *Chawton*, sailed into the harbour. Paddy and I had wondered who was going to man and drive the Z Craft on the operation, but a quick trip on board as soon as they came alongside sorted that one out. The Royal Navy immediately took charge of the situation, providing the minesweeper first lieutenants to command the craft, and engine room staff to ensure that they were both in working order.

The minesweeper captains, Lieutenant Harry Mucklow and Lieutenant Jeremy Black, came ashore and helped Captain Moore with the detailed planning. This was the first meeting between Moore and Black, and 20 years later they were to find

Above right: Equipment is loaded aboard one of the pair of lighters moored on the waterfront of Brunei Town. The craft used on the operation received an urgent overhaul by engineers from the Royal Navy to make them fit for their task. Below: Marines of 42 Commando ready themselves for battle.

themselves in action together again in the South Atlantic, when Moore was the land-force commander and Black the captain of HMS *Invincible*.

By late afternoon, both craft were mechanically ready and were being given protective 'armour' as far as possible, with large packs acting as sandbags. Meanwhile, Moore was collecting as much intelligence as he could, with no more than small-scale maps and an out-of-date air photograph to help him. He had been told that a small police launch which had approached Limbang town two days earlier had been driven off by heavy smallarms fire. Information on the strength of the enemy and his dispositions was virtually non-existent; estimates varied from 30 men to over 100, but it was known for certain that the rebels were there in some numbers and possessed captured police weapons in addition to their own. Even so, Moore assessed that their firepower would be fairly ineffective at over 100yds range, and at close quarters the firepower of the two sides would be about equal. He knew, therefore, that his highly trained marines would be more than a match for a poorly led enemy.

He anticipated that he might be able to bluff the rebels into surrendering by a show of force, but if that

Limbang raid
L Company, 42 Commando, RM
13 December 1962

In 1962 the North Kalimantan National Army launched a revolt in Brunei aimed at seizing power from the Sultan and scotching the proposed accession of Brunei to a Federation of Malaysia. The rebels moved on key positions in Brunei and in parts of Sarawak and North Borneo. In Limbang and Seria the insurgents seized British hostages. Seria was retaken on 10 December – and the stage was set for L Company's daring raid on Limbang.

Key
Marines ➡

From Brunei to Limbang

13 Dec 1203 L Coy, 42 Commando leaves Brunei for Limbang embarked in two Z Craft river lighters.
0200 L Coy's Z Craft reach the main Sungai Limbang (Limbang river) some five miles outside Limbang town. The marines remain hidden in the narrower channel under cover of darkness.

Into action

0430 The Z Craft begin the final stretch of their journey along the Sungai Limbang. As the craft round the final bend, rebels open fire. Marines storm ashore under covering machine gun fire. By afternoon, the rebels are routed and 14 hostages have been released.

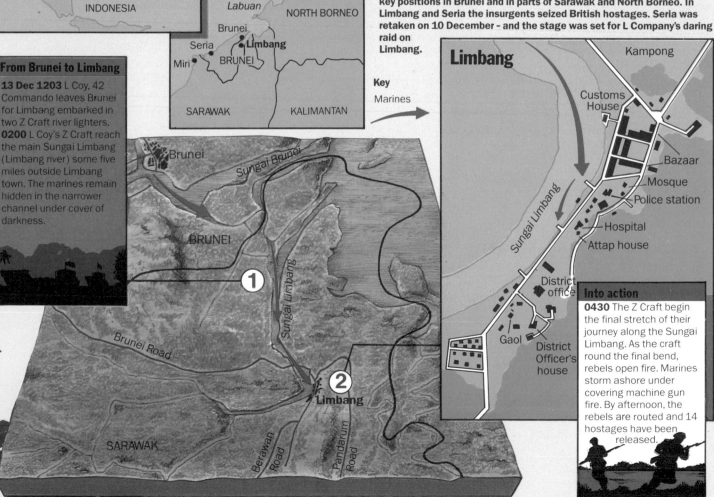

L2A3 Sterling SMG

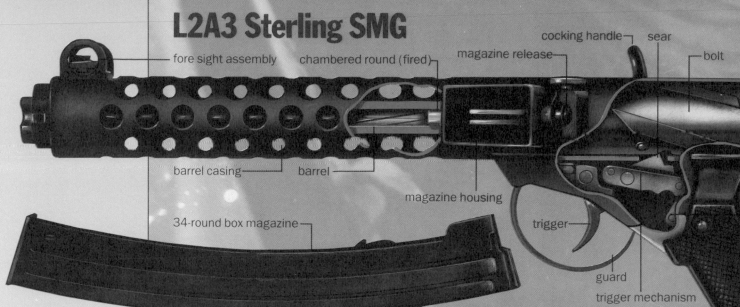

fore sight assembly

chambered round (fired)

cocking handle — sear

magazine release

bolt

barrel casing — barrel

magazine housing

trigger

guard

trigger mechanism

34-round box magazine

THE STERLING

The precursor of the modern Sterling sub-machine gun appeared in 1942 as a proposed replacement for the Sten gun. Designed by a Mr George Patchett and known as the Patchett machine carbine, the weapon underwent numerous trials and modifications and was finally introduced into service as the L2A1 in 1951. Manufactured by the Sterling Engineering Company, the gun soon became known as the Sterling. A modified version, the L2A2, arrived in 1953, but it was only with the introduction of the L2A3 in 1954 that the British Army deemed the Sterling a worthy replacement of the trusty Sten.

Since it has minimal recoil, the Sterling can be fired either from the shoulder with the stock extended, or from a crouching position with the folded stock resting in the pit of the stomach. Fired from below, the gun is aimed by 'walking' the rounds up to the target. The weapon uses low-powered 9mm ammunition and is generally preferred only for close-quarters fighting over a range of 30yds, beyond which it has uncertain stopping power. It functions well in poor conditions, due to the inclusion of a ribbed bolt which clears the gun while it fires and forces accumulated carbon out of the receiver.

failed, or if the operation was prolonged, they would probably either shoot the hostages out of hand or threaten to do so in order to make him withdraw. His prime concern was the safety of the hostages, but he did not know where they were being held. Several possible locations presented themselves: the police station, the hospital, the administrative offices and the British Residency, all separated by at least 300yds. He decided that the police station was the most likely place for the rebels to have set up their headquarters, and he planned to knock this out before they had a chance to harm their hostages. His simple plan was to go straight for the enemy and overwhelm their headquarters as fast as possible, each marine holding his fire until the rebels opened up. He intended to call on the enemy to surrender in the hope that, by a brave show, he could bluff his way in.

Under Lieutenant Paddy Davis, the other two subalterns and the troop NCOs, the depleted company prepared for action. Ammunition and equipment were checked, the medium machine guns were mounted forward on the Z Craft (where they would be most effective), and food and rest were hastily taken during what was left of the day.

In order to arrive off Limbang at dawn, it was decided to sail at about midnight, guided by the Brunei Director of Marine, Captain Muton, who had earlier brought the minesweepers up-river. Lieutenant David Willis, *Chawton's* first lieutenant, cast off the leading craft at three minutes past midnight. He was aided considerably by a clear night and a nearly full moon. His route lay in a series of complicated, winding channels varying from 30 to 100yds wide and flanked by the hideous Nipa swamp. The 100 marines on board, including members of L Company who had arrived just before nightfall, snatched whatever catnaps they could.

The two craft, keeping just within sight of each other, crept slowly down the narrow channels, keeping as silent as they could. No lights or noise emanated from their decks, and only the grinding engines might have announced their presence to a waiting guerrilla ambush. After half an hour the leading craft slewed across the river; one of her engines had decided that enough was enough and it had to be revived. Occasionally the craft bumped perilously against mangrove roots protruding into the narrower passages. By 0200 hours, both craft had reached the main Limbang river, and until 0430 they laid up,

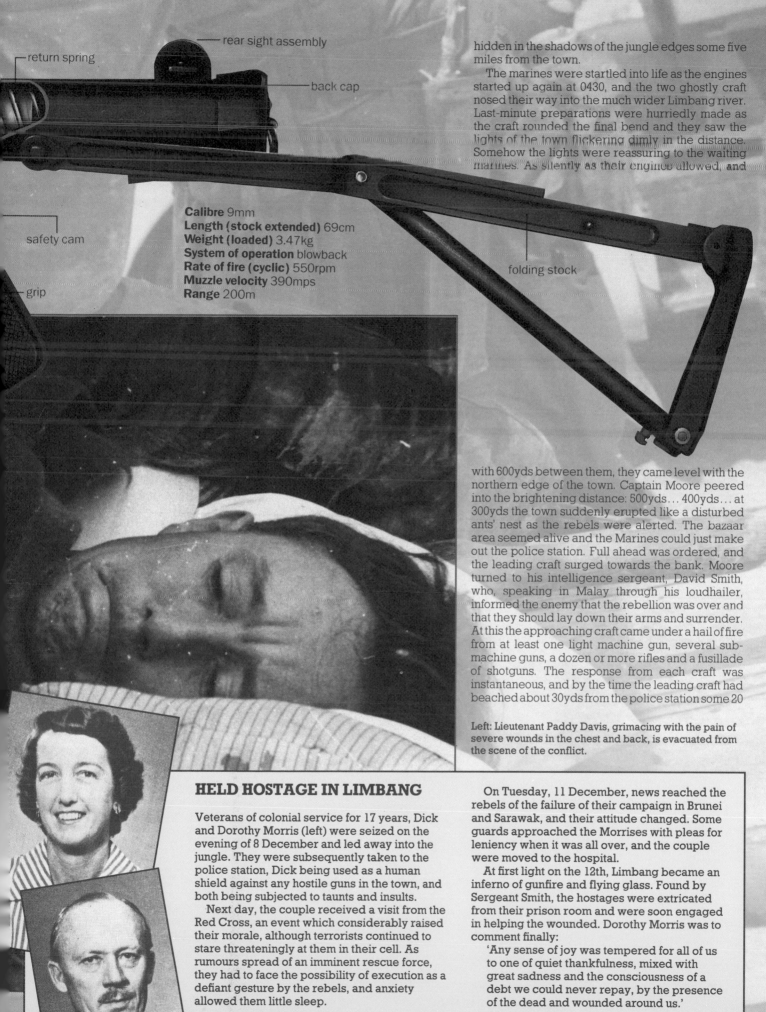

return spring

rear sight assembly

back cap

safety cam

Calibre 9mm
Length (stock extended) 69cm
Weight (loaded) 3.47kg
System of operation blowback
Rate of fire (cyclic) 550rpm
Muzzle velocity 390mps
Range 200m

folding stock

grip

hidden in the shadows of the jungle edges some five miles from the town.

The marines were startled into life as the engines started up again at 0430, and the two ghostly craft nosed their way into the much wider Limbang river. Last-minute preparations were hurriedly made as the craft rounded the final bend and they saw the lights of the town flickering dimly in the distance. Somehow the lights were reassuring to the waiting marines. As silently as their engines allowed, and

with 600yds between them, they came level with the northern edge of the town. Captain Moore peered into the brightening distance: 500yds... 400yds... at 300yds the town suddenly erupted like a disturbed ants' nest as the rebels were alerted. The bazaar area seemed alive and the Marines could just make out the police station. Full ahead was ordered, and the leading craft surged towards the bank. Moore turned to his intelligence sergeant, David Smith, who, speaking in Malay through his loudhailer, informed the enemy that the rebellion was over and that they should lay down their arms and surrender. At this the approaching craft came under a hail of fire from at least one light machine gun, several sub-machine guns, a dozen or more rifles and a fusillade of shotguns. The response from each craft was instantaneous, and by the time the leading craft had beached about 30yds from the police station some 20

Left: Lieutenant Paddy Davis, grimacing with the pain of severe wounds in the chest and back, is evacuated from the scene of the conflict.

HELD HOSTAGE IN LIMBANG

Veterans of colonial service for 17 years, Dick and Dorothy Morris (left) were seized on the evening of 8 December and led away into the jungle. They were subsequently taken to the police station, Dick being used as a human shield against any hostile guns in the town, and both being subjected to taunts and insults.

Next day, the couple received a visit from the Red Cross, an event which considerably raised their morale, although terrorists continued to stare threateningly at them in their cell. As rumours spread of an imminent rescue force, they had to face the possibility of execution as a defiant gesture by the rebels, and anxiety allowed them little sleep.

On Tuesday, 11 December, news reached the rebels of the failure of their campaign in Brunei and Sarawak, and their attitude changed. Some guards approached the Morrises with pleas for leniency when it was all over, and the couple were moved to the hospital.

At first light on the 12th, Limbang became an inferno of gunfire and flying glass. Found by Sergeant Smith, the hostages were extricated from their prison room and were soon engaged in helping the wounded. Dorothy Morris was to comment finally:

'Any sense of joy was tempered for all of us to one of quiet thankfulness, mixed with great sadness and the consciousness of a debt we could never repay, by the presence of the dead and wounded around us.'

seconds later, it was clear that L Company had the fire advantage, thanks largely to the heavy weight of lead pouring from their Vickers medium machine guns.

Two marines of the leading troop were killed even before they got to the bank, and Lieutenant Peter Waters was hit in the leg as he jumped ashore. The coxswain of the leading craft was also hit, as were Lieutenant Paddy Davis and a seaman in the second craft, which was still standing off and giving covering fire. No.5 Troop stormed ashore, clearing the police station in its stride, with Corporal Bill Lester taking his section across the road, mopping up and providing a cut-off to the rear. Sergeant Johnny Bickford, a corps footballer and physical training instructor, with his section commander, Corporal Bob Rawlinson, pressed home the attack though Rawlinson was soon wounded in the back.

Meanwhile, with its coxswain wounded, the leading craft had drifted off the bank. Lieutenant David Willis immediately took the wheel and drove it back into the bank again, although now the un-wieldy craft was beached half-way between the residency and the hospital, some 150yds from the initial landing.

Captain Moore now re-assessed the situation and ordered his troop sergeant, Sergeant Wally Mac-Farlane, ashore with the reserve section. Sergeant Smith, having decided that his loudhailer was no longer an adequate weapon, accompanied them. By this time there was only spasmodic fire, and Sergeant MacFarlane moved stealthily north, clearing the enemy from their hiding places in the jungle fringe. They reached the hospital without incident, and Sergeant Mac-Farlane decided to press on to join up with the force near the police station.

Suddenly, all hell was let loose as a group of determined rebels opened fire, killing the troop sergeant and two marines. The marines fought back, eliminating all the guerrillas in the area other than those who had fled into the jungle. Then, through the sounds of battle, Sergeant Smith heard some unharmonious singing from within the hospital. Recognising the tune as a version of *Coming round the mountain*, he called out to them in English and discovered Dick and Dorothy Morris, along with several other hostages, unharmed but severely shocked. Their guards had fled. Captain Moore, his main task of freeing the hostages now achieved, checked with Dick Morris that no-one was being held elsewhere.

During the whole of this time, the second craft had been manoeuvring in the fast-flowing river to give the best supporting fire possible. The company sergeant-major had taken command of the situation when Lieutenant Davis had been severely wounded. At this juncture the reserve sections on the second craft came ashore, the craft itself once again taking up a position in mid-stream to cover any eventuality with its medium machine guns.

A number of rebels were soon routed by 5 Troop in the area of the Attap House, whilst 6 Troop cleared the police station and 4 Troop moved north, past the mosque to the back of the bazaar. There, one of the rebels engaged them from a room full of women and children, but he was soon dislodged with no further casualties. From this time on most of the enemy resistance collapsed, although a number of rebels held out in the town and the jungle, and there was considerable movement and sniping for the next 24 hours.

As soon as the second craft beached, Terry Clark, the Royal Naval sick berth attendant, made his way to the hospital and set up a dressing station, treating the casualties while the released hostages helped him to prepare dressings. Four of his six cases of gun-shot wounds were in the legs. Sergeant Smith set about interrogating the hostages and other ex-prisoners, and discovered that more were being held in the gaol and in the southern area of the town. By late afternoon this area had been systematically cleared and a total of 14 hostages had been rescued.

Later in the morning, the Z Craft returned to Brunei, this time quickly and triumphantly, bringing the hostages and the casualties with them. L Company had lost five dead and five wounded, plus one sailor, and the wounded were quickly flown to La-buan and thence to Singapore. When L Company consolidated the next day, 15 rebel bodies were found and about 50 prisoners were taken. It was learned subsequently that many others died of wounds in the jungle. It transpired that initially nearly 350 rebels had held Limbang, many later discarding their uniforms and melting anonymously into the bazaar areas of the town.

Much later, Captain Jeremy Moore made the following observations:

'It is perhaps interesting to note that, though my assessment of where the enemy headquarters might be was right, I was quite wrong about the hostages. Furthermore, it was chance that the second beaching happened where it did, that resulted in us taking the hospital from the direction we did. It could be that this saved us heavier casualties, though I assess the most important factor in the success of the opera-tion was first class leadership by junior NCOs. Their section battlecraft was a joy to watch, and the credit for this belongs to the troop and section commanders.'

This action, along with others by the Queen's Own Highlanders at Seria, and by the Gurkhas at Tutong, crushed the revolt within five days of its breaking out. For the action at Limbang, Captain Jeremy Moore was awarded a bar to his Military Cross, and Corporals R.C. Rawlinson and W.J. Lester received the Military Medal. Lieutenant David Willis was awarded the Distinguished Service Cross, and Petty Officer D.J.D. Kirwin the Disting-uished Service Medal. Marine Barry Underwood was mentioned in despatches.

Top: Lieutenant Peter Waters, who was shot in the leg as he reached the shore at Limbang, tells the story of the assault as he awaits evacuation from Brunei. Above: Captain Jeremy Moore, MC, commanding officer of L Company on the Limbang raid. Twenty years later, Moore commanded the British land forces in the Falklands campaign of 1982.

THE AUTHOR Captain Derek Oakley, Royal Marines, was a staff officer of 3rd Commando Brigade, Royal Marines, in 1962. He was liaison officer to 99 Gurkha Infantry Brigade during the revolt in Brunei.

For 15 days, US Marines defended Wake Island against relentless Japanese attack. General James Devereux tells their heroic story

I ARRIVED ON WAKE ISLAND on 16 October 1941, and assumed command of the detachment of the 1st Defense Battalion. The atoll was a behive of constant activity as the civilian contractors and marines strove to convert a sleepy Pacific island, holding a Pan American Airways hotel and maintenance facilities, into a modern air base. As Marine historian Colonel Robert D. Heinl has written:

'In a broader sense . . . the Wake of autumn 1941 was literally in the image of America: an island in the path of inevitable war; an island vibrant with unceasing construction in an effort to recapture time lost; an island militarily naked.'

At the southernmost tip of Wake, one airstrip was operational, eight concrete magazines were nearing completion, and work on living quarters, warehouses and shops was well underway. On Peale Island, patrol plane facilities and a concrete ramp had been constructed, while in the lagoon a dredger was removing coral heads from the runways for the seaplanes that were to be based at Wake.

On 2 November we were reinforced by 200 marines led by Major George H. Potter, and at the end of the month Commander Winfield Scott Cunningham arrived at Wake and assumed command of the island. I remained in command of the Marine detachment, and was responsible for co-ordinating the operations of the defense battalion and the Marine Fighting Squadron (VMF) 211. The latter, commanded by Major Paul A. Putnam, flew in from the flight deck of USS *Enterprise* on 4 December. The 12 Grumman F4F Wildcats of VMF-211 were short-range fighters, but, as they were the only planes we had at our disposal until reinforcements arrived, they were forced to begin flying dawn and dusk patrols around the island almost immediately upon arrival.

My detachment – responsible for Wake's ground defence – consisted of 15 officers and 373 marines, together with six 5in seacoast guns and 12 3in anti-aircraft artillery pieces. Our strength was well under half that of a full defense battalion, however, and one 3in battery was entirely without guncrew. Only three out of four of the guns in the other two

In the early hours of 7 December 1941, the calm of Oahu Island was shattered by the whine of dive bombers and the chattering of machine guns. Using torpedoes and specially adapted armour-piercing shells, the Japanese aircraft crippled the might of the US Pacific Fleet. Not a single battleship escaped damage. As the torpedo planes and Zero fighters swooped low over the naval yard at Pearl Harbor, anti-aircraft guns, lacking any ready ammunition, pointed helplessly at the sky. Yet the rage to strike back was so intense that troops fired pistols at enemy planes as they strafed the island. Five hours later, and 2500 miles to the west, enemy bombers pummelled Wake Island and the Marines' heroic defence of the tiny atoll began. Below: USS *Pennsylvania* in the aftermath of the attack on Pearl Harbor. Although heavily damaged, the battleship was later repaired and rejoined the fleet.

CALL TO ARMS

WAKE ISLAND

In 1940, as war clouds began hovering over the Pacific, the US Navy initiated a belated but accelerated attempt to construct base facilities on several of the islands lying to the west of Pearl Harbor – as a security belt for America's major naval base in the Pacific. Midway Island was thus garrisoned by the 3rd Defense Battalion, and elements of the 1st Defense Battalion were sent to Johnston Island.

Wake Island, 2500 miles west of Pearl Harbor, is in fact an atoll of three islands – Wake, Wilkes and Peale – amounting to 2600 acres of sand and coral, most of which was covered with a low layer of bush.

The island was expected to become a forward base for US submarines and an operating base for Consolidated Catalina PBYs (US Navy flying patrol boats). Civilian workers and naval engineers began construction in January 1941. At Pearl Harbor, Admiral Chester Nimitz, Commander-in-Chief, Pacific Fleet and Pacific Ocean areas, directed that elements of the 1st Defense Battalion be sent to Wake to reinforce the island. His order specified that the

garrison was to comprise four 3in anti-aircraft artillery batteries (four guns each), three 5in coast artillery batteries (two guns each), and a variety of automatic weapons.

On 19 August 1941, commanded by Major Lewis W. Hohn, 5 officers and 173 enlisted marines of the 1st Defense Battalion arrived on the island.

batteries would be manned and firing in the event of combat. In addition, we had only half the number of marines needed to operate our 0.5in and 0.3in machine guns that were to be used for air and ground defence respectively. The SCR-270B search radar we had been promised had failed to arrive, and the eyes and ears of marines atop two 50ft-high water towers had to suffice as our air raid warning system.

Before I had left Pearl Harbor, I was told that my mission was only to withstand a 'minor raid', where the attacker might shell the island and attempt to land a small party to capture supplies. However, not even at full strength could we be expected to defend against a full-scale attack – in this eventuality, we would have to hold out until reinforcements could be sent from Pearl. This, then, was our condition when we went to war.

In the early hours of 8 December, an officer burst into my tent with an intercepted radio message that stated Pearl Harbor was under attack. I immediately ordered 'Call to Arms' sounded. By 0730, ammunition had been broken out of storage and distributed, and all Marine positions manned. Commander Cunningham informed me that he would set up his command post at Camp 2, and I decided to establish mine in the brush as soon as we could set up the necessary radio communication.

At noon, a flight of 30 Japanese bombers from the Marshall Islands emerged without warning from behind the cover of a rain squall to give the inhabitants of Wake Island their first taste of war. The Japanese crossed the beachline in waves between Camp 1 and Peacock Point, dropping a dense pattern of bombs in the face of heavy anti-aircraft fire. Seven Wildcat fighters were destroyed on the ground, and, when the squadron's 25,000-gallon fuel tank suffered a direct hit, it erupted in a ball of flame. Leaving a trail of death and destruction that left 23 marines dead and 11 wounded, the bombers crossed the lagoon and strafed Pan American's facilities, setting fuel tanks on fire and killing 10 American civilians. Ten minutes later the Japanese planes were gone, leaving us to clean up and tend to the

wounded. We removed our dead to a large empty refrigerator until such time that we could hack graves out of the coral.

Aware that the enemy could launch an assault at a variety of points along the shore, I created a mobile reserve by mounting four machine guns on a truck and assigning a dozen marines to man the vehicle. If the situation became desperate, these men would be pulled from their positions and sent to the area in gravest danger of being overrun. By nightfall, I had dispersed my guns as follows: a two-gun battery of 5in guns and a three-gun 3in battery at Peacock Point; another two-gun 5in battery and a four-gun 3in battery at Toki Point; and the third 5in battery and a 3in battery of four guns at Kuku Point. I also spotted machine guns around the airfield strip and emplaced four 0.5in guns on Wilkes Island, Peacock Point and Peale to provide anti-aircraft fire. Meanwhile, I had the airstrip mined with dynamite and placed generators for exploding the mines at three positions around the strip.

Both shells entered the port side of the cruiser amidships, closely followed by two more

Right on schedule, the Japanese bombers appeared over the horizon at 1145 the following day – 27 planes flying in from the south. This time, however, the Marine pilots were ready. We had four Wildcats in the air and awaiting the enemy's arrival. Although the bombers again gave the island a good pasting, the leathernecks claimed one kill and the 3in guns followed suit with some fine shooting. While we didn't know it at the time, we sent 14 bombers back to their base with flak damage.

That night I moved the 3in guns on Peacock Point 500yds inland in case they had been spotted. We placed dummy guns in the old positions, and these were dutifully destroyed the next day when the Japanese attacked at 1045, 18 strong. Nine of the bombers hit Wilkes Island, badly damaging the 5in guns and ammunition stores. The other nine bombers attempted an attack on Peale Island, but the fire from our 3in guns was heavy enough to keep the enemy too high to be accurate. Meanwhile, our four Wildcats jumped the bombers as they came in. Captain Henry Elrod, who was later to be awarded

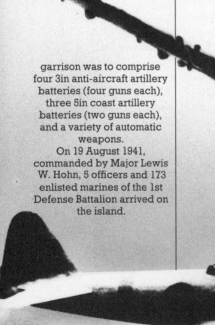

Left: The Grumman F4F Wildcat, an aircraft flown with remarkable tenacity by the pilots of VMF-211. Japanese bombers, escorted by the agile Zero fighter (below left) possessed an overwhelming numerical advantage – but the gallant Leathernecks fought on. Below: Using a 6.5mm machine gun, Japanese troops lay a deadly carpet of fire.

Wake Island
December 1941

On 19 August 1941 the first elements of the 1st Defense Battalion, USMC, arrived on Wake. This was part of a general strengthening of US defences in the Pacific as tension developed between the United States and Japan because of the latter's aggressive policies in the Far East. They received a further reinforcement on 2 November and on 4 December the men and aircraft of VMF-211 arrived.

By this time Japanese forces were already deployed for attacks across the Pacific. As part of this general offensive Wake was subjected to heavy air attacks on 8-10 December by Japanese bombers based in the Marshalls. At the same time, an assault force from the same islands was sailing towards Wake. They arrived on 11 December.

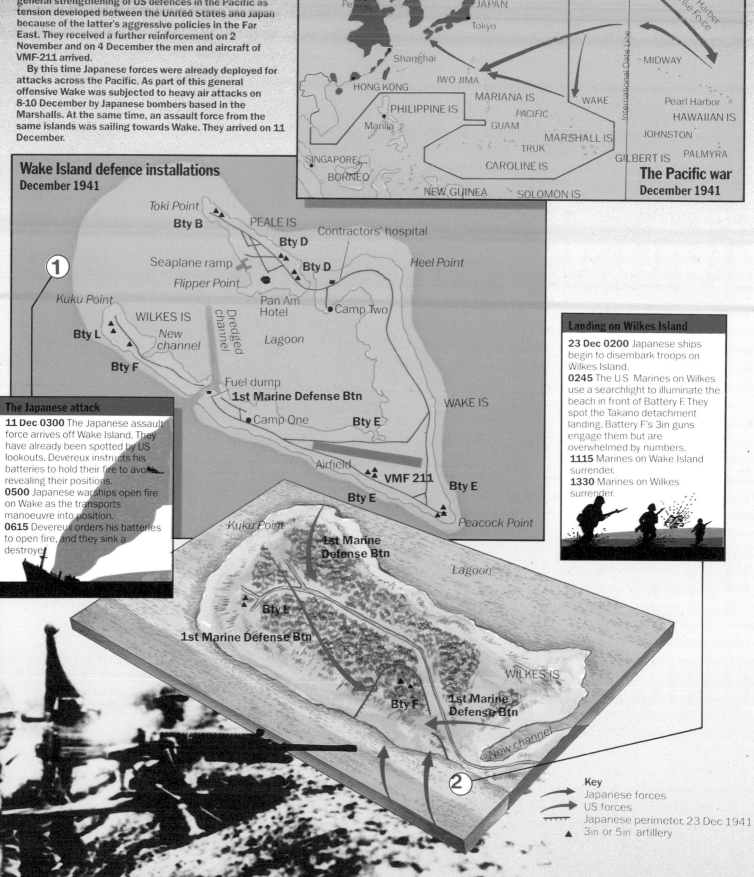

Key
- Extent of Japanese territory, Dec 1941
- Japanese carrier strike force

CHINA
Peking
JAPAN
Tokyo
Shanghai
HONG KONG
IWO JIMA
MARIANA IS
PHILIPPINE IS
Manila
GUAM
WAKE
PACIFIC
MARSHALL IS
TRUK
CAROLINE IS
SINGAPORE
BORNEO
NEW GUINEA
SOLOMON IS
MIDWAY
Pearl Harbor
HAWAIIAN IS
JOHNSTON
GILBERT IS
PALMYRA
International Date Line
Pearl Harbor Strike Force

The Pacific war
December 1941

Wake Island defence installations
December 1941

Toki Point
Bty B
PEALE IS
Bty D
Contractors' hospital
Seaplane ramp
Bty D
Heel Point
Flipper Point
Pan Am Hotel
Camp Two
Kuku Point
WILKES IS
Dredged channel
Bty L
New channel
Lagoon
Bty F
Fuel dump
1st Marine Defense Btn
WAKE IS
Camp One
Bty E
Airfield
VMF 211
Bty E
Bty E
Peacock Point

(1)

The Japanese attack

11 Dec 0300 The Japanese assault force arrives off Wake Island. They have already been spotted by US lookouts. Devereux instructs his batteries to hold their fire to avoid revealing their positions.

0500 Japanese warships open fire on Wake as the transports manoeuvre into position.

0615 Devereux orders his batteries to open fire, and they sink a destroyer.

Landing on Wilkes Island

23 Dec 0200 Japanese ships begin to disembark troops on Wilkes Island.

0245 The U S Marines on Wilkes use a searchlight to illuminate the beach in front of Battery F. They spot the Takano detachment landing. Battery F's 3in guns engage them but are overwhelmed by numbers.

1115 Marines on Wake Island surrender.

1330 Marines on Wilkes surrender.

Kuku Point
1st Marine Defense Btn
Bty L
1st Marine Defense Btn
Lagoon
WILKES IS
Bty F
1st Marine Defense Btn
New channel

(2)

Key
- Japanese forces
- US forces
- Japanese perimeter, 23 Dec 1941
- 3in or 5in artillery

the Medal of Honor posthumously, for valour in the air and on the ground, flew magnificently and splashed two of our attackers.

At 0300 on the morning of 11 December, I was awakened by the duty sentry and told that enemy movements had been detected offshore. I scanned the horizon and spotted them – a series of blurs only slightly darker than the night that surrounded them. We were to learn later that this Japanese force comprised three light cruisers, six destroyers, two destroyer transports carrying the landing force and two transports holding the Japanese garrison force.

I passed the word for all hands to prepare for battle and that not a shot was to be fired until I gave the order. I felt that our only course lay in playing a cat-and-mouse game – let the Japanese draw in close enough for our 5in guns to inflict some damage before the enemy knew what had hit him.

Minutes seemed like hours as the enemy ships drew closer and closer. At 0500 the flagship *Yubari*, a light cruiser, began her firing run, closely followed by two destroyers. Because of the casual way in which the ships were approaching the shore, I was convinced that the bombers had reported back to their base that everything on the island had been destroyed. When the Japanese began firing their guns, we were well dug in and had nothing to worry about except lucky hits.

Our 5in guns on Wilkes Island and Peacock Point had been tracking the enemy for 75 minutes as they closed on Wake, and at 0615, when they were 4500yds offshore, I gave the order – 'Commence firing.' The two batteries opened up as one. When the initial salvoes flew over their target, Lieutenant Clarence A. Barninger, commanding Battery A on Peacock Point, dropped the range 500yds and fired again with his two guns. Both shells entered the port side of the cruiser amidships, closely followed by two more that slammed into the ship slightly aft of the first hits. Smoke and steam poured from the jagged holes as the cruiser tried to get away, and a destroyer – attempting to lay a smoke screen between the cruiser and the shore – turned tail when a lucky 5in

shell exploded on her forecastle. On Wilkes Island, Battery L's commander, Lieutenant John A. McAlister, guessed the range and deflection well enough for his guns' next salvo to blow the leading destroyer out of the water – the *Hayate* was the first Japanese warship to be sunk by Americans in World War II. Our morale soared.

Flying through heavy flak thrown up by the enemy, the leathernecks managed to score a number of hits

On Peale Island, Battery B, commanded by Lieutenant Woodrow Kessler, finally got its chance to get into the war and opened up on the destroyers as they went by. Although some hits were scored, however, the enemy ships held their course and their return fire shot one of the 5in guns out of action. Meanwhile, three transports were hit and one blew up as the troops were clambering aboard one of the destroyers. All the remaining ships pulled out of range, and I ordered a ceasefire at 0700 hours.

Throughout this time, the Wildcats had attacked the enemy ships, despite being able to carry only two 100lb bombs and having to return to the airfield after each bombing run to re-arm. Nevertheless,

Above: Two months after being released from captivity, Colonel Devereux (centre) holds a reunion with fellow marines who had been with him on Wake Island. Below: A Japanese soldier captured at Wake presents a sullen face to the camera.

Left: Finally succumbing to wave after wave of enemy bombing, Wildcats lie helpless on the Wake airstrip following the Japanese invasion. Inset left: The VMF-211 squadron insignia, incorporating the Wake battle honour.

flying through heavy flak thrown up by the enemy, the Leathernecks managed to score a number of hits. At 0730, during his last sortie, Captain Elrod dropped one of his bombs on the destroyer *Kisaragi*, which sank almost immediately. There were no survivors.

Back on Wake, we were excited, happy but exhausted. We had sunk two enemy ships, hit eight more and killed some 700 Japanese soldiers and sailors – achieved at a cost of only four marines wounded and one aircraft lost. Colonel Heinl noted:

'US Marine gunners and aviators had accomplished a feat never again to be equalled by either side in World War II: the defeat of an amphibious assault.'

Even as this first Japanese force disappeared below the horizon, I knew that the enemy would have further plans for our destruction. Sure enough, we were hit by an air raid at 1000 hours. Our two remaining Wildcats went up against the 12 Japanese bombers and shot down two, while our gunners claimed one more and sent three home smoking badly. This day, 11 December, was the high point in our defence of Wake.

From this moment on, the Japanese began mounting two air raids each day, the first at midday by land-based bombers and the second at dusk by flying boats. Every raid took its toll in men and equipment, despite being stoutly opposed by our

anti-aircraft guns and planes. The bravery and extraordinary feats of professionalism exhibited by Major Putnam, his pilots and his groundcrew inspired us all. On 14 December the tail of one of the two remaining Wildcats was set on fire during an air raid. Three men from the squadron engineering section, Second Lieutenant John Kinney, Technical Sergeant William Hamilton and Aviation Machinist's First Mate James Hesson, left their cover and ran towards the burning aircraft. Working against time, they accomplished the remarkable feat of stripping the undamaged engine and dragging it clear. By cannibalising the damaged planes, the unstinting groundcrew performed miracles – three days later VMF-211 had four Wildcats that could do battle with the enemy.

The days dragged on, the bombings continued and still no word of relief. In our heart of hearts, I guess while we all hoped that we would shortly see a large relief force on the horizon, we knew it was not

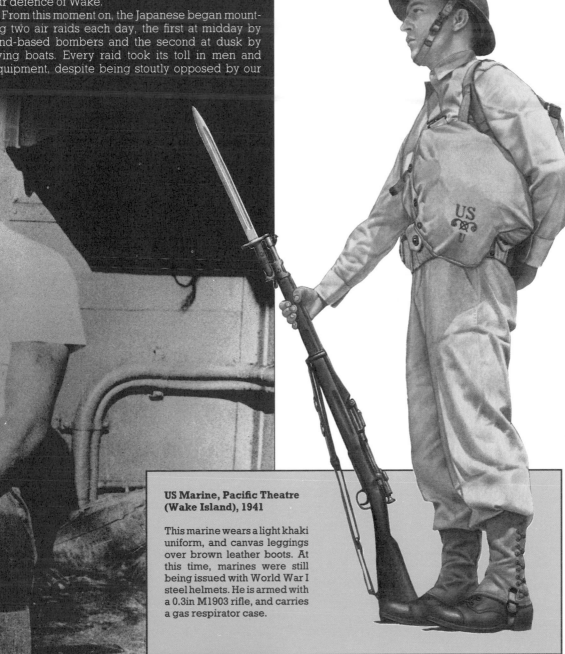

US Marine, Pacific Theatre (Wake Island), 1941

This marine wears a light khaki uniform, and canvas leggings over brown leather boots. At this time, marines were still being issued with World War I steel helmets. He is armed with a 0.3in M1903 rifle, and carries a gas respirator case.

MARINE DEFENSE BATTALIONS

After the formation of the Fleet Marine Force (FMF) in 1933, the islolationist attitude of the American people saw Congress extremely reluctant to appropriate money to any of the services. However, Thomas Holcomb, Major General Commandant of the Marine Corps, cleverly argued that an increase in Marine Corps manpower would actually constitute an increase in the defensive, rather than offensive, potential of the United States. Accordingly, the defense battalion programme began with the activation of the 3rd Defense Battalion on 10 October 1939. This was intended to provide the Marine Corps with a force capable of seizing and securing bases for the US Fleet.

On 2 October 1941, the tables of organisation for four different types of defense battalion appeared. Common to each were a Headquarters and Service Battery, and a 90mm or a 3in anti-aircraft artillery (AAA) group. The addition of two of the following components would complete the organisation of the battalion: a 155mm artillery group; a special weapons group; a 5in artillery group; a machine-gun group; or a 7in artillery group. The total strength of these battalions was generally in excess of 1000 officers and enlisted men, including a naval component of 25 doctors, dentists and hospital corpsmen.

It was originally intended that defense battalions would reach an objective after the assault troops had landed. However, in the case of Wake, Midway and several other Pacific islands, the defense battalions were already entrenched when America entered the war. In 1944, in an effort to boost the strength of the six Marine divisions, 17 of the 20 defense battalions were redesignated anti-aircraft battalions. Their personnel were transferred to the AAA units where possible, while the remainder were retrained as field artillerymen and transferred to line artillery regiments.

going to happen. I had passed the word around from the start that we were going to be reinforced – if I had not kept this hope alive in my marines, I would have encountered a severe morale problem with men who thought they had been written off.

On 20 December our battery positions were hit by 29 Japanese Navy bombers escorted by 18 Zero fighters. This was the first time that we had been attacked by carrier-based planes; it could only mean that an enemy task force was closing on Wake. Two days later, two Wildcats were in the air when 39 planes were spotted coming in from the north. Both pilots attacked from 12,000ft, and Captain Herbert Freuler claimed one kill before he was caught from behind by a Zero. Although shot in the back and shoulder, Freuler was able to bring his plane in for a crash-landing. The other Wildcat, flown by Second Lieutenant Carl Davidson, was never seen again. Now we had no planes left.

I realised that I had to organise the battalion to oppose any attempted landing. Since the airfield was undoubtedly going to be the primary enemy objective, I figured that he would hit us somewhere between Kuku and Peacock Points. I thus strengthened the southern shore, at the same time recognising that the Japanese could make feints elsewhere on the atoll and even enter the lagoon. I had 60 marines commanded by Captain Wesley McC. Platt on Peale Island, and a further 85 on the shore of Wilkes. To beef up my anti-aircraft defences, I concentrated my 3in guns on Wake itself and moved two more to new positions on Peale to act as beach defences. The 5in guns remained where they were.

At 0115 on 23 December, with all batteries and machine guns manned along the shore, observation posts reported small boats off the north shore of Peale and barges off Peacock Point. Five minutes later the machine guns on Wilkes Island opened fire and everything began to happen at once. About 1000 Special Naval Landing Force troops were coming ashore at four points between Kuku and Peacock Points. A fierce stream of machine-gun fire reached out towards the barges and a 3in gun, emplaced as an anti-boat weapon, slammed 14 rounds into one of two destroyer-transports. When one of these rounds exploded an ammunition magazine, the whole landing area, swarming with enemy troops, was turned into daylight. Before we knew it, there were 1000 Japanese on the southern shore of Wake. Defense battalion and squadron marines began fighting a desperate hand-to-hand delaying action while falling back to final positions.

As reports of the battle poured into my command post, our chances became grimmer by the moment.

Despite a stout defence by Captain Wesley McC. Platt's marines, Wilkes Island had been taken. At one point, Platt and nine others had charged a force of over 100 Japanese and launched a counter-attack, before realising that the situation was hopeless and marching east towards Wake Island. Meanwhile, the three-man detail under Lieutenant David Kliewer had failed to blow the airfield on Wake. They had reached the strip, despite being attacked en route, but discovered that rain had shorted out the generators.

The first streaks of daylight revealed 17 enemy ships surrounding Wake Island, and I received a message from Toki Point that three enemy destroyers were within range and closing. The two 5in guns opened up on the lead destroyer, scoring a direct hit with the fourth salvo and sinking it.

The message went out: 'Cease firing. Destroy all weapons. The island is being surrendered'

Throughout the battle, Commander Cunningham had left the defence of the island in my hands, keeping in contact by radio. At 0700, when I reported to him that Japanese flags covered Wilkes Island and that all our forward positions had been overrun, he replied, 'Well, I guess we'd better give it to them.' With no friendly ships within 24 hours of the island, I realised that Commander Cunningham's decision to surrender was inevitable and beyond any refutable argument. To continue fighting would entail a futile waste of life.

The message went out: 'Cease firing. Destroy all weapons. The island is being surrendered.' After performing these tasks, the marines sat down in their positions and began to eat as much as they could – somehow they knew what lay in store for them. We had not given up without a fight, and had held out for 15 days after the first air raid. During the raids, shelling and assault of the island we had lost 81 killed or wounded, but had inflicted 1000 casualties on the enemy. Four Japanese ships had been sunk and a further eight damaged, and our fighters and guns had shot down 21 planes – according to postwar reports we damaged 51 others.

For those of us who had survived the Japanese onslaught, a fresh ordeal was about to commence. After some atrocious treatment from our captors, on 12 January 1942 we were loaded aboard the *Nitta Maru* and shipped to Japan for four long years as prisoners of war. The prospect was grim, yet I could be proud of the marines. They were the best of the Old Corps.

The Marines' heroic example at Wake led President Roosevelt to declare that millions had 'been inspired to render their own full share of service and sacrifice.' Below: On 14 May 1944 US troops returned to the island with a vengeance.

THE AUTHOR Brigadier General James P.S. Devereux, USMC Retired, related the story of the Marines' heroic defence of Wake Island to the US military historian Benis M. Frank.

BRIGADIER GENERAL DEVEREUX

James Patrick Sinnott Devereux (above) was born on 20 February 1903 at Cabana, Cuba. The son of a US Army medical officer, he attended the Army and Navy Preparatory School in Washington D.C., and later entered Cornell University. Devereux enlisted in the Marine Corps in July 1923 and was commissioned two years later. Following assignments in Cuba and Nicaragua, and a period of sea duty, Devereux was detailed to China where he commanded the Mounted Detachment of the Marine Legation Guard in Peking.

In 1933 he was assigned to the US Army's Coast Artillery School at Fort Monroe, Virginia, and later became an instructor in the Defense Weapons School at Quantico Marine Barracks.

With the rank of major, Devereux was ordered to Pearl Harbor in January 1941, joining the 1st Defense Battalion. He then moved to Wake, as commander of the 373 marines who comprised the battalion's detachment on the island.

Upon his release from prisoner of war camp in 1945, Devereux was detailed as a student to the Amphibious Warfare School at Quantico, Virginia. Following graduation, he was assigned to the 1st Marine Division at Camp Pendleton, California. He retired from the United States Marine Corps on 1 August 1948, with the rank of Brigadier General. For his gallant leadership in command of the tiny garrison defending Wake Island, Devereux was awarded the Navy Cross.

TOP MALO

Where the Mountain and Arctic
Warfare Cadre of the Royal Marines
routed 602 Commando Company of
the Argentinian Special Forces
during the Falklands War

BY MARCH 1982, the Mountain and Arctic Warfare (M & AW) Cadre was a much-respected and highly professional part of the Royal Marines. Brigadier Julian Thompson, commanding 3 Commando Brigade at the time of the Falklands conflict, stated that the cadre was the best in the world at what it did. Indeed, he placed them above the SAS and SBS as far as long-range reconnaissance and patrolling were concerned in the most unforgiving of environments. In 1982, the cadre's annual winter deployment in Norway ended during the last week of March and its men had just returned home for a spot of Easter leave when, on 1 April, 3 Commando Brigade was alerted.

General Leopoldo Galtieri, the Argentinian president, made a number of planning mistakes before launching his invasion of the Falklands, but the worst was his choice of timing. The Antarctic winter was just about to begin; not only were the majority of his own troops totally unsuited to winter warfare, but the best arctic troops in the world had just completed their winter training. Moreover, having seen television pictures of their fellow marines surrendering in

WAR IN THE ARCTIC

The Arctic is an almost unbelievably harsh and very unforgiving environment; the problems faced by men in action are specific and solutions are not easily found. However, trial and error over some 16 years has proved to the Mountain and Arctic Warfare (M & AW) Cadre that specific drills, if correctly followed, can offset the worst of the prevailing conditions.

The basic needs for survival are warmth and dry clothing. Heat is generated by the consumption of rations which provide 5500 calories for each man per day. Adequate food is essential in a region where over 1500 calories can be expended in sleep. It is difficult to stay dry in the snow, so M & AW-trained men accept getting wet and only change into dry clothing at night, after getting into their bivouacs. Once inside, they can put on thermal underwear, quilted over-suits, windproofs, and duvet-type overboots to keep their extremities warm.

The Arctic environment also places tight constraints on the type of military hardware that can be used in action; many conventional weapons are inappropriate, and specific modifications have been developed to overcome this problem. In particular, the Northern Lights prevent or dislocate communications; mortars and field guns cannot be dug into soft snow; and air-burst shells have been substituted for conventional impact shells which may not explode under such circumstances.

From the medical point of view, two things contribute to the mens' health: the legendary physical fitness of the Royal Marines, which makes sure that men are never quite pushed to the limits of their endurance and, secondly, the very high standard of survival training. Simply, a high degree of professionalism counts for more in the Arctic than almost anywhere else.

Although the Mountain and Arctic Warfare (M & AW) Cadre of the Royal Marines has been in existence for just over 10 years, its origins can be traced back to the end of World War II. In 1945, groups of instructors in the Commandos, known as cliff leaders, taught combat survival and rock climbing skills to recruits. In action, these leaders were attached to rifle companies and led cliff assaults or advised officers on living rough under difficult conditions.

In the mid-1960s, cliff leaders were renamed recce leaders and taught members of Recce Troops the techniques needed for operations in difficult environments.

With the deployment of 45 Commando to Norway in 1970 as part of Britain's NATO commitment, the instructors became known as mountain leaders.

Over the next two years the mountain leaders and other volunteers were trained in arctic warfare by the Norwegians at their school in Rjukan, to the west of Oslo.

In recognition of their role as guardians of NATO's northern flank, these specialists became known as the M & AW Cadre of Instructors during 1972. The team was based at HMS *Condor*, a shore installation in Scotland.

When 42 Commando went 'whiteshod' in 1978, the cadre was under the control of HQ Commando Forces. Since 1981, however, the cadre has fallen under the operational control of the commander of 3 Commando Brigade.

The exact composition of the cadre varies with the time of year and the number of recruits, but a rough order of battle might include two officers, and 15 NCOs. Other mountain leaders, up to 100, are attached to Marine units as advisers.

Previous page: A deadly combination – a sniper of the Mountain and Arctic Warfare Cadre and the powerful Individual Weapon Sight Type SS20. Left: The men of the M & A W Cadre must learn to adjust to a frozen environment, and they must be prepared for the effects ice and cold can have on their equipment. Here they are operating a Milan missile launcher (top left), an 81mm mortar (bottom left) and a GPMG (left).

Port Stanley, they were thirsting for revenge. General Galtieri had also forgotten that a great many of these arctic-trained marines had served in the Falklands in the recent past and knew the islands' terrain and weather conditions intimately. While 3 Commando Brigade might not enjoy home advantage in any attempt to wrest the Falklands back from Argentina, they had plenty of local knowledge.

While SAS and SBS teams were inserted at the beginning of May to check possible landing sites and enemy dispositions, the M & AW Cadre bided their time. Their job was tactical recce: they would go in with the rest of 3 Brigade on D-day and, as the three Commandos and two battalions of paras dug in at the San Carlos beach-head, they would move out and check the ground over which any break-out would take place.

The M & AW Cadre consisted of 35 men under the command of Captain Rod Boswell, RM. He divided his team into four-man patrols and sent them out to the east and southeast of the beach-head. On 21 May, the main landings began and the cadre teams moved out on foot, by helicopter and in the rigid raiders of No. 1 Raiding Squadron RM, to their pre-designated patrol areas.

By 30 May the men had been out on patrol for nearly 10 days and badly needed a rest. Boswell

called in 16 of them and was on the point of telling them to stand down for a few hours when Lieutenant Frazer Haddow, the commander of a four-man patrol in an observation post (OP) some 20 miles northwest of Bluff Cove, sent in a contact report. He had spotted 16 men of the Argentinian Special Forces, from 602 Company, making their way in tactical formation down a valley in the vicinity of a deserted farm building called Top Malo House. The group had crossed a river and then entered the house without leaving any trace behind them. Haddow and his men had an ugly few minutes wondering if the Argentinians were after them.

They decided they were not and sent back a report to Boswell at his temporary base near San Carlos. Boswell's first thought was to call in an air strike, but his request was turned down; 42 Commando were about to be lifted by helicopter onto Mount Kent that night and all the available Harriers were needed for air cover.

Boswell thought again. All other British forces were heavily tied up: 2 Para were licking their wounds after their victory at Goose Green, 45 Commando and 3 Para were resting after their epic march across East Falkland, 40 Commando was badly needed at San Carlos in case of an Argentinian airborne counter-attack, and 42 Commando was on

TOP MALO HOUSE

Corporal J. K. Nicoll, section signaller with the M & AW Cadre, recounts the attack on Top Malo:
'The plan to attack Top Malo House was simple, using two groups: a fire group and an assault group. Deploying 66mm shoulder-launched anti-tank rockets, the fire group would initiate the attack and then use their personal weapons at opportune targets. Once the rockets had struck their targets, the assault group would sweep through the area at right angles to the covering fire provided by the fire group. My job was to fire two 66mm rockets, the first at a small wooden out-house, roughly the size of a garden shed, and the second at Top Malo House itself. I also carried an AR15 (Armalite) rifle and, being a section signaller, a radio.

'As planned, we left the Community Hall at San Carlos and moved to the landing strip in darkness, settling down to wait for our Sea King. Unbeknown to us at that time, our helicopter was delayed and would eventually arrive in broad daylight. The cover of darkness, which would have provided an element of surprise, was lost. At one stage, I began to think that the helicopter might not arrive at all....

'Other men were also expressing their doubts over the Sea King, yet, the marshaller consistently maintained that it was on its way. A black speck appeared in the distance, gradually increasing in size as it drew closer; it was a Sea King and it was for us. We all realised that, despite the delay and the daylight, the attack would now go ahead as planned. Once we had all crammed into the helicopter, we were soon airborne and flying at a very low level to avoid detection. With the door half open, the ground seemed uncomfortably close, as the pilot concentrated on finding and using folds in the terrain to provide cover from view.

'Time and time again, I ran over my responsibilities: what I had to do, when to do it, who was on my left and on my right. As I mentally rehearsed my actions, the Sea King slowed and then landed. The crewman had the door completely open and we spilled out of the helicopter and onto the damp grass. During our few minutes of flight, the roar of engines had partially deafened us all and the Sea King wasted no time getting airborne. As it vanished over the horizon, I remember being struck by the sudden silence as we all made the final adjustments and preparations before moving off.

'We had landed relatively close to the house, but had not had an update on the Argentinians since the initial sighting by Haddow's OP. We did not know if the enemy had been reinforced or had left the area altogether. Would they have sentries out? Were there other enemy groups in the area? All these questions were unanswered and would remain that way. After a few hundred yards, we reached the point where both groups separated and moved into their final positions. Each team had a few moments to prepare the 66mms before a single green mini-flare from the assault group would signal 'open fire'. We hurriedly extended and primed the rockets. Finally, I caught sight of the pale green flare as it arced over the building. My rockets were by my right side and, in order to get a better view of the buildings, I was forced to adopt a kneeling position. Taking aim, I lined the foresight up on the wooden out-house and gently squeezed off the first rocket. I watched in disappointment as it crashed through the flimsy wall and exited at the far end without exploding. Throwing the empty launcher to one side, I snatched the second and concentrated on the main building; being two stories high it filled the foresight.

'We were no more than 130 yards from the building, and I used a window as an aiming mark, before firing the second rocket. Other men in the group were firing 66mms and one fell short, bouncing off the turf 20 yards from the building before exploding harmlessly. Three other rockets hit the corrugated walls of the house and punched a hole through, before exploding inside. After two or three muffled bangs, the entire building erupted in one almighty explosion. The force of the blast sent the roof hurtling skyward and all four exterior walls peeled back like a banana skin. The only part of the house left standing was the brick chimney which refused to collapse into the surrounding debris.

'I had still not seen the Argentinians as I had

Left: Corporal S.K. Nicoll (who was promoted to sergeant in 1984) photographed during a training exercise in Norway. Below: Lieutenant Callum Murray, commander of Boswell's fire group. Bottom inset: Top Malo House, devastated by a tremendous explosion triggered by the LAWs of the M&AW Cadre. Background: A Wessex helicopter approaches Top Malo to evacuate the casualties after the raid.

been wholly absorbed in firing the two rockets, but I dropped flat, picked up my Armalite and prepared to advance. Directly in front of the house was a stretch of 'dead ground' which effectively hid anyone from my view. However, the men on my left could see the enemy moving across this ground, armed with SLRs and M79 grenade launchers. I was not aware of any return fire from the Argentinians until Corporal Steve Groves was hit in the side, only ten feet away from my position.

'By now, the enemy had come into my view, by a small bank, and the whole weight of our fire was brought to bear on them. Some fell instantly but others ran to find some form of cover before being hit or dropping to the ground. To our right, I could see the assault group charge downhill and suffer two casualties: Sergeants Chris Stone and Terry Doyle. As the assault group moved in front of us, we switched our fire to the left until they were on top of the enemy. One man remained with Steve Groves while we all moved down...

'It was a strange sensation to confront the enemy after the battle. The majority were injured, some had sustained several gunshot wounds. All the enemy were disarmed and searched before we moved. The seriously injured were treated with dressings and morphine. This done, they were brought together and guards were placed. With three casualties of our own, the priority was to get them back to Ajax Bay for treatment. After an agonisingly long wait a Wessex appeared and lifted all the injured out.

'Eventually everyone was lifted out but, instead of returning to San Carlos, the uninjured were flown forward to Teal Inlet where the prisoners were questioned. Events had moved so quickly that no-one had had the opportunity to sit down and gather their thoughts. None of us fully realised the difficulties and importance of the battle. It only became apparent later, when we found out that the Argentinians were part of 602 Commando Company, a unit of special forces. Other Argentinian patrols either surrendered or returned to Stanley after hearing of our attack, and the valuable intelligence we gained from the prisoners gave a detailed picture of Stanley, the enemy's poor morale and, more importantly, the news that the airfield was still open and operating. Ours, were the first prisoners to be captured who had recent information and gave a valuable insight into what was happening.

the point of making a highly dangerous low-level flight across hostile country.

However, the enemy were Special Forces and they had to be neutralised or 45 Commando, 3 Para and 42 Commando might be at serious risk. The only answer was to put elements of the cadre into an assault on the building. Ordering Haddow's patrol to remain where it was, Boswell tried to recall the rest of his men, but radio contact was impossible due to interference from the Aurora Australis. He enlisted the administrative section and that night gave his orders to only 19 men to take on a similar number of the enemy.

The operation, as Boswell planned it, was very simple. Before first light, he and his men would be dropped by a Sea King helicopter some distance away from Top Malo House itself. The party would then divide into two groups: a seven-man fire section and a 12-man assault group. On Boswell's command the fire group would flatten the building, hopefully with the enemy still inside, and then the assault group would skirmish down the hill from their startline to finish off any surviving defenders.

The dull, misty weather at first light on 31 May promised to be of some help to the Royal Marines, but the shortage of available helicopters meant that their transport was delayed and it was not until about 1230 hours GMT (about an hour-and-a-half after first light), that they finally took off. According to Sergeant Derek Wilson, the pilot did not fly the big Sea King at all, but 'drove' it at an average altitude of less than eight feet, with the main landing gear brushing crest lines and rippling the surface of the rivers that they followed along the valleys of no-man's-land.

The marines touched down in a knee-deep bog about one mile to the southwest of Top Malo House and began to move in. Boswell was pre-occupied; were the enemy still there? There was no reason for them to have moved on and, since he had heard nothing from Haddow's patrol, he kept his own counsel. However, he had other more immediate worries: had the enemy placed any sentries out in the field? He would know soon enough. Then, the marines stampeded a flock of sheep. It was a bad omen, some thought, but still they pressed on.

On Boswell's signal – a green flare – they would open fire with four LAWs and automatic rifle fire

Finally, they got to their assault base, a ridge line overlooking the four buildings and small corral which made up the Top Malo settlement. Only one of the buildings, a white-painted two-storey house, could contain the enemy; the others were dilapidated wooden out-houses, deserted by the look of it. All was quiet. They had achieved total surprise.

The fire group would open the batting for the cadre. Between them, the seven men had an L42A1 sniper rifle, three SLRs and three Armalites. In addition, they carried three M79 grenade launchers ('bloopers') and eight 66mm LAW rocket launchers. On Boswell's signal – a green flare – they would open fire with a salvo of four LAWs, pepper the building with automatic rifle fire, and then send off the next four rockets. The assault group would then skirmish in tactical formation (divided into pairs, with one man running five steps then dropping to cover his 'oppo' with aimed rifle fire, while he moved forward in turn) and clear the building. Boswell took one last long look, searching for dead ground and possible enemy escape routes, then he ordered his men to fix

The qualification that sets a member of the Mountain and Arctic Warfare (M & AW) Cadre apart from other marines is the Mountain Leader badge. There are two levels of skill: ML1 and ML2. Any marine must have passed a junior command course before he would be considered for the ML2 training.

This course lasts for 11 months and begins each September with a few weeks' rock climbing at St. Just in Cornwall. From there, the trainee mountain leader is sent to Capel Curig in Snowdonia, where the rock climbing is harder and the conditions harsher.

If successful, he is then sent to the Hebrides to learn combat survival skills and, after an evasion and escape course, is taught how to resist interrogation.

From January to March, the men are taken to Norway for a skiing course and to develop snow and ice climbing skills.

Other mountaineering exercises are carried out in Scotland and the Alps. They then go to RAF Brize Norton, to learn the finer points of parachute techniques.

If successful, the trainee will be allowed on the ML1 course, after passing the senior command course at Lympstone. Promoted to sergeant or higher, the aspiring ML1 then returns to Cornwall and Wales to train a new batch of ML2s.

After this, he is sent to Norway as a Military Ski or Arctic Survival Instructor, attached to a rifle company. He then rejoins the cadre for more training, before ending the ML1 course on Ben Nevis.

bayonets and he fired the flare.

The firepower was devastating. The first salvo of LAWs took the enemy completely by surprise, three of the rockets hitting the building and blowing great holes in it. All hell broke loose. Contrary to British press reports of the time, all Argentinians were not incompetent half-trained conscripts. These men came out fighting, and they shot straight. Some sprinted for the river gully in front of the house while others made for the dead ground in front of, and slightly to the left of, the fire group.

The second salvo of LAWs went in, but only three this time – the fourth was shot from Sergeant McLean's hand by an enemy bullet. Three were enough, however, to blow the roof right off the building. While the fire group was blazing away, Boswell ordered two LAWs to be fired by the assault group; he then gave the order for his men

Below: Any ground force operating in the Arctic would be hamstrung without highly developed skills in snow and ice climbing. Bottom: A cunningly camouflaged M&AW Cadre field base in the Falklands.

to start skirmishing down the hill.

In the event, the assault group charged down the hill straight towards the house, firing from the hip. Sergeant Derek Wilson remembers a 'text book' right-flanking assault, but saw little of it. As the assault group's M79 gunner, he was running, lobbing grenades over the building into the enemy beyond the house, then dropping down to reload. The 100 yards down to the building took some time to cover as the Argentinians were putting up a hard fight and two Royal Marines went down in quick succession: Sergeant Terry Doyle of the assault group was wounded in the right arm as he got up to throw a grenade, while Sergeant Stone, who had moved round with the rest of the fire group to get a better field of fire, took a round in the chest from an FN FAL rifle. Corporal Holleran took his courage in both hands and went to the aid of Terry Doyle, ignoring the bullets which were churning up the soft peat all around him.

The Argentinian refused to give up until he had been hit for the fourth time by Boswell's 5.56mm rounds

By this time the ground was littered with spent cartridge cases and the wounded of both sides. The Argentinians, after a bitter firefight, had retreated back to the river and some had surrendered. As the assault group swept through the settlement and moved towards the gully, the fire group moved round to their left and started bringing enfilading fire down on the Argentinians' right flank. But many of the enemy fought on; another marine, Corporal Steve Groves, went down, shot in the chest, and lay in full view of the enemy, propped up to prevent congestion of his lungs, with bullets striking the ground inches away from him.

Boswell led from the front and was one of the first to come to close quarters with the enemy. The Argentinian second-in-command was firing his FN at Boswell, who returned fire with his own Armalite. The two confronted each other, and, while Boswell was unscathed, the Argentinian refused to give up until he had been hit for the fourth time by one of Boswell's 5.56mm rounds which ricocheted off the man's rifle and cut his forehead. For Boswell, this was confirmation of the lack of real punch of the Armalite 5.56mm round compared with that of the 7.62mm ammunition fired by the FN rifles used by both British and Argentinian forces.

The man hit by Boswell was the last of seven Argentinians to be wounded. Five had died. Like the others, he had fought bravely, and his example was to be followed by other Argentinians during the night battles around Port Stanley. Like 2 Para at Goose Green, the M & AW Cadre had discovered just how brave and skilful the Argentinians could be – the good ones, at any rate.

But 602 Company made several mistakes; the bitingly cold weather had, in the opinion of their now-dead commander, made the likelihood of a British attack very remote and for this reason he had not placed sentries on the high ground covering the house. This was explained to Boswell by the second-in-command who went on to say that he had English relatives and had been on specialist courses in England. According to M & AW Cadre folklore, Boswell exploded: 'Why the hell didn't you apply some of the bloody lessons you learned, then?'

After the battle, the cadre and Argentinian casualties were taken to Ajax Bay while the uninjured

Top Malo House
Mountain and Arctic Warfare Cadre RM
31 May 1982

At Top Malo, an isolated farm some 20km northwest of Bluff Cove, 19 men of the Royal Marines Mountain and Arctic Warfare Cadre took on a group of Argentina's elite Special Forces, surprising them with a rocket attack and routing them in a classic right-flanking assault.

Key
- Mountain and Arctic Warfare Cadre
- Argentinian Special Forces unit
- Argentinian defensive position during firefight
- Line of fire

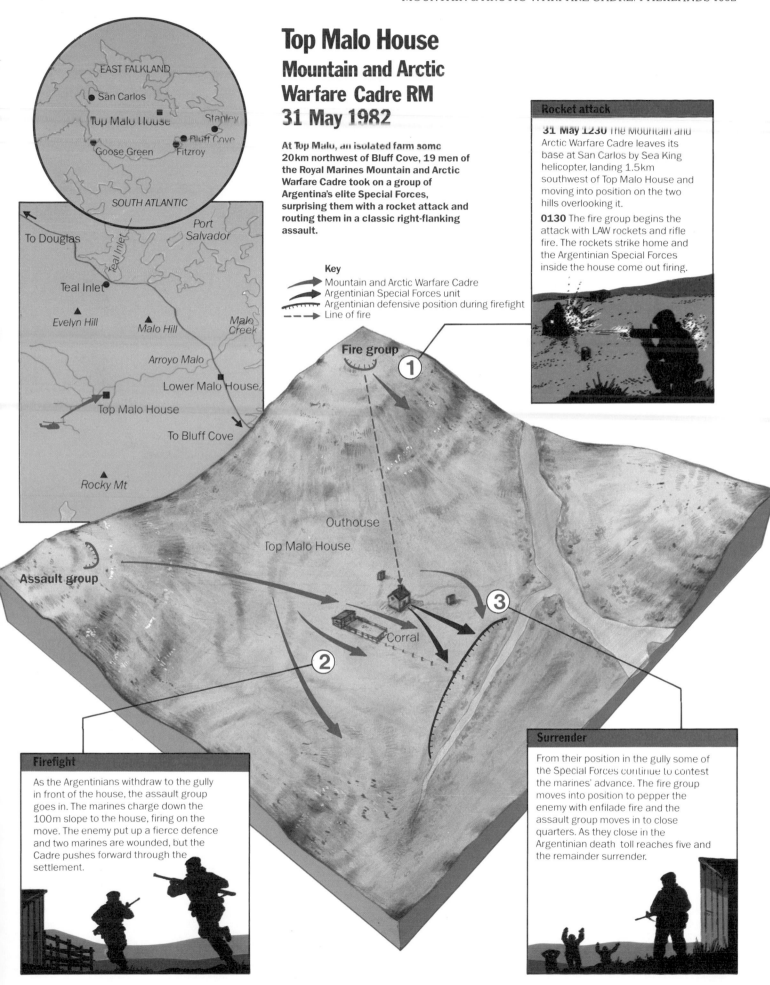

Rocket attack

31 May 1230 The Mountain and Arctic Warfare Cadre leaves its base at San Carlos by Sea King helicopter, landing 1.5km southwest of Top Malo House and moving into position on the two hills overlooking it.

0130 The fire group begins the attack with LAW rockets and rifle fire. The rockets strike home and the Argentinian Special Forces inside the house come out firing.

Firefight

As the Argentinians withdraw to the gully in front of the house, the assault group goes in. The marines charge down the 100m slope to the house, firing on the move. The enemy put up a fierce defence and two marines are wounded, but the Cadre pushes forward through the settlement.

Surrender

From their position in the gully some of the Special Forces continue to contest the marines' advance. The fire group moves into position to pepper the enemy with enfilade fire and the assault group moves in to close quarters. As they close in the Argentinian death toll reaches five and the remainder surrender.

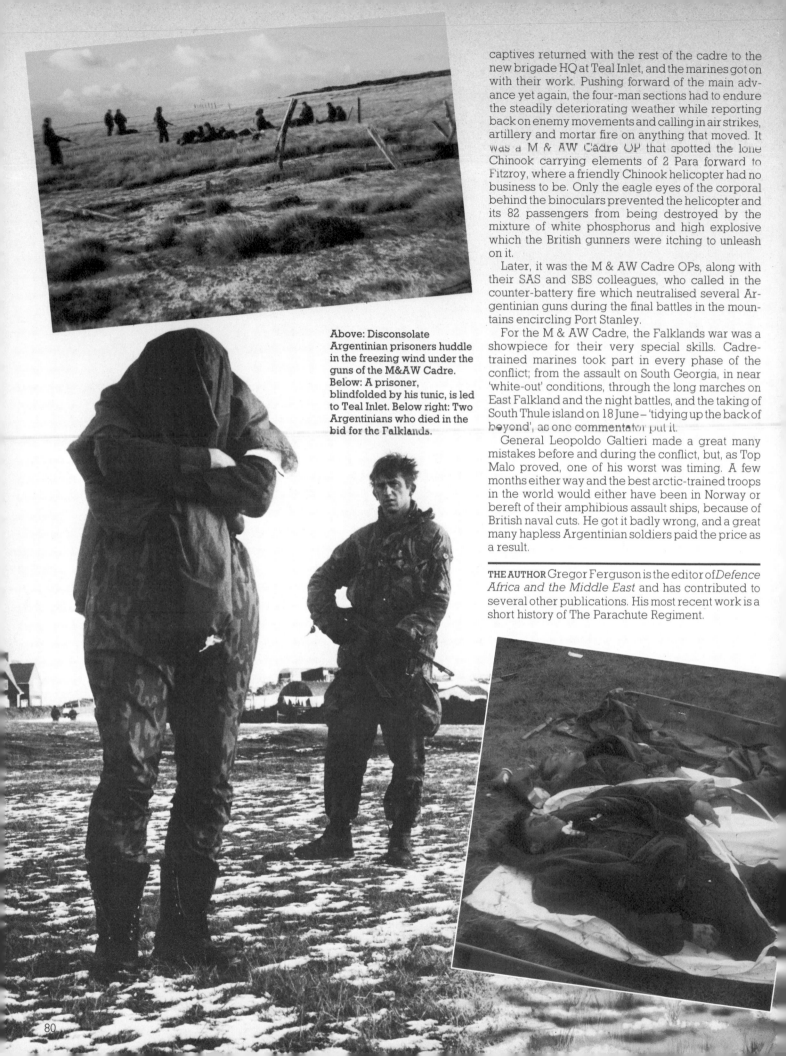

captives returned with the rest of the cadre to the new brigade HQ at Teal Inlet, and the marines got on with their work. Pushing forward of the main advance yet again, the four-man sections had to endure the steadily deteriorating weather while reporting back on enemy movements and calling in air strikes, artillery and mortar fire on anything that moved. It was a M & AW Cadre OP that spotted the lone Chinook carrying elements of 2 Para forward to Fitzroy, where a friendly Chinook helicopter had no business to be. Only the eagle eyes of the corporal behind the binoculars prevented the helicopter and its 82 passengers from being destroyed by the mixture of white phosphorus and high explosive which the British gunners were itching to unleash on it.

Later, it was the M & AW Cadre OPs, along with their SAS and SBS colleagues, who called in the counter-battery fire which neutralised several Argentinian guns during the final battles in the mountains encircling Port Stanley.

For the M & AW Cadre, the Falklands war was a showpiece for their very special skills. Cadre-trained marines took part in every phase of the conflict; from the assault on South Georgia, in near 'white-out' conditions, through the long marches on East Falkland and the night battles, and the taking of South Thule island on 18 June – 'tidying up the back of beyond', as one commentator put it.

General Leopoldo Galtieri made a great many mistakes before and during the conflict, but, as Top Malo proved, one of his worst was timing. A few months either way and the best arctic-trained troops in the world would either have been in Norway or bereft of their amphibious assault ships, because of British naval cuts. He got it badly wrong, and a great many hapless Argentinian soldiers paid the price as a result.

THE AUTHOR Gregor Ferguson is the editor of *Defence Africa and the Middle East* and has contributed to several other publications. His most recent work is a short history of The Parachute Regiment.

Above: Disconsolate Argentinian prisoners huddle in the freezing wind under the guns of the M&AW Cadre. Below: A prisoner, blindfolded by his tunic, is led to Teal Inlet. Below right: Two Argentinians who died in the bid for the Falklands.

UNDER SIEGE

US MARINES VIETNAM

Between 1954 and 1962, the US Marines (whose insignia is shown above) had provided only a small advisory group to work with the South Vietnamese Marine Corps, but as US concern over the situation in South East Asia mounted in the early 1960s, a Marine helicopter squadron was deployed to Vietnam to support South Vietnamese forces in their war against the Viet Cong. Over the next three years, individual marine squadrons were rotated for six-month tours until February 1965 when President Lyndon Johnson made the decision to commit ground troops to Vietnam. A month later elements of the 3rd Marine Division were landed at Da Nang and throughout the summer of 1965 further units, including elements of the 1st Marine Division, continued to arrive. In August the 3rd, 4th, 7th and 9th Marine Regiments, supported by four Marine Air Groups, were operating in Vietnam and their first major operation – Starlite – was launched; over 1000 Viet Cong were killed. In January 1966 the remainder of the 1st Division was deployed and the Marines continued to support South Vietnamese forces in large pacification operations. 1966 also saw the arrival of the 5th Marine Division, including the 26th Marine Regiment who were to bear the brunt of the fighting at Khe Sanh. By the end of 1967, 21 battalions from three marine divisions were active in Vietnam.

In 1968, 6000 US Marines were besieged at the combat base of Khe Sanh. William Dabney, then a captain in charge of a vital hill near the main position, describes how his men held on grimly, as the pressure increased and the bombardment intensified.

THE SNIPER was well-concealed on a hill about 400m to the north, the only hill high enough and close enough to our positions on Hill 881 South to offer a vantage point for effective rifle fire. He had been there about a week. He fired only rarely, when visibility was good and a clear target was offered, and he was deadly. With a total of perhaps 20 rounds, he had killed two marines and wounded half-a-dozen others. He was patient, waiting for an artillery mission that would force the gunners into the open, or a 'medevac' helicopter mission to evacuate wounded – the stretcher bearers made easy targets as they stumbled across the rough landing zone to the chopper with their burdens – and he was careful. On the one day that was not overcast, we had directed napalm strikes to blanket the area where we knew he must be, but the next cloudy day he was back, and still deadly. He knew very well that our jets could not be used so close to friendly lines through clouds.

But he was not careful enough. On a still afternoon, a machine-gunner, one of a dozen marines who patiently kept watch on the hillside, saw a slight movement in a bush. We had reckoned that the sniper had a hole, and was well-protected from smallarms fire, and so the gunner fired to pin him in the hole, while he called for something heavier. A 106mm recoilless rifle, our primary mid-range anti-tank gun, was brought laboriously along the trench from the south side of the hill (where it covered the only feasible tank approach to our position) and sighted onto the gunner's target. Following his precise directions, a high-explosive plastic round, designed to blow a track or turret from a tank, crashed through the bush, making a crater of the hole and formless pulp of its occupant.

The sniper's hill was too far away for us to maintain an outpost on it safely, and since the North Vietnamese could move with relative impunity at night and in fog, he was soon replaced. Over the next 10 days, this second sniper killed one and wounded several other marines. Inevitably, he too was spotted. Again the 106, a crater, and a pulpy mess.

We settled in to wait. It was a short wait, for within two days, the sniping began again. By now, the artillerymen and stretcher bearers were very worried. Any exposure for more than a few seconds invited the sharp crack of a rifle round. It was especially bad during the medevacs, because the crack of the bullet going by would cause the stretcher bearers to hit the deck, dropping their wounded comrade with an agonising jar. But the new sniper was soon located, and the crew again wrestled the 106 around the hill. As its gunner patiently adjusted it onto the point described by the spotter, a young private approached me. Crouched in the trench, he observed that this third sniper had been in position a week, had fired about as many rounds as his predecessors, but hadn't hit a damned thing. He suggested that we leave him be, for if we blew him away, the North Vietnamese would surely replace him, and his successor might be better. This idea made sense, and the 106 was moved back.

For a time, the marines amused themselves by waving 'Maggie's drawers' – a red cloth that is the traditional signal for a miss on the rifle range – every time the sniper fired, but it eventually occurred to us that this sniper was perhaps not so poor a marksman as he was crafty. He knew the fate of his predecessors, and would logically do whatever he could to avoid it. He had to fire regularly to satisfy his superiors, but since they could never determine whether he hit or not, his most sensible course was to miss deliberately, keeping his officers happy without provoking our response. So to support what we assumed to be his ruse, we quit taunting him, and sometimes even faked casualties. He stayed there for the remainder of the battle – about two months – fired regularly, and never hit a man.

Hill 881 South (881S) was one of several high hills

Page 81 : Marines on the main base at Khe Sanh dive for cover, ready to bear the brunt of yet another North Vietnamese artillery barrage. At times during the siege, Khe Sanh withstood the impact of more than 1000 incoming shells per day. Below left: A detachment manhandles a heavy 106mm recoilless rifle into position on a hill outpost. Normally deployed as an anti-tank weapon, the 106 proved extremely valuable for knocking out enemy snipers hidden deep in burrows in the hillsides facing the Marine hill positions. Below right: While the main base was never assaulted by massed infantry, the hill posts saw a great deal of close-quarters infantry fighting as the North Vietnamese attempted to wrest these crucial positions from the company-sized Marine units holding them. So heavy was the fighting for these hills that the marines holding Hill 881S sometimes suffered a 50 per cent casualty rate during the battle for Khe Sanh.

overlooking Khe Sanh Combat Base, the remote marine regiment outpost in the northwest corner of South Vietnam that came under attack from two divisions of North Vietnamese in early 1968. The marines at Khe Sanh had made a detailed study of the battle for Dien Bien Phu where the French forces in Indochina had suffered a devastating defeat in 1954 at the hands of the Viet Minh. The French had made the grave mistake of allowing the Viet Minh to bring up massive quantities of artillery, that wreaked havoc on the French defences, and the marines recognised that denial of the hills surrounding Khe Sanh to the enemy was crucial to a successful defence of the low-lying base.

This was 'Indian Country', in the parlance of the young marines at Khe Sanh

Not all of the hills offered defensible terrain, but there were sufficient to enable us to engage the enemy and to provide observation positions for the marines over the likely North Vietnamese routes of advance on the base from their staging areas to the west in Laos. None was more critical, nor more exposed, than 881S, a steep-sided hill rising 500m from its surrounding valleys, some 8km west of the base. It had been the scene of a bloody fight a year before, when the North Vietnamese holding it had chosen, uncharacteristically for that time in the war, to stand and fight. The attacking marines had finally seized it after several costly assaults, and the massive bombing and artillery barrages that helped them carry it had left its slopes devoid of vegetation, pocked with craters, and littered with collapsed bunkers in which the remains of North Vietnamese

soldiers were still entombed.

The hill overlooked Route 9, the old French highway that wound its way west from Khe Sanh across the Laotian border to Tchepone. This was 'Indian Country', in the parlance of the young marines at Khe Sahn, and crawling with enemy troops.

There was also a road running east from the base to the marine coastal bastions near the Demilitarized Zone; but this route twisted for 24km through narrow gorges and across several bridges and the North Vietnamese Army (NVA) had closed it several months earlier. All supplies for both the main base and the hill positions had to be brought in by air. The base had a runway of steel matting, and for a time, even after the so-called 'siege' had begun, four-engined C-130 cargo planes landed regularly with supplies. After NVA anti-aircraft fire had become too intense to permit such landings, the base had to be resupplied by paradrops. Water was available from streams and a well at the base.

The tactic was to direct massive fire to attack every observed or suspected enemy position and formation

The surrounding occupied hills, however, with their small perimeters, could be served only by helicopter, and constant resupply was necessary, for the marines held only the crests, which meant that they had no access to fresh water. To send a water party down the exposed slopes to the nearest streams was to invite a major skirmish with the surrounding North Vietnamese. If the water party suffered casualties – which it almost certainly would – it required reinforcement to fight its way back up the hill with its wounded, and the only source of reinforcement available was the unit holding the top of the hill; this, in turn, meant denuding the defences, and as the prime mission of these units was to hold their assigned hills, getting to water was too much of a risk to contemplate.

In any case, it was not tactically sensible to engage in firefights lower down the slopes, since the marines' main advantage lay in their occupation of fixed positions with everything around them a 'free-

fire' zone. With virtually unlimited artillery and air support available, it was unnecessary to manoeuvre on the ground to dispose of enemy formations, and to do so only complicated the co-ordination of supporting arms. The simple, and ultimately successful, tactic was to hold to the hills, whose locations were well-known to the artillerymen and aviators, and direct massive fire, using everthing from B-52 strategic bombers to 60mm mortars, and, close in, machine guns and hand grenades, to attack every possible observed or suspected enemy position and formation.

Each hill was held by a company-sized unit, all part of or attached to the 26th Marine Regiment that had overall responsibility for the defence of Khe Sanh. Hill 881S, being the most distant and most difficult to reinforce, had all of Company I ('India') and two platoons and the headquarters of Company M ('Mike'), 3rd Battalion, 26th Marines. With a section of 81mm mortars (2 tubes), 106mm recoilless rifles (2 guns), and a detachment of 105mm howitzers (3 guns), on 20 January 1968, the defenders under my command totalled some 400 marines.

Intelligence had accurately predicted the NVA's intention to besiege or attack Khe Sanh, and three battalions of about 1000 marines each had been flown to the base during December and January to reinforce the battalion already in place. With a 300-man battalion of South Vietnamese Rangers and normal supporting units, the garrison totalled about 6000 men, deployed on the base itself and in the surrounding hills.

Although there had been no major engagements before 20 January, we had been patrolling aggressively around 881S, and, on the 18th and 19th, had fought skirmishes with North Vietnamese soldiers to the north of the hill, where patrols had previously passed unmolested. Concerned about an enemy build up to the north, I sought permission to take India

Below: One of the main problems facing Colonel David E. Lownds, commanding officer at Khe Sanh, was keeping a flow of supplies and equipment coming into the base. By mid-February it had become too costly to land fixed wing transports (they were sitting ducks for enemy fire) on Khe Sanh's exposed airstrip. Supplies were then dropped by parachute into a drop-zone at the northwestern corner of the base using LAPES and GPES procedures. With LAPES (low altitude parachute extraction system), the delivery transport came in low and a parachute dragged the cargo across rollers and out of the rear doors. GPES (ground parachute extraction system) utilised an arresting line that was snagged by the aircraft on its low-level approach, and then pulled the crates of supplies out of the rear. During the siege some 11,250 tonnes of cargo were delivered to the beleaguered marines at Khe Sanh – without this the base could not have held out.

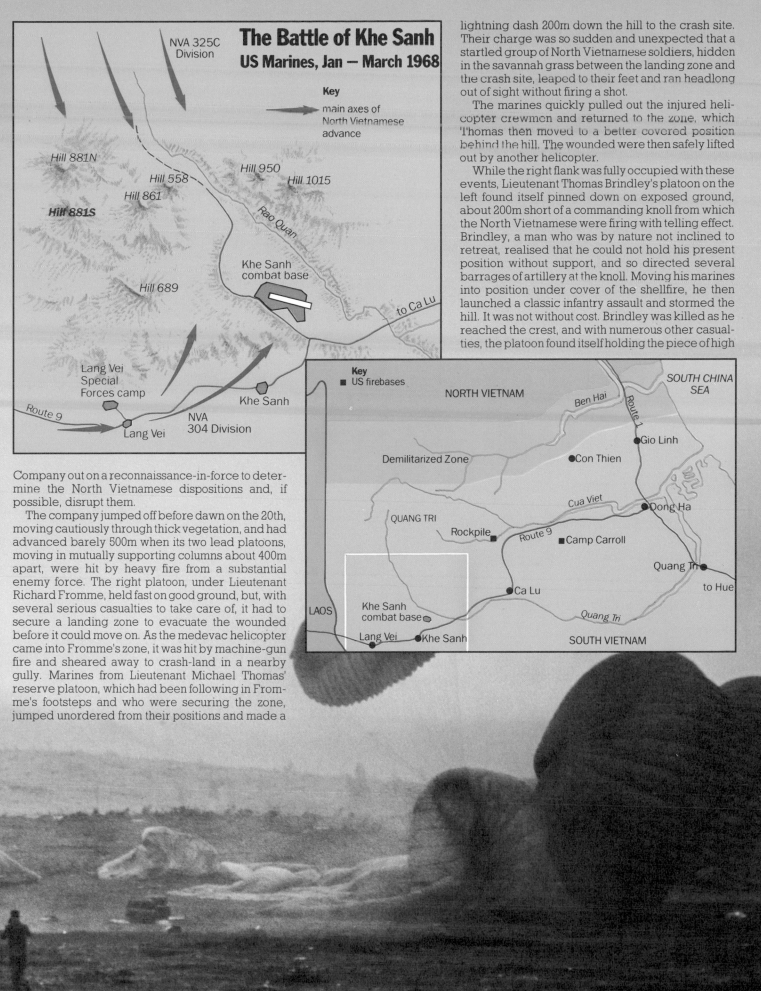

The Battle of Khe Sanh
US Marines, Jan — March 1968

NVA 325C Division

Key

→ main axes of North Vietnamese advance

Hill 881N

Hill 558

Hill 950

Hill 1015

Hill 861

Hill 881S

Rao Quan

Khe Sanh combat base

to Ca Lu

Hill 689

Lang Vei Special Forces camp

Khe Sanh

Route 9

Lang Vei

NVA 304 Division

Key
■ US firebases

NORTH VIETNAM

SOUTH CHINA SEA

Ben Hai

Route 1

Gio Linh

Demilitarized Zone

Con Thien

Cua Viet

Dong Ha

QUANG TRI

Rockpile

Route 9

Camp Carroll

Quang Tri

to Hue

Ca Lu

LAOS

Khe Sanh combat base

Quang Tri

Lang Vei

Khe Sanh

SOUTH VIETNAM

lightning dash 200m down the hill to the crash site. Their charge was so sudden and unexpected that a startled group of North Vietnamese soldiers, hidden in the savannah grass between the landing zone and the crash site, leaped to their feet and ran headlong out of sight without firing a shot.

The marines quickly pulled out the injured helicopter crewmen and returned to the zone, which Thomas then moved to a better covered position behind the hill. The wounded were then safely lifted out by another helicopter.

While the right flank was fully occupied with these events, Lieutenant Thomas Brindley's platoon on the left found itself pinned down on exposed ground, about 200m short of a commanding knoll from which the North Vietnamese were firing with telling effect. Brindley, a man who was by nature not inclined to retreat, realised that he could not hold his present position without support, and so directed several barrages of artillery at the knoll. Moving his marines into position under cover of the shellfire, he then launched a classic infantry assault and stormed the hill. It was not without cost. Brindley was killed as he reached the crest, and with numerous other casualties, the platoon found itself holding the piece of high

Company out on a reconnaissance-in-force to determine the North Vietnamese dispositions and, if possible, disrupt them.

The company jumped off before dawn on the 20th, moving cautiously through thick vegetation, and had advanced barely 500m when its two lead platoons, moving in mutually supporting columns about 400m apart, were hit by heavy fire from a substantial enemy force. The right platoon, under Lieutenant Richard Fromme, held fast on good ground, but, with several serious casualties to take care of, it had to secure a landing zone to evacuate the wounded before it could move on. As the medevac helicopter came into Fromme's zone, it was hit by machine-gun fire and sheared away to crash-land in a nearby gully. Marines from Lieutenant Michael Thomas' reserve platoon, which had been following in Fromme's footsteps and who were securing the zone, jumped unordered from their positions and made a

An extract from the Times-Herald of February 1968 provides an insight into the high morale on Hill 881S: 'The flag is battered, heads are bloody, but "the colors" still sound on Hill 881. A tough Marine company led by Capt. William H. Dabney is today showing the Viet Cong how American fighting men respond to the rigors of the battle in the much beleagured Khe Sanh Combat complex. Each day, a torn and bullet riddled American flag is hauled up an improvised flag pole on Hill 881, and then the muted tones of a bugle sounding "to the colors" echoes through the trenches and earthworks. Captain Dabney and his men stand at attention during the brief ceremonies, although enemy guns are trained on them every moment. They hit the dirt as soon as the last note is sounded. India Company now has the unique position of performing the "most dangerous flag-raising ceremony in the world", according to reports from the battle zone. Officially, the American flag is not supposed to be raised alone over South Vietnamese territory, but in this instance the Marines feel strongly that it is a right they have fought hard to get.

'The Marines argue that since it was their blood alone that bought the hills around Khe Sanh, it is the American flag that belongs there.

Captain Dabney has been described by on-the-scene reporters as one who "is known for his dash and his flair for the unorthodox".

Captain Dabney has also put in another requisition for "supplies" on 881. This time he wants more musical instruments. His request to headquarters said: "Need saxophone and trombone to fill out Trench Foot Trio. Technicians for the instruments available this position." An AP news story says that the instruments haven't arrived on the hill, but it would be interesting to see the Viet Cong's reaction to an American jazz session along with the flag-raising ceremonies.'

Khe Sanh Combat Base

SUPPLY DROP ZONE

RED SECTOR

to Khe Sanh village

4.2in mortar bty

155mm howitzer bty

BLUE SECTOR

105mm howitzer bty

Marine air traffic control unit

GREY SECTOR

control tower

fire support coordination centre and 26th Marines command post

water point

main ammo dump

airstrip

105mm howitzer btys

main perimeter

77 DAYS AT KHE SANH

The US combat base at Khe Sanh was situated in the northernmost province of South Vietnam, some 23km south of the Demilitarized Zone and 10km east of the border with Laos. Khe Sanh was established as one of a series of firebases, known as the McNamara Line, that stretched from the coast to the Laotian border. Its purpose was to cut troop and supply infiltration into South Vietnam from the North and to block North Vietnamese incursions from Laos along the strategically important Route 9. In early January 1968, US intelligence sources pointed to signs of a mounting North Vietnamese offensive in the northern provinces and two North

Vietnamese Army (NVA) divisions, 324B and 325C, were identified in the area.

On the base the Marine commanding officer, Colonel David E. Lownds, had at his disposal the 1st, 2nd and 3rd Battalions, 26th Marine Regiment, and an artillery unit, the 1st Battalion, 13th Marines. As the siege developed, the battalions of the 26th and 13th Regiments were reinforced by the 1st Battalion, 9th Marines and the 37th Rangers (a South Vietnamese battalion), bringing the total number deployed to some 6000 men.

It soon became clear that the NVA intended to hit Khe Sanh in strength. The battle for Khe Sanh opened on 22 January 1968 with a massive rocket, artillery and mortar bombardment that

ground with depleted ammunition stocks and only a lance-corporal in command.

An enemy skirmish line then charged up the rear slope to retake the hill but was annihilated by a napalm drop so close to the marines' lines that several soldiers had their eyebrows singed. The situation, however, was still desperate, and, with Fromme holding on the right, I took Thomas' reserve platoon across the intervening gully to relieve the marines on the knoll and move the wounded back for medevac.

I soon discovered that an eight-man reconnaissance team attached to Brindley's platoon had become disoriented during the assault and had strayed off into a gully to the left, where it was pinned down and under attack by enemy soldiers withdrawing from Brindley's hill. Thomas, in a move typical of his aggressive brand of leadership, volunteered to find them and lead them back to the lines. He got about 20m before he was felled by an enemy bullet. His platoon sergeant, David Jessup, immediately replaced him, located the team, and after several trips carrying wounded marines, had them all back to relative safety.

By now, with the enemy forces located, India was bringing heavy supporting fire to bear, but, with darkness approaching and its mission still the defence of 881S, it could advance no further. Under cover of artillery fire, the withdrawal was uneventful, and Company India rejoined Company Mike on the hill as darkness fell, weaker by 50 marines than it had been that morning.

Large-calibre rocket and artillery fire created havoc along the runway and exploded the main ammo dump

At about 0200 hours the following day, the North Vietnamese simultaneously assaulted several of the outlying positions with massed infantry. Hill 881S, however, was not attacked. The lightly-manned position at Khe Sanh village, a few hundred metres outside the base perimeter, had to be evacuated but the others repulsed the assaults, and constant artillery concentrations on North Vietnamese reserve staging areas and approach routes prevented their exploitation of their initial successes. Why 881S, the most vulnerable position, was not assaulted is a mystery, but it was probably because India's fighting reconnaissance the previous day had revealed the NVA force moving into assault position against it, and had hurt it enough to discourage the attempt.

During the battle of the 21st my 81mm mortarmen had fired nearly 700 rounds at near-maximum range from their two tubes to seal off the breach in the perimeter of Hill 861, our neighbouring position 3km to the northeast. The mortar tubes got so hot that the propellant ignited as the rounds slid down the tubes, causing the bombs to go unpredictably astray, and the tubes had to be cooled. The marines used their precious water, but soon exhausted that and a meagre cache of canned fruit juice. Finally, a 'daisy chain' of marines was formed to urinate on the tubes, and the fire mission continued until, with the coming of dawn, we were no longer needed. The smell was unpleasant, but the job was done.

With the opening round over, the units on the hill positions settled in for a prolonged contest. It began in earnest the next morning, on the 22nd, when, shortly after dawn, the main base was struck by several hundred rounds of large-calibre rocket and artillery fire, creating havoc along the runway and

blew up 1340 tons of munitions in the main ammo dump. Throughout February the enemy continued to pour heavy fire into the base and onto the Marine positions on Hill 881S. Infantry attacks were mainly confined to the outposts on the hills which saw some of the heaviest fighting in the war, but throughout the siege the US hammered the investing NVA with bombs, cannon and napalm, culminating in March with massive close-in B-52 strikes. By the beginning of April, NVA attacks on the base began to fade as the US relief operation – Pegasus – came into effect. Khe Sanh was relieved on 8 April although skirmishing in the surrounding country continued to the middle of the month. Estimates place the North Vietnamese strength during the siege at between 15,000 and 20,000 men. From 19 January to 31 March the Marines lost 199 men killed and 830 wounded while General Westmoreland's staff put NVA losses at between 10,000 and 15,000 in the most heavily barraged and bombed target area in the history of modern warfare.

Above: Under constant threat of mortar fire, marines extend the slit trench earthworks along the crest of a hill outpost.

exploding the main ammunition dump. The shells came from two sources. The first was the line of deadly accurate artillery pieces – 152mm howitzer and 130mm guns – positioned in Laos to the west and southwest of the base. The second source, far greater in volume, consisted of sheaves of 122mm Russian-made rockets, fired 30 to 50 at a time from several positions at once, that had a devastating effect upon a target as large as Khe Sanh.

Having lost the element of surprise on 881S when we attacked north on the 20th, and faced thereafter with alert and well-emplaced defenders, ready to throw back a ground assault, the North Vietnamese decided to force us off the hill by cutting off our resupply. But for the unique structure of the Marine Air-Ground Team, they might have succeeded.

The NVA began by positioning their 120mm mortars about 5000m west of the hill, emplaced deep in the ground with narrow tunnels dug at the proper angle for the rounds to shoot out on the required trajectory. These mortars were impossible to detect from the air and impervious to anything short of a direct hit down the hole from a heavy bomb or large-calibre shell. Since 881S was a fixed target, such underground positions were entirely feasible, because, at that range, a minute change in the horizontal or vertical alignment of the tube was enough to ensure that any point on the hill could be fired on. Even the thud of a mortar firing was muffled by the depth of the emplacement, so that a report, readily audible had the tube been out in the open, could only be heard on the hill by a practised ear and only when all else was quiet – a rarity on the Khe Sanh plateau.

At first, our resupply was provided by a single helicopter from Khe Sanh. The pilot would ask that the troops be up in the trenches, firing to suppress the numerous anti-aircraft guns whose rounds swept across the hilltop landing zones from north and south. The result, however, was catastrophic, for, as soon as the pilot committed the helicopter to a zone, the North Vietnamese forward observer relayed the zone location to his mortarmen, who knew from long practice the exact range to each zone, and were able to fire precisely-aimed rounds in seconds, unheard on the hill because of the noise of the helicopter. The time of flight for the rounds was about 25 seconds, and to unload supplies and load up the wounded within that time was impossible. With so little time in hand, the landing zone was crowded with men, and the effect of those impacting rounds was devastating.

On the 22nd, two rounds bracketed the zone just as

Bottom: A US Skyraider blasts a North Vietnamese position, dangerously close to the perimeter of the base. Such close air support was crucial to Khe Sanh's defence but could also be very un-nerving to its defenders. Below: Fire extinguisher at the ready, marines surround a pilot in the wreckage of his crashed spotter aircraft. Right: Evacuation of casualties from the hill posts was an extremely hazardous operation. When the C-46 helicopters came in, the wounded had to be loaded at break-neck speed before the landing zone was deluged with enemy mortar fire.

FIRE FROM THE SKY

On 26 February 1968 a single US Air Force B-52 strategic bomber took off from U Tapao airbase, destination Khe Sanh. Its bomb bays contained 108 500lb bombs and its mission was to test a close-in attack on North Vietnamese positions around the besieged combat base. The marines on the base were naturally jumpy at the prospect of such massive ordnance being unloaded within 1000m of their own lines. The test, however, was a success. The next day, using Combat Skyspot, a computer system that guided the incoming bombers onto their targets, four more close-in missions were flown. All the bombs fell within the designated target boxes and as the detonations of hundreds of bombs exploding simultaneously shook the earth at Khe Sanh, marines emerged from their shelters to cheer the passing B-52s. This new tactic was to have a devastating effect on the North Vietnamese investing the base. During March B-52 close-in strikes became routine and the records of the USAF 3rd Air Division indicate that during the siege some 2548 sorties were flown, with 59,542 tons of bombs dropped. Photo reconnaissance showed 274 North Vietnamese defensive positions totally destroyed and 67 damaged, while 17 weapon positions were annihilated and a further eight put out of action. Bomber crews reported 1382 secondary explosions and 108 secondary fires. To estimate the number killed by B-52 bombardment would be impossible. In the words of General Westmoreland, it was the B-52s that 'broke their backs' at Khe Sanh.

the last wounded man was being loaded aboard a medevac helicopter, and 22 men were killed or grievously wounded, including the helicopter crew. The plane, with its cargo of wounded marines, was completely destroyed.

By early February, the combined effects of the mortars and the incessant anti-aircraft fire had cost the marines of Companies India and Mike 150 casualties and six helicopters. Including the toll of men shot by snipers, the casualty rate was over 50 per cent, with no end in sight. At that rate, the position would soon have become untenable, for replacements were sometimes hit before they even got off the incoming helicopters, and the troops were down to one quart canteen of water per day, an unacceptable level for the climate. When NVA anti-aircraft guns were destroyed, as they frequently were by air attacks or fire from our own guns, they were replaced as quickly as were the snipers.

The solution was unusual, probably impossible for any other military service in the world, and was instantly and consistently effective. A carefully rehearsed, perfectly timed and co-ordinated air-ground resupply operation, known as the 'Super Gaggle', was mounted on the first clear day in mid-February. On a pre-arranged signal, the mortar tubes on 881S opened up with white phosphorus shells, pre-registered against known anti-aircraft emplacements. Within seconds of the rounds' impacts, a flight of four Marine A-4 Skyhawk attack jets, each with several 5in anti-tank rockets mounted beneath its wings, dived from altitude and systemati-

STOPPED BY A BULLET

'It is night and the sky is burning with slowly dropping magnesium flares. Heaps of equipment are on fire, terrifying in their jagged black massiveness, burning prehistoric shapes like the tail of a C-130 sticking straight up in the air, dead metal showing through the grey-black smoke. God, if it can do that to metal, what will it do to me? And then something very near me is smouldering, just above my head, the damp canvas coverings on the sandbags lining the top of a slit trench. It is a small trench, and a lot of us have gotten into it in a hurry. At the end farthest from me there is a young guy who has been hit in the throat, and he is making the sounds a baby will make when he is trying to work up the breath for a good scream. We were on the ground when those rounds came, and a marine nearer the trench had been splattered badly across the legs and groin. I sort of took him into the trench with me and he kept swearing and shouting until someone told him that I wasn't a grunt but a reporter. Then he started to say, very quitely, "Be careful, Mister. Please be careful." He'd been wounded before, and he knew how it would hurt in a few minutes. Far up the road that skirted the TOC (tactical operations centre) was a dump where they burned the gear and uniforms that nobody needed any more. On top of the pile I saw a flak jacket so torn apart that no one would ever want it again. On the back, its owner had listed the months that he had served in Vietnam. *March, April, May* (each month written out in a tentative, spidery hand), *June, July, August, September, Octobler, Novembler, December, Janurary, Feburary,* the list ending right there like a clock stopped by a bullet.' Michael Herr, freelance journalist, Khe Sanh.

cally attacked the emplacements, using the smoke from the phosphorus shells as a marker.

As soon as the first aircraft had unleashed their rockets and departed, a second flight of four A-4s, this time carrying napalm, bracketed the hill, close in, with sheets of fire to kill or discourage the North Vietnamese who in the past had frequently lain on their backs in shallow holes, just outside the defensive barbed wire, and fired automatic weapons into the bellies of the approaching helicopters. Close behind came two more A-4s, one on either side of the hill, dropping canisters of delayed-fuse bomblets which scattered the length of the flanking valleys and detonated at irregular intervals for several minutes thereafter.

There was then a momentary pause during which each mortarman fired several more rounds of white phosphorus in quick succession to blind whatever anti-aircraft guns the air attacks might not have destroyed. No fire from the hill, other than the mortars, was attempted. All other troops stayed under cover in individual man-sized holes dug into the uphill side of the trench bottom, with two or three metres of dirt and rock over their heads.

Below: North Vietnamese rockets pour into the base. Life for the marines consisted of long periods of boredom shattered by devastating artillery and rocket barrages. Shelters had to be constantly reinforced and living quarters were cramped and primitive (left above). Left below: Marines take coffee from old tin cans. Right: Tension shows on the face of an incoming helicopter crewman.

Left: Memories of World War I – marines huddle in a trench under a rain of enemy mortar bombs. Left below: Molikau Niuatoa (left), the Samoan marine whose painstaking watch on Hill 881S led to the destruction of five North Vietnamese 130mm artillery pieces.

Below: Armed with an M16 and a Colt Commando, US Marines keep a close watch for signs of North Vietnamese infantry as they patrol the battered and denuded slopes of a hill post. While the marines held the crests, the lower slopes often swarmed with North Vietnamese.

Through the haze of dust and smoke that constantly shrouded the plateau, there would then appear 10 Marine CH-46 medium helicopters, each bearing an externally slung load of 1500kgs of supplies. As the helicopters neared 881S, four more A-4s would scream by, two on either flank, laying a screen of thick white smoke between 881S and the ridges to the north and south on which the NVA anti-aircraft guns were positioned. The effect was to create a narrow valley of visibility over the hill, into which the 10 helicopters descended, in echelons of five, to release their loads and climb out quickly, into the smoke on the upwind side and away.

Usually, in the rear echelon of helicopters that followed a few seconds behind the first, one aircraft would land in a predetermined zone with replacement men, prepared to pick up the waiting casualties. The position of the aircraft in the echelon and the zone it would use, were varied constantly, and the blinded North Vietnamese mortarmen could only hope for luck in choosing the right zone to bombard. They were never again successful in hitting a zone with a helicopter and men in it.

The entire Super Gaggle operation took less than five minutes, and from the laying of the shielding smoke to the departure of the last helicopter was never more than 30 seconds. Anti-aircraft fire still swept the hill, but in substantially less volume, unaimed, and therefore ineffective. Mortar rounds still rained down, often for up to an hour after the aircraft had departed, but they were at most a nuisance, for the marines in their burrows kept their heads down. Some 15,000kgs of supplies were scattered across the hill, replacement troops were in, and the wounded were out, usually without a casualty. The entire operation was controlled from a two-seat TA-4 jet, flown by the A-4 squadron commander with the helicopter squadron commander in the back seat and radio contact with myself on the hill. These were all marines who had trained, marched and partied together for years, and so could make such a complex, split-second operation work.

After dark, when the North Vietnamese could no longer observe us, we gathered the supplies, which were often riddled by shrapnel from the post-Gaggle mortaring, distributed them, and set the watch to ward off any attack. The night watch was 50 per cent until midnight and all hands thereafter until dawn. The enemy could not set up for an attack until dusk without risk of detection, and movement to assault positions up the slopes of the hill would have taken until midnight. The marines knew – they'd climbed it often enough themselves.

Suddenly, the excited voice of the observer came over the radio: 'We found the bastards! We've got 'em!'

Hill 881S was never assaulted. There were occasional probes to the outer defensive wire, but these only served to prove that a marine could throw a hand-grenade downhill far better than a North Vietnamese soldier could throw one uphill – and ours didn't come rolling back down on us.

Both to conserve water and to avoid casualties, the marines worked at night, with only small observation posts and the supporting-arms controllers about in daylight. Casualties, after the Gaggles began, were steady but light, for few marines were above ground. An occasional unheard round would land in a trench, or catch a soldier crossing an open area, but even this firing decreased as the opposing commanders realised that their efforts had been foiled.

As their rate of fire decreased, so ours accelerated. The weather was improving, and attack aircraft could fly almost daily. Rocket sites were regularly attacked, and in an awesome display of patience and visual acuity, a young American Samoan, Lance-Corporal Molikau Niuatoa, using 20-power naval binoculars, spotted the flash of an artillery piece at a range of over 15,000m to the west. He'd been watching for weeks, orienting on the boom of the guns as they fired over 881S onto the base, impervious to sniper fire, heat, thirst, or any other distraction. Corporal Robert Arrotta, India's forward air controller, quickly sent an airborne observer to the area, but neither he nor Niuatoa could see the aircraft at that distance to guide it to the target.

With NVA artillery as the prize, the observer soon

had several flights of bombers orbiting over him, waiting to receive his target data. He fired a white smoke marking rocket, but it could not be seen from Niuatoa's position on the hill through the haze. Finally, his bombers running low on fuel, the observer proposed that he unload a planeload of 500lb bombs on a prominent ridge. He did, and we saw their impact. Niuatoa's first correction, given in his typical laconic voice, would qualify as bold in any armed force: 'Left 1000 yards, add two ridgelines.' Patiently, using bomb strikes as marking rounds, he closed the bracket, and suddenly, the excited voice of the observer came over the radio: 'We found the bastards! We've got 'em!' By day's end he was able to report the destruction of five 130mm Soviet field guns, whose accuracy and 27,000m range had been so damaging to Khe Sanh.

In March, as the siege of Khe Sanh wound down, Captain Harry Jenkins (commanding Mike Company) and I acted as the conductors of an orchestra. With radios as our 'batons' we orchestrated the unlimited and instantly available artillery and aircraft ordnance upon any movement, or sound, or smell, or hunch. The noise was constant. What had been a green rolling plateau three months earlier now looked more like the surface of the moon, with long series of overlapping craters and blasted stumps where before there had been lush forests.

The siege did not end abruptly. Rather, the North Vietnamese simply melted away, with an occasional small pocket of diehards left behind for the relieving forces to mop up. A full-scale attack on the Khe Sanh base was never mounted. An incident on 881S, around 1 April, as the relieving forces arrived, perhaps shows why. Two naked North Vietnamese soldiers ran up to our wire in broad daylight, waving propaganda leaflets to indicate surrender. One was

Above: Heads bowed around a makeshift sandbag altar, marines attend a service at Khe Sanh in February 1968, at the height of the battle. Maintaining a high level of morale among the defenders is a crucial aspect of any siege and regular religious services, in conjunction with demonstrations of undefeated patriotism such as Dabney's flag-raising ceremonies on Hill 881S, kept spirits high in the emotionally pressurised environment at Khe Sanh.

shot in the back by his comrades, and the other went to ground outside the wire until a marine, under our covering fire, crawled across and led him to the safety of the trench. He was an impressive man, almost six foot tall, healthy looking, and of imposing physique. We began to question him, but were interrupted by his amazing transformation as a marine jet passed overhead. He literally lost complete control of himself – his muscles, his eyes, even his bowels – and fell in a quivering heap to the bottom of the trench. Even a loud handclap behind him would produce that same petrified reaction. The man had been psychologically destroyed by the awesome pounding he and his comrades had been subjected to during the preceding 77 days. If he was anywhere near typical of the soldiers surrounding us, and in the rare moments when he was lucid he said that he was, it was no wonder they could not mount an assault. More tonnage of bombs was dropped within a 25km radius of Khe Sanh during those 77 days than had been dropped on all of Germany in the bombing raids of 1943.

India returned to the coast with only 19 of the 200 original marines who had taken up the defence of 881S. Mike had fared little better. And sent to a supposedly secure cantonment at Quang Tri the night we flew east, we lost six more of those 19 from India Company when a rocket struck the ridgepole of a tent to which they had been assigned. The defence of Khe Sanh had been successful but it had been costly.

THE AUTHOR Colonel William H. Dabney attended Virginia Military Institute and received his commission in 1960. As a captain, he commanded India Company, 3rd Battalion, 26th Marines at Khe Sanh. It was his company that held Hill 881 South.

MARINE ASSAULT

COLONEL NICK VAUX, DSO.

Born in London in 1936, Colonel Nick Vaux spent the first 10 years of his life in central Africa where his father was a British Government official. In 1946 he returned to England and was educated at Stonyhurst College until 1953.

In November 1954 he was commissioned into the Royal Marines and, whilst still under training, took part in the Anglo-French operations at Suez in 1956. In 1963 he took command of the RM detachment HMS *Ursa* and served at sea until 1965, on the West Indies station.

After attending the Army Staff College at Camberley, he became GSO2 in Military Operations (MOD Army). Subsequently, he was posted on exchange to the US Marine Corps, where he served as Special Adviser to the Commanding General, Marine Corps Development and Education, at Quantico, Virginia. Later, Colonel Vaux returned to England to command 42 Commando in the Falklands campaign.
Below: Colonel Vaux (foreground).

From his Tac HQ on the slopes of Mount Challenger, Lieutenant-Colonel Nick Vaux directed 42 Commando in the attack on the Argentinian defences around Mount Harriet. Here he tells the story of their hard-fought victory

IT WAS 0400 hours when my telephone shrilled at home. As I fumbled for the receiver, I concluded that the call must have something to do with my RAF flight to Washington later that morning. The urgent, familiar voice that briefed me, however, belonged to Colonel Ian Baxter from HQ Commando Forces. He ordered me to cancel all previous arrangements and return to base, because my unit had been recalled from leave. It was Friday, 2 April 1982 and I was then commanding 42 Commando Royal Marines, an Arctic-warfare-trained unit that had just completed three months' arduous training in northern Norway. Suddenly, all our professionalism, tradition and commitment was to be put to the test, because Argentina had invaded the Falklands and we were to form part of the force that would spearhead a British recapture of the islands. The call to arms produced a flurry of hectic activity. What most pleased me, more than all else, was the personal response of each individual to the urgent recall and the orderly preparations they made in the limited time available.

Less than eight weeks later, at dawn on 21 May 1982, I was standing on *Canberra's* bridge, watching the final wave of landing craft return from successfully putting ashore two RM Commandos and 2 and 3 Para, when the first wave of Argentinian Skyhawks and Mirage bombers swept over the Task Force in San Carlos Bay. At Suez in 1956, I had experienced air strikes, but then the devastating destruction was being brought down against the enemy by our forces. Now, it was the other way round and I watched with increasing horror as ship after ship was enveloped in clouds of spray, smoke and flames. Although the Royal Navy's air defences took a heavy toll of the Argentinians, the latter resolutely persisted with their attacks and it seemed inevitable that the largest target of them all, the *Canberra*, in which the whole of 42 Commando remained, must be hit.

Large stocks of explosives were stacked up in her stern: three battalions' worth of anti-tank missiles, as well as our own first line of HE, phosphorus and illuminating mortar bombs together with tens of thousands of rounds of assorted smallarms ammunition. One direct impact from bomb or rocket would probably have blown the *Canberra* in half. Our last line of defence was nothing more than the 7.62mm GPMGs mounted on the ship's guard rails but, with tracer, these proved an effective deterrent as the enemy pilots were wary of their flashes.

Even so, I was desperate to get my unit ashore before we sank without a fight, but this was not achieved until early afternoon. We disembarked before the last air raids, but were very relieved to hear that the *Canberra* had survived and was to be withdrawn that night. At last we were on *terra firma* and our friends on board were safe for the moment.

For the next few days, air attacks delayed the amphibious off-load and forced some fundamental changes of plan

For the next few days Argentinian air attacks delayed the amphibious off-load and forced some fundamental changes of plan. The headquarters of 3 Commando Brigade had hoped to resupply over the beach, leaving our stocks afloat in the logistic ships. After two of these ships were hit – luckily the bombs did not explode – it became clear that this was too hazardous, and that all the equipment needed for the breakout from the beach-head must be landed and stockpiled ashore. Another planning assumption was that troop movement across the appalling terrain would be heliborne by night in the four giant Chinooks aboard SS *Atlantic Conveyor*. When an Exocet missile destroyed her, even though one Chinook miraculously survived, major troop lifts were no longer possible. In fact, our precious, remaining helicopters could hardly be risked outside the protective envelope of air defence within the beach-head until the out-numbered air-defence Harriers and Sea Harriers had broken their opponents.

A few days later, 2 Para moved down from Sussex Mountain on foot to rout gloriously the Argentinians at Goose Green after a desperate battle. But ammunition shortages and the loss of light helicopters supporting them in daylight only underlined our Brigade's limitations without air superiority. 42 Commando actually 'stood to' as reinforcement during the battle but, eventually, only J ('Juliet') Company was flown down that night. The next day, those Royal Marines forced to surrender in Stanley to the enemy's invasion force, had the satisfaction of escorting over 1000 Argentinians into captivity.

During this period, 42 Commando had been tasked to fly forward to seize Mount Kent as soon as the brigade HQ considered the risk was justified. It was certainly a bold concept, because this objective was nearly 50km forward of our lines and well within range of enemy artillery and open to counter-attack. Teams of the SAS, who had been operating in the area for some time, suspected that the enemy positions on Mount Kent might have been reduced to reinforce Goose Green, but nobody was really sure. I could only plan on sufficient airlift for a rifle company with limited artillery support. Our eventual 'orbat' (order of battle) consisted of K ('Kilo') Company, three light guns with limited ammunition from 29 Commando Light Regiment, a section of our 81mm mortars and a team of Blowpipe air-defence missiles, with my Tac (Tactical) HQ in command. We knew that we could not be reinforced until the following night.

Against the roar and buffet of the Sea Kings, poised and loaded for action, I discussed the crisis with the flight leader

Our first attempt to fly forward failed when the Sea King helicopters were caught by a 'white out' in the mountains. Despite passive night-goggles, the pilots lost all vision and our first wave spent a harrowing period hovering at ground level before a break in the blizzard permitted recovery. The following night, 30/31 May, we succeeded, although this operation was full of drama. As the leading elements of K Company consolidated a perimeter around the landing zone, a fire-fight developed with an Argentinian patrol. Although the SAS confidently moved out to deal with this threat, the helicopter pilots were not impressed and the crucial build-up was halted.

In the darkness of San Carlos airstrip, against the roar and buffet of the Sea Kings, poised and loaded for action, I discussed this crisis with the flight leader. We had operated together before, of course, be-

Opening page: Major Guy Sheridan's assault force boards one of HMS *Antrim*'s Wessex helicopters for the flight to South Georgia. The recapture of Grytviken, the island's main settlement, was accomplished without loss to 42 Commando's M Company. To celebrate the victory, the company flag (above) was raised over the whaling station. Below left: 42 Commando come ashore at San Carlos. Above left: Consolidating the beachhead. Trenches gave protection against air strikes.

THE ROYAL MARINES

Although members of the present-day Royal Marine Commandos can trace their unit's history back to 1664, the corps did not receive its 'Royal' title until 1802, and was not deployed in the commando role until World War II. Indeed, the Royal Marines did not take sole responsibility for Britain's Commandos until 1945.

In the post-war era, the corps has undergone several reorganisations, and today consists of 3 Commando Brigade and support units. The brigade itself comprises 40, 42 and 45 Commandos. Each has a strength of 650 men, divided between three rifle companies of three troops, a support company and headquarters.

The support company is equipped with mortars, machine guns and Milan anti-tank missiles. Snipers and assault engineers are also attached to the company. The rifle companies are equipped in a similar fashion to other infantry units.

The Brigade is supported by 29 Commando Light Regiment RA with 18 105mm guns, the Commando Logistic Regiment, an air squadron of 18 helicopters, and a Blowpipe-equipped air defence troop. Other units integral to the Royal Marines include the Special Boat Squadron; 59 Independent Commando Squadron, Royal Engineers; the Mountain and Arctic Warfare Cadre, and 1 Raiding Squadron.

Since 1974, 3 Commando Brigade has formed part of Britain's NATO commitment to the defence of Norway and Denmark.

cause RN Commando squadrons accompany us to northern Norway each winter. Only a few weeks earlier, in fact, we had been intercepting a Norwegian advance across moonlit Arctic terrain, so mutual confidence was a bond. I knew he would not lightly risk his precious assets, but he knew how vulnerable the leading elements of K Company Group would be on their own. In keeping with Royal Navy tradition, we agreed to 'give it a go' and the next wave went in.

On the way back, however, the Chinook took a 'birdstrike' through the RAF pilot's windscreen and, while he was regaining control, his huge machine bounced off the surface of a lake, smashing the undercarriage. Fortunately the guns and some ammunition were now in, but I realised that further

sorties must be curtailed and so, in one final wave, we piled on top of one another, among missiles, bombs, grenades and flares, with safety belts and weight restrictions ignored, until the helicopters could barely achieve lift-off. Smuggled in with us was Max Hastings, the well-known war correspondent, who shouted to the SAS Squadron Commander with him, 'Will we make it?' To which came the predictable reply, 'Who dares wins!'

We landed during the final stages of that firefight which soon terminated unhappily for the enemy. K Company had already set off up the long, steep slopes of Mount Kent, where they occupied abandoned Argentinian positions just after midnight. Apart from dealing with some stragglers the next morning, it was a bloodless victory for one of the key

features in enemy-dominated terrain. At first light on 31 May, I arrived up there with the cumbersome Blowpipe missiles, one of which was carried by the lofty Hastings, to enjoy the welcome sight of Stanley town and harbour several kilometres below us. Psychologically, it was a real morale booster to see our goal within striking distance! We decided to employ a little psychology ourselves, at the suggestion of Chris Romberg, K Company's Forward Observation Officer, by bringing down salvoes of 'Supercharge' onto the old Royal Marine barracks at Moody Brook. This target was on the outskirts of the town so every Argentinian in Stanley knew we were on our way!

However, revenge was still some time away because 45 Commando and 3 Para were still completing the famous 'Yomp' into the mountains, across nearly 80km of tussock and slush, shouldering their heavy burdens through the howling gales of sleet and rain. The rest of 42 Commando flew in on subsequent nights, but now we had to endure the diabolical weather for the next fortnight until preparations for the major assault on the Argentinian strongholds around Stanley could be completed.

It was the most arduous experience of more than 20 years of field soldiering around the world. In freezing temperatures, across bleak slopes, the icy gusts that constantly change direction created a wind-chill factor which menaced the soaked troops with exposure. To begin with, we did not even have rucksacks, and there were only a handful of small tents for the HQ. Everyone had a wet sleeping bag

and sometimes resupply of food and fuel was delayed by other priorities. The decisive factors ensuring that the marines survived in such adversity were the superb cold-weather clothing and the Commando's many winters of Arctic experience.

Regimental Sergeant-Major Dave Chisnall, BEM, was a typical example. An instructor in mountaineering and cross-country skiing, he had spent 13 winters in Norway and climbed regularly in the Alps. His toughness and know-how were an inspiration and reassurance to those younger and less experienced, but there were many more officers and NCOs of similar calibre. At one stage, I was asked if the unit should be withdrawn to 'dry out', but we never doubted morale and resilience, even though 'trench foot', particularly, was taking an increasing toll. Most nights, fighting patrols probed forward from the Mount Challenger feature where L ('Lima') and J Companies had now been established. Brigadier Julian Thompson, with 3 Commando Brigade HQ, had joined all three units in the mountains and he had warned me that Mount Harriet would be our objective.

This feature, which I code-named 'Zoya' after my eldest daughter, rose approximately 300m above the plateau skirting Harriet Sound. Along the base of the mountain ran the track between Stanley and

Far left: Surrounded by the clutter of war, the author (right) confers with his second-in-command, Major Guy Sheridan, and Ian McNeil, an OPS officer, below Mount Kent. Centre left: L Company deploying onto Mount Challenger during the preparations for the attack. Left: Two heavily-laden members of 42 Commando move down from Mount Kent. Below: The airlift that helped to bring victory. Sea King and Wessex helicopters being boarded by Royal Marines.

CASUALTY EVACUATION

Despite losing only one man killed during the attack on Mount Harriet, 42 Commando did suffer several casualties, mainly from smallarms fire and mines. The survival of often badly wounded men owed much to the well-oiled machinery for dealing with the injured. The instant a man was hit or stepped on a mine, the treatment began. His 'oppo' would administer rudimentary first aid: applying a dressing to the wound and giving a pain-killing injection of morphine, if needed.

From this point on, the casualty passed through a number of hands, receiving more sophisticated treatment at each stage. A company medic would give more advanced first aid, before the man was transferred to a regimental aid post, where he would be seen by a Regimental Medical Officer. Here, the precise nature of the wounds would be established and the casualty's condition stabilised. Once able to withstand further movement, the man would be casevaced (lifted by helicopter) to a battlefield hospital.

During the early stages of the campaign, facilities were available at Ajax Bay but, as the area of fighting moved eastward, the theatre was moved to Teal Inlet and then Fitzroy. Many life-saving operations were carried out in these surgeries.

After surgery, a man's vital signs would be monitored until he was considered fit enough to be moved to the next link in the chain, the hospital ships with the Task Force.

Goose Green. It was the most southerly peak of the high ground dominating Stanley, but separated from the Challenger feature by a rocky chasm, across which we could observe enemy positions from a jumble of crags called Wall Mountain. The latter became 'Tara', after my second daughter, and was precariously occupied by a daring band of forward observers, fire controllers and their protection party, who remorselessly harassed the Argentinians with naval gunfire, artillery and mortar fire, in return for which they were regularly bombarded them-selves with everything the enemy had.

But long-range surveillance can be no substitute for the close reconnaissance required for a night attack. The crucial factor in this type of operation is often the route chosen to the objective, so we had to establish that first. By now we knew that the enemy had laid mines and our suspicions that these were unmarked became confirmed when Marine Curtis of L Company had his foot blown off in a defile lying northwest of Wall Mountain. Unfortunately, he was one of the heaviest men in the patrol, and it took over eight hours to carry him back across the precipitous 'stone runs' since the foul visibility and darkness prevented lifting him out. To our amazement, he lived through this ordeal to reach the hospital ship *Uganda* soon enough for surgery and blood transfusions to sustain him. So many other British casualties were to survive thanks to the skill of our surgeons and

Far left: In a campaign where even the most basic creature comforts were often denied the men in the field, a steaming mug of tea was always a welcome sight. Here, two marines make the best of a lull in the fighting. Left: Intelligence gathering was a vital part of the build-up to the main assault on Mount Harriet. The author (right) chats to a group of marines on their return from a night patrol. Below: Fire support was provided by the 105mm guns of 29 Commando, Light Regiment RA.

J ('Juliet') Company

As the men of 42 Commando were making their final preparations before travelling to rendezvous with the *Canberra* at Southampton, urgent orders arrived at their headquarters requesting that M Company, under Major Guy Sheridan, be sent to RAF Brize Norton. From there, it was to fly to Ascension Island and join a small force earmarked for the recapture of South Georgia. On 25 April South Georgia was retaken in a text-book operation: over 150 Argentinian prisoners were captured.

Despite the importance of Sheridan's mission, the temporary loss of one of 42 Commando's three rifle companies was a major headache: the unit was no longer a balanced combat force. The most serious problem was likely to be that the unit would not be able to put in co-ordinated attacks. However, the problem was solved with typical Royal Marine ingenuity, and when 42 Commando landed at San Carlos on 21 May it was at full strength.

The solution to the difficulty revived memories of World War II. During that conflict units were sometimes raised by sending out volunteers to recruit men from other formations with the right qualities and qualifications. Major Mike Norman was appointed to find recruits to fill the gap left by the departure of M Company.

Within 40 hours of being approached, Major Norman was able to report that he had raised more than 75 men of the different ranks and specialisations needed in a rifle company. The 'recruits' came from various groups and individuals rushed on board the *Canberra* without a specific role. However, all were marines and had trained to be fighters above all else. With traditional Royal Marine cunning they were equipped with all the weapons needed, and J Company was ready for action.

It was fitting that Major Norman was tasked with finding replacements for M Company. In early April he had led the Royal Marine unit that had given the original Argentinian invasion force a bloody nose at Port Stanley.

medical staffs, although what also saved Mark Curtis, was the first-aid rendered by his companions, especially Leading Medical Attendant Hayward, RN, during the protracted casevac. Commandos are most fortunate in having a number of these highly trained 'medics', who can accompany the troops anywhere because they are 'Green-Beret' trained.

By now, I knew that a frontal assault would be suicidal because this was clearly what the Argentinians expected. Apart from minefields, heavy machine guns covered the forward slopes of Mount Harriet, and the track below. To the south, the ground was ominously open, so 'right flanking' did not appear particularly feasible either. North, towards Two Sisters, seemed to offer a covered approach around Goat Ridge, but 45 Commando's objective was Two Sisters and we might be dangerously restricted with two major units manoeuvring in

the dark. Something original was clearly called for, so we decided to see if the enemy could be surprised from the rear. Led by the resourceful Sergeant Collins of K Company, a patrol moved out one night to seek a route looping south across the plateau, then approaching the enemy from behind. Not long after crossing the road, however, they too hit an unmarked minefield and Marine Patterson lost a leg. This time, a light helicopter, flown by Captain Nick Pounds, RM, surmounted appalling weather to meet the patrol back at the track and Patterson lived to tell his tale as well.

In the meantime, Sergeant Collins resolutely continued with his task until his small group suddenly observed a large Argentinian patrol approaching from Mount Harriet. They quickly went to ground in a water-filled depression, which caused the enemy to seek cover as well. It was a desperate situation as the

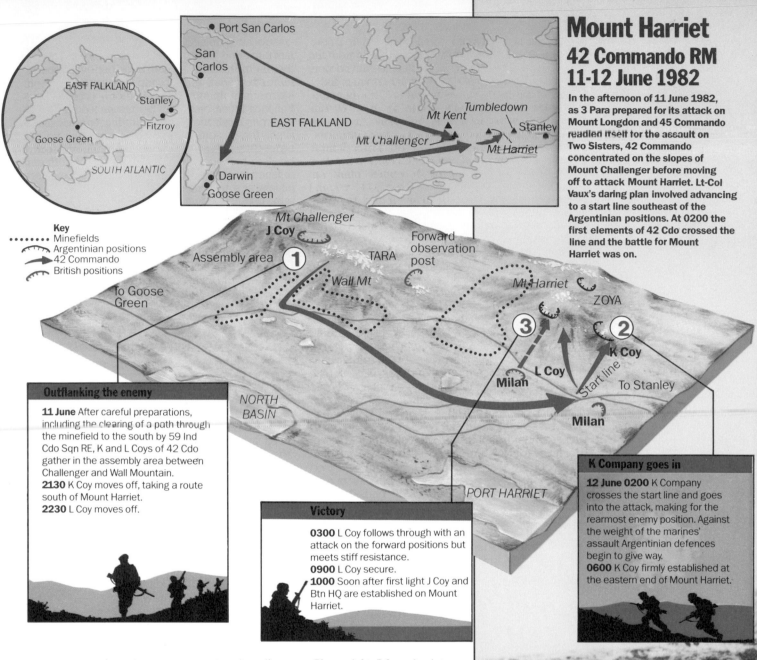

In the afternoon of 11 June 1982, as 3 Para prepared for its attack on Mount Longdon and 45 Commando readied itself for the assault on Two Sisters, 42 Commando concentrated on the slopes of Mount Challenger before moving off to attack Mount Harriet. Lt-Col Vaux's daring plan involved advancing to a start line southeast of the Argentinian positions. At 0200 the first elements of 42 Cdo crossed the line and the battle for Mount Harriet was on.

Key
- ••••••• Minefields
- Argentinian positions
- → 42 Commando
- British positions

Outflanking the enemy

11 June After careful preparations, including the clearing of a path through the minefield to the south by 59 Ind Cdo Sqn RE, K and L Coys of 42 Cdo gather in the assembly area between Challenger and Wall Mountain.
2130 K Coy moves off, taking a route south of Mount Harriet.
2230 L Coy moves off.

Victory

0300 L Coy follows through with an attack on the forward positions but meets stiff resistance.
0900 L Coy secure.
1000 Soon after first light J Coy and Btn HQ are established on Mount Harriet.

K Company goes in

12 June 0200 K Company crosses the start line and goes into the attack, making for the rearmost enemy position. Against the weight of the marines' assault Argentinian defences begin to give way.
0600 K Coy firmly established at the eastern end of Mount Harriet.

marines were heavily outnumbered and totally unsupported. Collins recognized, however, that their training and discipline might prevail in this 'Mexican stand-off' and he was absolutely right because, an hour or so later, the disgruntled enemy succumbed to cold and impatience by withdrawing back to their positions. These were all plotted by the patrol incidentally, and savagely shelled by our guns the next day. The following night, with an outstanding display of courage and determination for which he was awarded the Military Medal, Sergeant Collins finally established a route to the south which led to the fence east of Mount Harriet that we had earmarked as our start line.

Although we now knew how to get there, I was still unhappy about the very open ground to be crossed by hundreds of heavily-laden troops, possibly under the light of the moon. The brigadier and I discussed this problem and agreed that, although other unit attacks were to be 'silent until detected', 42 Commando could bring down distracting fire whenever we considered it prudent. To accustom the enemy to this we harassed the wretched Argentinians each night with every gun or mortar that could spare some of the ammunition being hoarded for the attacks.

Above right: Advancing into Port Stanley, a pair of marines of K Company, 42 Commando armed with GPMGs, patrol through the settlement. **Right:** A column of very dejected Argentinian prisoners, some of the 300 captured by 42 Commando on Mount Harriet, are escorted into captivity. Speed was vital; when this picture was taken the battle for the feature was still raging.

The fighting patrols that now nightly took their toll of the nervous enemy, discovered how easy it was to pinpoint machine guns by goading inexperienced defenders to react to our provocations with fire. This gave us the idea of a pre-emptive strike on the most dangerous ones, if only we could get them to fire as the attack commenced. The Milan seemed the obvious weapon to use, because of its long range and precision accuracy providing the aimer can see the target throughout the flight of the missile. Our problem was that Milan in the Falklands did not have a nightsight. The Royal Marines are not more than 300 years old for nothing, however, and soon a solution was devised. At the crucial moment, a troop on Tara would simulate a major engagement with explosions, lights, shouts and smallarms fire. This seemed certain to prove an irresistible lure to the trigger-happy gun teams on Zoya but, as soon as their tracer betrayed each position, our 81mm mortar troop would illuminate the area. Milan teams, pre-positioned up to a mile away, could then use their weapons to reach out to eliminate them.

The final decision to be made was one of command and control, because I had to decide where Tac HQ should be situated during the battle. A crucial factor was obviously going to be reliable communications. Throughout the attack, co-ordination of movement between sub-units and the control and direction of supporting fire from two ships, up to three batteries and our own Support Company, had to be centralised and uninterrupted. Tac HQ was therefore positioned high above the plateau, on the shoulder of Tara, from where we could observe the facing and southern slopes of Zoya and maintain reliable communications in all directions.

Each man was camouflaged, blacked out, bowed down with ammunition and equipment, and festooned with deadly weapons

On the afternoon of 11 June I flew forward onto the reverse slope of the Challenger feature where most of 42 Commando were 'grouping up' in a concentration area. Moving with each rifle company would be guides from Recce Troop, sappers to breach minefields, artillery observers, snipers, medics, signallers – all the specialist components of modern infantry warfare. In the twilight of the late afternoon they began to move purposefully forward in long, single files, menacingly silhouetted against the waning light. Each man was camouflaged, blacked out, bowed down with ammunition and equipment, and festooned with deadly weapons. As we approached the saddle behind Tara, enemy 155mm shells struck the mortar line, killing a popular young corporal and wounding several marines. Now no-one needed reminding that this was going to be a dangerous business.

Several hours later we stood shivering uncontrollably in the freezing wind, anxiously awaiting progress reports from the companies as they stealthily crossed the plateau. Preceded by Sergeant Collins and Lieutenant Colin Beedon, hundreds of men were tiptoeing along a narrow, meandering track, which they knew led between deadly minefields. Anything that compromised their presence would bring down a hail of machine gun and artillery fire and, with that, essential surprise would be lost. On several occasions the moon perversely peeped out from behind the scudding clouds and our battery commander, Major David Brown, RA. or Captain Nigel Bedford.

RA, swiftly distracted the Argentinian lookouts with harassing fire.

We agonised for several minutes when Captain David Wheen, commanding L Company, reported that they had strayed off the marked path; but, finally, marvellously, the laconic voice of Captain Peter Babbington of K Company told me they were at the start line. It was time for Lieutenant Tony Hornby's diversion and the radios began to crackle, '31, this is Nine. Vesuvius. I say again, Vesuvius.' The reply came, '31, Wilco. Out'. Over the crags in front of us, the night erupted with the crash and flash of explosions that were followed almost immediately by the gratifying sight of Argentinian tracer arching into the sky over Tara. Night turned to day as the mortar troop illuminated the slope in front of us and several Milan missiles streaked vengefully towards those dangerous machine gun nests, exploding with a shattering impact that was followed by a heartening silence.

A mile away, on the Stanley side of Mount Harriet, K Company had crossed the start line at 2200 hours and was advancing undetected towards its objectives. In the meantime L Company, that I had always kept an hour behind in case things went wrong, was moving into the forming-up position. Its mission, as Phase 2, was to capture the western strongpoints on Zoya, once K Company was established on the far end. Peter Babbington's leading troop advanced for almost 700m before 'contact' in my headphones told me the fight was on. By then, they were almost on top of the bewildered Argentinians who were overwhelmed by the momentum and ferocity of the attack.

The assault was pressed home by gallant section commanders like Corporal Lawrence Watts who was killed at point-blank range

The assault was pressed home, regardless of personal danger, by gallant section commanders like Corporal Lawrence Watts who was killed at point-blank range leading his section against the heavily fortified positions. Within minutes, K Company had captured a command post, several 0.5in machine guns and four 120mm mortars. As the defences began to crumble, the marines leapfrogged in groups along the spine of the ridge, using 66mm LAW, or 88mm MAW with fearful effect amongst the rocks. Now was the moment to release L Company, who set off towards their objective 600m away, but surprise was lost and they quickly came under effective fire.

This caused several casualties including the second-in-command, Lieutenant Ian Stafford, on secondment to us from the Argyll and Sutherland Highlanders. David Wheen now had a difficult task on his hands that was to take nearly five hours of resolute skirmishing and heavy supporting fire to complete. For a while the enemy seemed to rally amongst their almost impregnable defences, until our superior courage and professional experience wore them down.

But now we had a new problem, as more and more Argentinians were coming forward in the darkness to surrender. Luckily, we had formed a special follow-up group, sardonically nicknamed 'Porter Troop'. Their role was to carry up the GPMG sustained fire kits, and extra ammunition for use in the event of an enemy counter-attack; this equipment would have weighed down the assaulting troops. In fact, Porter Troop proved equally useful for collecting in the casualties and escorting prisoners.

Left: Despite claims that the Argentinians were poorly led conscripts, some fought with great tenacity to hold the ring of hills around Port Stanley. Many, like this man, paid the ultimate price. Below left: The strain of the march across the island and the battle for Mount Harriet clearly shows on the face of this marine. The certain knowledge of final victory did much to ease the feeling of fatigue. Right: Celebrations began as soon as the battle ended. Men from K Company, who led the attack on Mount Kent, pose for the camera on Mount Harriet.

Marine, 42 Commando, Falklands 1982

Marching into Stanley, this Royal Marine commando wears kit typical of the conflict: DPM trousers and jacket with 58-pattern web equipment. In contrast to the standard DMS boots worn by most Army troops in the Falklands, the Marines favoured superior civilian models or the high leg boots worn here. Steel helmets were rarely worn by the Marines and while one is carried on his waist belt, pride of place is given to the green beret, upon which is affixed a bronze Marine Badge. Alongside a 7.62mm SLR this Marine is also armed with a 66mm LAW rocket launcher, a highly effective weapon for dealing with Argentinian bunkers.

From the Brigade radio net, we knew that our friends in 45 Commando and 3 Para were on their objectives and, in the remaining darkness, each unit now consolidated and co-ordinated defences against possible counter-attacks. Tac HQ had to get forward as rapidly as possible onto the summit of Mount Harriet, but this was several kilometres away from us. There was certainly no time to follow the winding path through the minefields! Knowing that, the risk was outweighed by the urgency, and we lurched down Tara's slope and turned sharp left along the Stanley/Goose Green track. Once again Argentinian ineptitude saved us – it was clear!

As dawn broke and enemy shells rained sporadically down, Tac HQ reached the summit of Mount Harriet. On the way up the steep, rocky slopes we had passed the grim testimony to 42 Commando's courage and shock action. Dazed groups of prisoners were descending its slopes, often escorted by our own 'walking wounded'.

Abandoned weapons abounded: helmets, equipment, supplies and tentage were littered around apparently impregnable strongpoints. In these positions, bodies lay sprawled in the violent contortions of death, because the enemy had resisted fiercely to begin with. Later, an officer in 45 Commando commented: 'if Royal Marines had defended these mountains, we'd have died of old age there.' Luckily, it was the other way round.

THE AUTHOR Colonel N.F. Vaux, DSO, was the Commanding Officer of 42 Commando Royal Marines during the Falklands campaign and a book on his experiences in the conflict, *Still Winds from the South Atlantic*, will be published in 1986.

HUE

Fighting at close quarters in the streets of the 'Imperial City', the US Marines took on a foe that would not budge an inch. Thrown unexpectedly into action after the communist Tet Offensive of 1968, US Marines were plunged into deadly house-to-house fighting through the war-torn streets of Hue.

DURING THE afternoon of 31 January 1968, Lieutenant-Colonel Marcus Gravel, commander of the 1st Battalion, 1st Marine Regiment, led his men across the fire-swept Nguyen Hoang bridge, into the Old City of Hue. Supported by tanks (which were unable to follow because of their vulnerability in close-quarters urban fighting), Gravel found that he was facing far more enemy firepower than he could cope with. Commandeering some trucks, he pulled back with his wounded. The involvement of the US Marines in the fighting for Hue had begun.

Hue was the most important city in the northern provinces of South Vietnam. It was often called the 'Imperial City' because it had formerly been the capital of the state of Annam and the seat of govern-ment of the emperors who had ruled the area. So far during the Vietnam War, Hue had been relatively unaffected by the fighting raging over much of the country, although it was close to North Vietnam itself – less than 50km south of the Demilitarized Zone (DMZ). Many refugees had moved in, swelling the 100,000 permanent population, most of whom lived in the Old City, a part of Hue surrounded by thick walls, lying north of the Perfume river.

The decision to attack Hue had been taken the previous summer. The North Vietnamese and their southern allies, the Viet Cong, had made up their minds to undertake a large-scale offensive against the major towns in the South, in an attempt to destroy the morale of the South Vietnamese Army (ARVN) and provoke an uprising against the government.

The Tet offensive, as the series of attacks in late January 1968 became known, was not entirely unexpected, but the scale and intensity of the attacks was. Not only that, but the attention of all US troops in Vietnam, and especially the Marines, was concentrated on Khe Sanh, the beleaguered combat base that had been under siege since 21 January. Indeed, on 25 January, the US forces in the northern provinces had begun planning the relief of Khe Sanh, not preparing to defend against assaults on key urban areas.

The crump of mortars and the roar of rockets heralded the opening of an assault against Hue

---

In the early morning of 31 January, the crump of mortars and the roar of rockets heralded the opening of an assault by North Vietnamese Army (NVA) forces against Hue. The few ARVN forces that were stationed in the city belonged to Brigadier-General Ngo Quang Truong's 1st Division and were of good quality. They had realised that there was the possibility of an attack, and so were at full alert; and the 'Black Panther' Company managed to slow considerably the advance of two NVA infantry battalions and their sapper support as they drove into the Old City from the southwest. With solid support from local Viet Cong units, however, the NVA troops soon controlled almost all the Old City. Only the far northern corner, the site of Truong's divisional head-quarters, still held out by the time dawn broke.

Meanwhile, in the part of Hue south of the Perfume river known as the 'New City', the attacking troops were also successful. Viet Cong squads took over key government buildings, and although the Americans in the headquarters compound of the MACV (Military Assistance Command Vietnam, the official title of the US command in Vietnam) held out, there were only a few other isolated pockets of resistance. The attack on the Imperial City had been a great success. Well-armed, well-trained, and knowing exactly what they had to do, the communist forces had taken most of their objectives, and NVA battalions now began to fan out, to take up blocking positions to the north and south of the city, while the Viet Cong flag, gold stars on red and blue, was soon flying defiantly over the old Imperial Palace.

The nearest US Marine units were at the Phu Bai combat base, some 12km to the south. There, Task Force X-Ray, under Brigadier-General Foster Lahue (a veteran of the Marine Raiders of World War II and a battalion commander in Korea) was com-posed of the headquarters detachments of the 1st and 5th Marine Regiments, and three understrength battalions (at full strength, Task Force X-Ray should

---

PLANNING THE OFFENSIVE

In July 1967, a high-level conference was convened in Hanoi under the auspices of Ho Chi Minh, the President of North Vietnam, and his military commander, General Vo Nguyen Giap. Its brief was to consider the means of breaking the current military stalemate in the Vietnam War.

After protracted discussion, it was decided that a massive offensive should be launched against South Vietnam in early 1968 using the combined might of the regular North Vietnamese Army (NVA) and the Viet Cong, the military arm of the National Liberation Front (NLF). The attack was designed with three aims in mind: to encourage a popular anti-government rising in the South, to bring about the collapse of the South Vietnamese government and to seriously undermine the military and political standing of the US in Vietnam. A less obvious element in North Vietnamese thinking was concerned with the Viet Cong, whose leaders were increasingly dissatisfied with Hanoi's commitment to the war. It was, therefore, both a military and political decision to launch the offensive.

The assault was planned to be as widespread as possible with the NVA attacking the northern provinces and the Viet Cong striking at every major town and village in South Vietnam. The decision to attack during the Tet (Lunar New Year) celebrations at the end of January 1968 was signficant. Giap believed that, with many soldiers on leave, the South Vietnamese would be caught off balance and that bad weather might make it impossible for the US to fly close-support missions.

In the weeks prior to the New Year, the NVA and Viet Cong continued to mount their regular operations to disguise the concentration of their forces but, by the end of January, all was ready and on the 31st the Tet offensive began. Over 84,000 NVA and Viet Cong troops attacked 36 provincial capitals, 64 district capitals and 50 villages in South Vietnam. The focal point of the attack in the northern coastal provinces was the old imperial city of Hue.

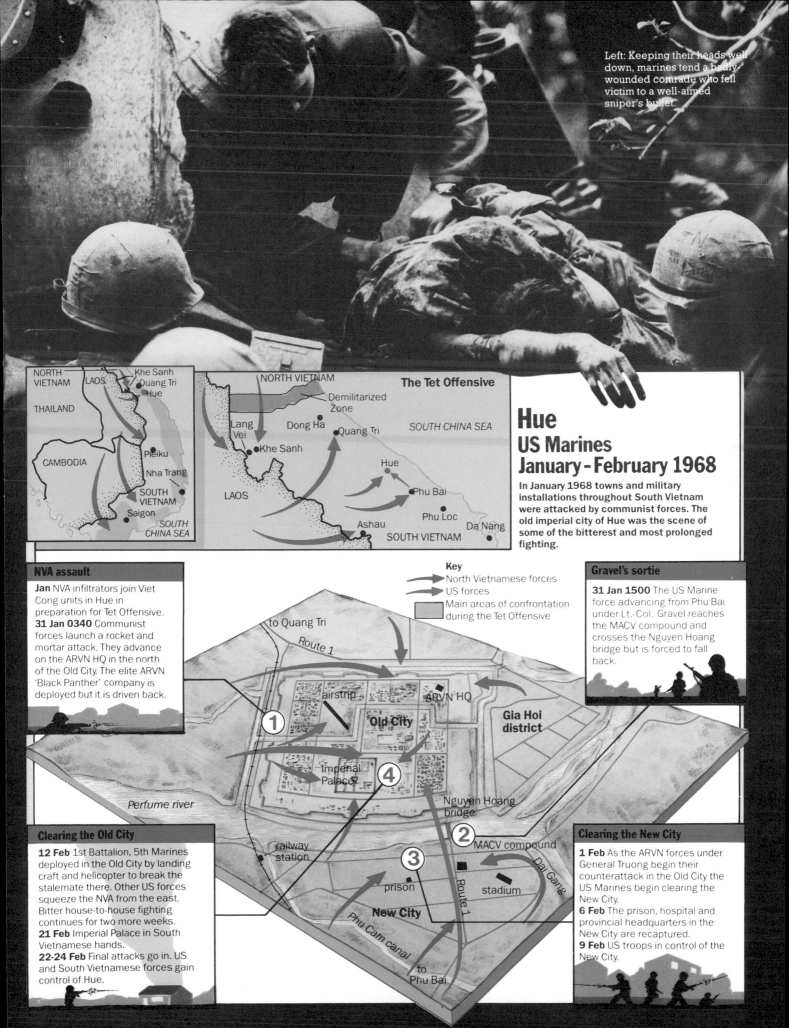

Left: Keeping their heads well down, marines tend a badly wounded comrade who fell victim to a well-aimed sniper's bullet.

The Tet Offensive

NORTH VIETNAM · LAOS · Khe Sanh · Quang Tri · Hue · THAILAND · CAMBODIA · Pleiku · Nha Trang · SOUTH VIETNAM · Saigon · SOUTH CHINA SEA

NORTH VIETNAM · Demilitarized Zone · Lang Vei · Dong Ha · Quang Tri · SOUTH CHINA SEA · Khe Sanh · Hue · LAOS · Phu Bai · Phu Loc · Ashau · Da Nang · SOUTH VIETNAM

Hue
US Marines
January – February 1968

In January 1968 towns and military installations throughout South Vietnam were attacked by communist forces. The old imperial city of Hue was the scene of some of the bitterest and most prolonged fighting.

NVA assault

Jan NVA infiltrators join Viet Cong units in Hue in preparation for Tet Offensive.
31 Jan 0340 Communist forces launch a rocket and mortar attack. They advance on the ARVN HQ in the north of the Old City. The elite ARVN 'Black Panther' company is deployed but it is driven back.

Key
North Vietnamese forces
US forces
Main areas of confrontation during the Tet Offensive

Gravel's sortie

31 Jan 1500 The US Marine force advancing from Phu Bai under Lt.-Col. Gravel reaches the MACV compound and crosses the Nguyen Hoang bridge but is forced to fall back.

to Quang Tri
Route 1
airstrip
ARVN HQ
Gia Hoi district
Old City
Imperial Palace
Perfume river
Nguyen Hoang bridge
railway station
MACV compound
Dai Gang
prison
Route 1
stadium
New City
Phu Cam canal
to Phu Bai

Clearing the Old City

12 Feb 1st Battalion, 5th Marines deployed in the Old City by landing craft and helicopter to break the stalemate there. Other US forces squeeze the NVA from the east. Bitter house-to-house fighting continues for two more weeks.
21 Feb Imperial Palace in South Vietnamese hands.
22-24 Feb Final attacks go in. US and South Vietnamese forces gain control of Hue.

Clearing the New City

1 Feb As the ARVN forces under General Truong begin their counterattack in the Old City the US Marines begin clearing the New City.
6 Feb The prison, hospital and provincial headquarters in the New City are recaptured.
9 Feb US troops in control of the New City.

M16A1

rear sight adjustor
charging handle
foreward bolt assist
buffer tube
gas tube
bolt assembl
hammer
firing pin
auto sear
selector cam
disconnect
grip
trigger
magazine release spindle
magazine
sling swivel
stock

In the early 1950s the US Infantry Board announced its requirements for a new, lightweight service rifle: the weapon had to be accurate up to 460m and be capable of penetrating steel helmets and body armour at that range; it also had to be able to fire single shots and have an automatic capability, but weigh no more than 2.72kg. Eugene Stoner, then chief designer with Armalite Incorporated, a US smallarms research company, began work on a new weapon. In 1958 Stoner's rifle, known as the AR-15, was recommended as a possible replacement for the standard service M14. After encouraging initial sales to the US Air Force and to South Vietnam, the US government began to favour Stoner's design and by 1966 the army had purchased over 400,000. Shortly afterwards it was designated the M16. When the M16 came into service, much was made of the overall simplicity of its design and of the fact that it required only minimal cleaning. Unfortunately, this was often taken to mean that it needed no maintenance at all, and this led to a spate of complaints as weapons began to malfunction. Consequently, several small changes were made to the chamber and barrel. With these alterations the weapon was designated the M16A1. Constructed of aluminium alloy and light-weight plastic, it was easy to handle and its short length, coupled with a high rate of fire, made it ideal for fighting at close quarters. The M16A1 remains the standard US service rifle.

have included two whole regiments). Lahue's 4000 men were tasked with the defence of Phu Bai itself, the screening of the western approaches to Hue, and the maintenance of traffic along Route 1, from Hai Van Pass to Hue. Route 1 was the key north-south land communications route from Da Nang to Hue; it had already come under rocket and mortar attack during the night of the 31st.

Reports were flowing in of a major offensive throughout South Vietnam, including an assault on the US embassy in Saigon, and that morning Lahue had to take some critical decisions. He sent A Company, 1st Battalion, 1st Marines, towards Hue to investigate the situation on Route 1 and to link up with the MACV compound in the New City. A Company quickly ran into trouble, however. NVA troops were waiting in ambush, and the Marines had barely covered half the distance to Hue when they became pinned down.

By mid-morning on the 31st, Lahue had realised that A Company needed support, and so Lieutenant-Colonel Marcus Gravel, with the command group of 1st Battalion, 1st Marines, and G Company, 2nd Battalion, 5th Marines was sent out. A tank platoon and some engineers provided support. Gravel was able to use this small force to push a way through the NVA screen and, although under fire from Viet Cong and NVA elements within Hue itself, he crossed the bridge over the Phu Cam canal and entered the MACV compound just before 1500 hours.

Having got this far, Gravel was ordered to try to make contact with the ARVN units under Brigadier-General Truong who were holding out in the northern corner of the Old City. His men moved over the Nguyen Hoang bridge, but without heavy support they could make little headway in the Old City, and pulled back.

That night the chaotic situation all over Vietnam

Above: Armed with M16s, a group of marines awaits the order to join battle.

became clearer; and within Hue itself the possibility of further large-scale communist assaults began to recede. The next day, therefore, Gravel again tried to force a way through to Truong's headquarters, only to meet renewed resistance from the NVA troops digging in within the walls of the Old City.

Meanwhile, more Marine forces were arriving: by 4 February, Colonel Stanley Hughes, the regimental

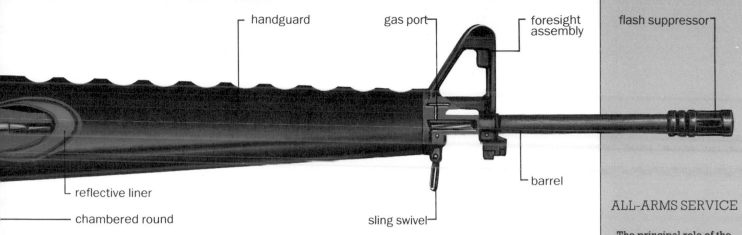

handguard   gas port   foresight assembly   flash suppressor

reflective liner

chambered round

barrel slip ring

take down hinge

barrel

sling swivel

Calibre 5.56mm
Length 99cm
Weight (loaded with 30 rounds) 3.82kg
Magazine 20 or 30-round box
Maximum effective range 400m
Rate of fire (auto) 150-200rpm
Muzzle velocity 990mps

Above: the US M16A1 rifle. This model is fitted with the current-issue curved 30-round box magazine and closed flash suppressor.

ALL-ARMS SERVICE

The principal role of the United States Marine Corps (USMC) is to maintain an amphibious capability for use in either the seizure and defence of forward bases in a war zone, or the conduct of land/sea operations.
A key feature of the USMC's position within the US military establishment is that it remains the only service to have its basic structure enshrined by law. In January 1951, Congress passed the Douglas-Mansfield Bill which formalised the Marines' separate identity, and fixed the Corps' strength at four divisions and four air wings. The Commandant of the Marines was made a member of the US Joint Chiefs of Staff. The USMC's powerful lobby in Congress ensures that the Corps retains it unique identity.
The active strength of the USMC is currently around 194,000 men. As they are required to carry out independent action, it was recognised that the service required its own organic air and ground support.
The four Marine Air Wings (MAWs), with a total of 286 to 315 aircraft each, have between 18 and 21 squadrons. The squadrons are used to fulfil a variety of battlefield roles; including close support, transportation and combat air patrols. Mobility is provided by helicopter units capable of lifting men and equipment both into and out of action. MAWs also contain early-warning observation and reconnaissance aircraft.
The concept of an all-arms force is also reflected in the structure of the Marine division. Apart from three rifle regiments, each division has an artillery battery, a tank battalion, an armoured amphibian battalion, a light armoured assault battalion, and other support and ancillary units.

battle that was to follow was in many ways more like some of the more gruelling episodes of the war against the Japanese on the Pacific Islands than anything that had been experienced in Vietnam so far. For the communist forces holed up in the city were not going to slip away to fight another day. They had been ordered to hold on until the bitter end, and they would have to be winkled out, house by house, bunker by bunker.

Most of the Marines at Hue were short-term enlistees, and, although they had been trained to operate in a number of environments, they expected to fight the Viet Cong in the countryside where they could call upon enormous resources of firepower and had the great advantage of superior mobility. Now, however, they faced a different kind of warfare: close-quarters, almost hand-to-hand combat with movement confined to swift dashes across fire-swept streets, dodging from one scrap of cover to another, with enemy snipers liable to pick off anyone careless enough to show himself, and with heavy support sometimes an irrelevance. Heaps of rubble were just as useful as complete buildings in providing shelter for the defenders, and so blanket shelling was of limited value. Just as in the great close-quarters battles of World War II – Stalingrad, Cassino, or Iwo Jima – the attacking infantry had to fight their way in and pull out the defenders one by one.

The attacking infantry had to put up an enormous weight of covering fire to support even short advances, and the dull pink buildings characteristic of Hue were soon pockmarked by the deluge of fire that the Marines put up to keep the heads of the NVA down while the American troops moved forward. The M16 assault rifle, which many Marines had regarded somewhat dubiously when it first came into service, proved invaluable in Hue, as its fully automatic mode gave a powerful burst that could

commander of the 1st Marines, had come in to take charge of the two battalions of Marines who had been ordered to clear Hue south of the Perfume river. The battalions consisted of those units from the 1st Marines that had already gone into action with Gravel, and three rifle companies, F, G and H, from the 5th Marines, now under their own battalion commander, Lieutenant-Colonel Ernest Cheatham. Hughes was an officer with considerable World War II experience, having won both a Navy Cross and a Silver Star for his service in that conflict; and the

Left, main picture: Festooned with M60 ammunition belts, a marine crouches warily in the yard of a bullet-riddled building in the Old City of Hue. Following the initial success of their assault on the city, NVA and Viet Cong troops dug in and fortified many of the buildings they had captured. The Marines were tasked with rooting them out, house by house, and encountered bitter resistance at every turn. Right: Drawn and haggard with battle fatigue, a marine takes a short break from the rigours of the close-quarters infantry fighting that characterised the battle for Hue.

US Marine, Vietnam 1968

This marine wears olive-drab drill fatigues and, for protection against blast weapons, he has an M1955 armoured vest. Footgear consists of nylon and black leather tropical boots, while his M1 steel helmet has a camouflage cover (complete with typical 'grunt' comment) and a bottle of insect repellent in the helmet band. Armament comprises the 5.56mm M16 assault rifle, the standard smallarm of US troops in Vietnam by 1968. Spare magazines are carried in the cotton bandolier slung over his left shoulder.

LEAVING HUE

During the fighting for Hue, landing craft became a major form of transport in and out. But the communist forces controlled key areas on the banks of the Perfume river, and enemy mortar spotters would quickly call up fire when the landing craft docked. Here, a journalist describes leaving Hue under fire:

'The mortar men were lousy shots. Two shells fell in the river, kicking up small geysers of water. A third one hit a packing crate, well away from the landing craft and the waiting passengers......

'When the last crate was hauled from the craft, the passengers rushed aboard. The women, children and the stretcher cases were taken below the main deck. The others, including wounded Marines who could still walk, squatted on the deck in the rain. It was a strange cargo. There were two priests, who had been held captive by the Viet Cong; the bodies of six Marines in green plastic bags; and a group of teachers who had found themselves trapped for nine days in Hue while artillery and mortars boomed around them.....

'"If you've got weapons, you ought to get them ready," one crewman told the passengers. "It will be a miracle if we don't have to use them." There was no miracle. Ten minutes out of Hue, Viet Cong troops ran along the riverbank firing rifles and rockets at the lumbering landing craft. The wounded Marines rushed to the railing, firing steadily...

'Bright red tracer bullets zipped over the cabin of the landing craft, a rocket shell struck a river patrol boat that had come along for protection.

'A half-an-hour later, when the shooting had subsided, one of the passengers reached under his coat, pulled out a bottle of Ambassador Scotch and passed it around to the Marines. They emptied it in four minutes. He passed around another bottle...'

Cam canal was rebridged on 12 February, and they suffered heavily. Two loaded with petrol, oil and lubricants caught fire and sank under enemy attack from the banks of the Perfume river and an LCU loaded with ammunition blew up when communist troops managed to get it in their sights. South of the river, helicopters were able to alight at relatively protected Landing Zones (LZs), but in the Old City there was always a problem. The only effective LZ was at the hospital, and craft landing there were always liable to be fired on. Only one Marine helicopter was actually lost in a total of 823 sorties, but many received multiple hits.

The fighting in Hue was the bitterest that any of the rank and file marines had experienced

The problem of moving supplies and reinforcements into Hue were mirrored by the difficulties of shifting wounded men to safety. The prospect of being lifted out by a helicopter vulnerable to enemy smallarms fire, or travelling on an LCU after the episode of the blown-up ammunition carrier was far from welcome.

The Marines had some support from M48 tanks (which did remarkably well in the street fighting – only one Marine tank was lost) and the 'Ontos', a thinly armoured, tracked vehicle mounting six recoilless rifles, proved an invaluable asset, deploying a great weight of firepower against defensive positions at close range. The Ontos could enter areas that the larger, heavier tanks could not; it would dart out, send in a shattering salvo, and then pull back under cover.

One Marine unit, Major Robert Thompson's 1st Battalion, 5th Marines, was deployed into the Old City to support Truong's ARVN force operating there; and this battalion had an even more difficult task than those south of the river. For the greater density of buildings and the greater determination of the defenders made this part of the fighting a grim struggle indeed.

The period of the battle for Hue coincided with the northeast monsoon. The skies were generally overcast and the atmosphere heavy, severely hindering any close air support. For the Marines, the days spent fighting in Hue under these grey, leaden skies

keep defenders under pressure.

For their part, the communist forces had turned all the government buildings they had occupied in the New City into strongpoints. Snipers took to the upper stories, while machine-gun nests were set up lower down. Mortars were carefully sited to cover approach routes, and dug in to avoid detection while the infantrymen settled into small 'spider holes', nursing extra magazines for their AK-47 assault rifles and waiting for any US soldier unlucky enough to let them get a shot in.

There was no 'front line' as such when the fighting began in Hue; Viet Cong sabotage squads and courageous solo snipers were an ever-present threat. Indeed, soon after the Marine clearing of the New City began, saboteurs blew up the bridge over the Phu Cam canal, which meant that supplies had to be brought in by helicopter or up the river. Both of these methods were fraught with peril. Slow-moving helicopters were vulnerable to ground fire if they strayed over a communist-held area, while shipping coming up the Perfume river had to run the gauntlet of NVA gun positions sited along the banks.

Five Landing Craft, Utility, (LCUs), brought the bulk of equipment and ammunition in until the Phu

WOUNDS AND AWARDS

The Marines at Hue fought in one of the hardest infantry battles of the Vietnam War. Inevitably, in the close-quarters street fighting they suffered very high casualties: helicopters evacuated just under 1000 wounded during the recapture of the Old City and 142 Americans were killed in the action.

In Vietnam the proportion of fatal wounds from smallarms fire averaged at around 51 per cent, a much higher figure than in World War II or the Korean War where artillery and aerial bombardment accounted for the majority of fatal casualties. The light-weight bullets fired by modern assault rifles caused large entry and exit wounds that resulted in severe, often fatal, tissue damage. Their rapid-fire capabilities also resulted in a higher level of multiple wounds. Some 36 per cent of wounds were, however, caused by artillery and mortar fragments, while booby traps and mines accounted for another 11 per cent of fatalities.

Those marines that survived the trauma of being wounded, in fact the majority, received speedy and first-rate medical attention, and only 2.6 per cent of those casualties that reached US hospitals died after admission. America has always honoured those wounded in the line of duty and the Purple Heart (shown above) is awarded to those men who have received injuries in action.

assumed a kind of routine. They would force their way forward during the day, struggling to prise the communist forces out of their concealed defences, bringing up what support weapons they could and then hope to catch a hot meal at night. But during the night, the NVA and the Viet Cong would launch local counter-attacks, and individual communist troops who had remained hidden would emerge to set lethal booby traps.

Crouching behind walls, setting up as much covering fire as they could, the Marines inched forward, haggard with fatigue. In the New City, the US forces began to assert control within a week: the building housing the administrative headquarters of the province was retaken by 6 February, as were the prison and the hospital. By 9 February, all organised resistance south of the Perfume river had been crushed. For Thompson's 1st Battalion, 5th Marines, on the northern bank helping Truong's forces in the Old City, things were more difficult. But by 21 February the flag of South Vietnam was flying again over the Imperial Palace, and on 22 February the final series of attacks went in, with Marine aircraft using the opportunity of a break in the cloud cover to deliver a devastating weight of ordnance on the southern corner of the Old City in support of Thompson's troops, dropping 115kg 'Snakeye' bombs and 225kg napalm canisters.

In spite of the fact that close support was always difficult, the Marines had used their superior firepower wherever possible. Marine artillery fired 18,091 rounds during the battle: high explosive, smoke, white phosphorus, illumination and CS gas. The accuracy of the 8in howitzer made it the most

Above: One of the many casualties receives first aid on the battlefield. Below: Marines in action with the M60.

effective artillery piece. From the Seventh Fleet, three cruisers and five destroyers expended 5191 rounds, and, although the weather limited their effectiveness, Marine aircraft flew 113 sorties.

The unexpected determination of Viet Cong and NVA forces to fight to the last inch, and the fact that street fighting was an unusual problem in the Vietnam War, made the fighting in Hue the bitterest that any of the rank and file marines had ever experienced; and they suffered 142 dead in the struggle to reclaim the city. But they had proved yet again the fighting qualities of their Corps, in adverse conditions and against a determined enemy.

THE AUTHOR Ashley Brown has contributed to various military publications and books, and edited *War in Peace*, a study of post-war conflict.

CARLSON'S

RAIDERS

MARINE RAIDERS

During the 1930s, the US Marine Corps experimented with the idea of using raider forces to carry out unconventional activities behind enemy lines, and in January 1942 the concept reached fruition when the 1st Battalion, 5th Marines was retitled the 1st Separate Battalion; a month later, a Marine officer, Lieutenant-General Evans F. Carlson, was ordered to raise men to form the 2nd Separate Battalion. Lieutenant Merritt A. Edson, a World War I veteran and ex-pilot, was placed in charge of the 1st Battalion.

In the following month, the units were redesignated the 1st and 2nd Raider Battalions, and prepared for action. Each battalion consisted of over 850 officers and men divided between six rifle companies, and a small headquarters. Apart from standard infantry weapons and equipment, the raiders used shotguns, bangalore torpedoes, chainsaws and rubber dinghies.

The raiders were formed to carry out three specific types of operation: spearheading amphibious landings; undertaking hit-and-run attacks on enemy-held islands; and launching long-term guerrilla-style sorties behind enemy lines. By mid-1942 both battalions were in the field. In August Carlson's raiders hit Makin Island and Edson's men fought on Tulagi. The success of the raiders encouraged certain officers to request the formation of other units. Although there was official opposition to the creation of further 'elites within an elite', other units were raised and formed into the 1st and 2nd Raider Regiments. Above: The badge of the 1st Raider Regiment.

In November 1942 the 2nd Marine Raider Battalion landed on Guadalcanal to begin a savage month-long battle against the Japanese

ON 20 SEPTEMBER 1942, Carlson's Raiders, the 2nd Marine Raider Battalion, landed at Espiritu Santo in the New Hebrides, some 400 miles short of their destination, the embattled island of Guadalcanal, part of the Solomon Islands in the south Pacific. After a final reconnaissance flight over the area, Carlson briefed his company commanders on their mission:

'Soon, my small command group and two companies, C and E, will board two destroyers and sail for Aola bay, 40 miles east of the island's Lunga river. From there, we will advance inland and provide security for a naval construction battalion building an airfield. This mission is to last two days and then we will return to Espiritu Santo.'

Nobody at the meeting believed that the job would be over so quickly, as the forces on the island needed all the help they could get in the face of a stubborn foe. US troops had been on Guadalcanal since early August when, in the first American offensive of the Pacific campaign, the 1st US Marine Division under Major-General Alexander Vandegrift had made a relatively unopposed landing. Since then, however, the Japanese had flooded the island with reinforcements, and launched a series of counter-blasts to throw the Americans back into the sea.

The raider companies earmarked for the job reached Guadalcanal on 4 November, a day later than planned as the Japanese had landed a strong body of reinforcements in the area on the previous day. On the 5th, Carlson's men were relieved by army units and ordered to patrol inland to the village of Reko, lying some 16 miles away. In the meantime, my company, B, and D Company had sailed for Aola, landing on the 7th. There were now four companies ashore and these would soon be reinforced by A and F Companies.

Ordered to join Carlson, B and D Companies set off

RAIDERS ON MAKIN

At 0300 hours on 17 August 1942, two US submarines, *Nautilus* and *Argonaut*, hove to some 500m off the shore of Makin, a tiny atoll in the Gilbert Islands. Aboard the boats were 13 officers and 200 men of the 2nd Raider Battalion under the command of Evans Carlson; their mission was to hit the Japanese garrison, estimated at 70 men, gather intelligence, destroy installations and then withdraw.

The landings on the south shore of Butaritari Island in the atoll were unchallenged and Carlson ordered A Company to push inland where they seized key buildings and dock facilities. The company then moved south, but ran into stiff opposition.

By early afternoon, Carlson ordered his raiders to fall back on the re-embarkation beaches. However, heavy surf prevented the assault teams from reaching the subs and Carlson was forced to stay on the island. On the following morning, resigned to another day ashore, Carlson despatched patrols to scour the island. One team uncovered an enemy supply cache, which they destroyed. Other patrols recovered the bodies of 11 raiders and polished off the remnants of Japanese resistance. By nightfall, the raiders were reunited with the submarines. Mission accomplished.

Page 115: A month after landing on Guadalcanal (below), members of Carlson's Raiders display their captured war trophies (above). Above, far left: Marines escort Japanese prisoners back to base. Far left: Prior to Guadalcanal, Carlson's men hit enemy installations on Makin. Top: The objective seen through the periscope of the US submarine *Nautilus*, used to carry the raiders to Makin. Above: A gruelling pre-raid route march. Left: Carlson (left) is congratulated after the Makin mission.

Evans F. Carlson, (below) the famed leader of the 2nd Raider Battalion in World War II, was born in 1896 and enlisted in the US Army at the age of 16. Seeing action in the Great War, he was awarded the Purple Heart for battle wounds.

He joined the Marines as a private in 1922 and was commissioned as a second lieutenant during the following year.

During a tour of duty in China at the end of the decade, he was awarded the Yangtze Service Medal and the Expeditionary Medal. In 1930 he was ordered to Nicaragua where he won his first Navy Cross for leading a dozen men against 100 bandits. Carlson left the Marines briefly in 1939 after a particularly hazardous third tour of duty in which he won the China Service Medal. Recommissioned as a major in 1941, Carlson was placed in charge of the 2nd Raider Battalion, a unit he led until its disbandment in 1944.

Carlson won a Gold Star in lieu of a second Navy Cross for his part in the attack on Makin Island in 1942. Three months later, a further Gold Star was awarded for his heroism and leadership on Guadalcanal.

After being forced to retire on 1 July 1946 as a result of wounds received on Saipan, where he won a second Purple Heart, Carlson was promoted to the rank of brigadier-general on the retired list, for his outstanding combat record.

into the jungle only to be hit by enemy smallarms fire. D Company deployed to deal with the threat while the other raider company continued to Reko. After four hours of hard going, we crossed the Bokokimbo river, the last barrier between us and Carlson's base.

During the night, a few Japanese tried to penetrate our lines, but all were shot. On the morning of the 8th, three raider companies were sent out on patrol to the north, west and south of our base and all had brushes with the enemy. The next day the raiders moved up to the village of Kema. From there were sent out the usual patrols, but one company was sent to the village of Tasimboko to pick up much-needed supplies delivered by sea from Aola. Escorted by parties of raiders, local natives back-packed the rations to our camp. Each man filled his extra socks with food and blocks of thick chocolate.

At dawn on the 9th, we moved forward to Binu, a village on the Balesuna river, south of where the Japanese were engaging the 7th Marines and 164th Infantry. Although exhausted, our gourmet cooks put some spark in the air with their activities. Rice was prepared with raisins, fatback and chocolate – every way a raider could dream up. That night was a really special occasion: the 167th anniversary of our corps' foundation.

We had several encounters with the enemy on the next day. It was B Company's turn to provide base security and stand ready to assist any raiders in trouble, other companies were sent out on the usual patrols. It was not long before they bumped into the Japanese. C Company had hardly cleared our lines before one Japanese soldier ran into our outpost and got killed for his pains. He seemed healthy, unlike the weak and anaemic Japanese we had seen before, and was probably a member of the reinforcements that had just landed on the island. Within the hour, all the patrols were engaged and our base was under direct attack.

D Company ran into trouble. Pinned down by accurate mortar fire, casualties mounted

The first radio message came in from C Company. The CO reported that his men had run into a battalion-sized enemy unit armed with machine guns and mortars. Although the raiders had surprised the Japanese, inflicting heavy casualties, they had lost five men killed and several wounded. Carlson believed that the enemy was moving south from the mouth of the Metapona river, where the 7th Marines and 164th Infantry had given them a bloody nose. Carlson ordered Captain R.E. Washburn, the leader of E Company, to move his men south along the river, and moved C Company along the river's eastern bank. Both company commanders were told to rendezvous at a point north of Asamana village.

Washburn was fortunate. Catching two Japanese companies in the process of crossing the river, he ordered Lieutenant Evans Carlson, the CO's son, to position his heavy weapons on the river bank in plain view of the unwary enemy. Opening fire, his men inflicted heavy casualties, but after a few minutes they came under accurate machine-gun fire. Washburn then committed Lieutenant Clelland Early's platoon to the fight and it quickly silenced the Japanese fire.

Elsewhere, D Company ran into trouble as it was crossing a wide, flat clearing. Pinned down by accurate mortar fire, casualties mounted. After much scurrying around, identifying the dead and admi-

nistering first-aid to the wounded, Platoon Sergeant George Schrier began to evacuate his men. Carlson ordered my men to assist the withdrawal, but we had gone less than 100yds before we sighted Schrier leading the remnants of D Company back to base.

During the night I received orders to move the rest of B Company up to Washburn's position. A heavy rain was falling and, although the first leg of our journey was less than two-and-a-half miles, it was through thick jungle. The trail wound around banyan trees and briars, but just after daybreak we left the jungle and entered Carlson's base, sited in a coconut grove. After a short break, Carlson and Major John M. Mather, an Australian officer in charge of Sergeant-Major Vouza and his natives, joined B Company and we continued on into Asamana. F and C Companies returned to Binu, where E Company was preparing to join us for the march into Asamana.

Near the river, some raiders spotted three Japanese in a canoe. As it reached the right spot, the lead team jumped the canoe, killing one man and capturing the other two. A short time later, Lieutenant Bill Does' platoon skirmished through the village, receiving sporadic smallarms fire. The rest of my company came up and was assigned defensive positions; Washburn's men took charge of the other half of the village. With Corporal McCall's squad, went back across the river to organise some defences and then hiked back to my command post.

Dead tired, I ate a D-bar, unrolled my shelter, poncho and blanket, and then fell into a deep sleep. About midnight, a rifle shot cracked through the hut, but I was too tired to be bothered. Later, however, several rounds came through the walls and I got on my knees to dig a prone foxhole. Whilst digging, I uncovered the body of a dead Japanese. Firing was pretty general by this stage; most of it came from around McCall's position.

At daybreak, Gunnery Sergeant Cone, Corporal Needham and I made our rounds of the village. Because of heavy rainfall during the night, the river was too swollen to wade. Captain Green gave it a try and almost drowned, but Private Royal, our best swimmer, swam across with a rope in his mouth and tied it to a boat. We ferried across the river; later, our demolition experts felled a tree to make a permanent bridge. McCall's squad had killed 13 Japanese during the night, and by the afternoon of the 13th Green's platoon had accounted for seven and Doe's nine. Washburn had also killed a similar number.

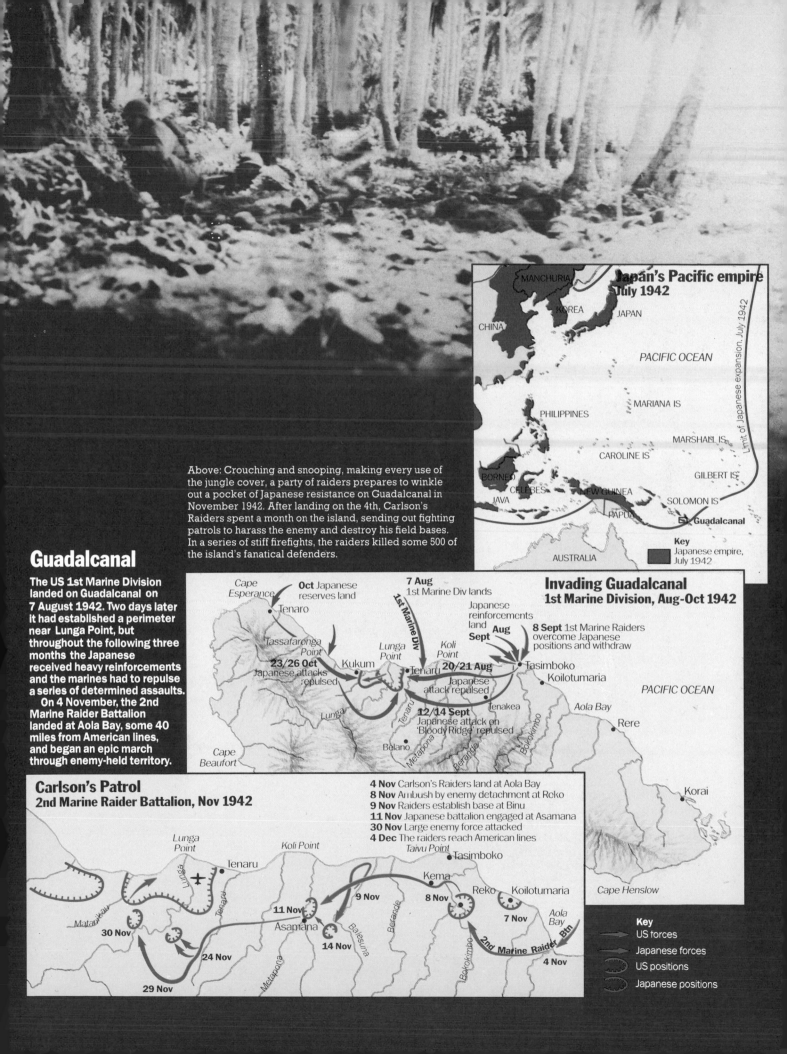

Japan's Pacific empire
July 1942

MANCHURIA
KOREA
JAPAN
CHINA
PACIFIC OCEAN
PHILIPPINES
MARIANA IS
MARSHALL IS
CAROLINE IS
GILBERT IS
BORNEO
CELEBES
NEW GUINEA
SOLOMON IS
JAVA
PAPUA
Guadalcanal
AUSTRALIA

Limit of Japanese expansion, July 1942

Key
Japanese empire,
July 1942

Above: Crouching and snooping, making every use of the jungle cover, a party of raiders prepares to winkle out a pocket of Japanese resistance on Guadalcanal in November 1942. After landing on the 4th, Carlson's Raiders spent a month on the island, sending out fighting patrols to harass the enemy and destroy his field bases. In a series of stiff firefights, the raiders killed some 500 of the island's fanatical defenders.

Guadalcanal

The US 1st Marine Division landed on Guadalcanal on 7 August 1942. Two days later it had established a perimeter near Lunga Point, but throughout the following three months the Japanese received heavy reinforcements and the marines had to repulse a series of determined assaults.

On 4 November, the 2nd Marine Raider Battalion landed at Aola Bay, some 40 miles from American lines, and began an epic march through enemy-held territory.

Invading Guadalcanal
1st Marine Division, Aug-Oct 1942

Cape Esperance
Oct Japanese reserves land
Tenaro
7 Aug 1st Marine Div lands
Japanese reinforcements land **Aug Sept**
8 Sept 1st Marine Raiders overcome Japanese positions and withdraw
Tassafaronga Point
Lunga Point
Koli Point
23/26 Oct Japanese attacks repulsed
Kukum
Tenaru
Tasimboko
Koilotumaria
PACIFIC OCEAN
20/21 Aug Japanese attack repulsed
Aola Bay
Rere
Lunga
Tenakea
12/14 Sept Japanese attack on 'Bloody Ridge' repulsed
Metapona
Berande
Bokokimbo
Bolano
Cape Beaufort
Korai

Carlson's Patrol
2nd Marine Raider Battalion, Nov 1942

4 Nov Carlson's Raiders land at Aola Bay
8 Nov Ambush by enemy detachment at Reko
9 Nov Raiders establish base at Binu
11 Nov Japanese battalion engaged at Asamana
30 Nov Large enemy force attacked
4 Dec The raiders reach American lines

Lunga Point
Koli Point
Taivu Point
Tasimboko
Ienaru
Kema
Lunga
Tenaru
Reko
Koilotumaria
11 Nov
9 Nov
8 Nov
Asamana
7 Nov
Aola Bay
Matanikau
30 Nov
24 Nov
14 Nov
Balesuna
Berande
2nd Marine Raider Btn
4 Nov
29 Nov
Metapona
Bokokimbo
Cape Henslow

Key
→ US forces
→ Japanese forces
US positions
Japanese positions

Just after noon, we saw a flight of enemy dive-bombers and fighters overhead; our naval and shore-based anti-aircraft shells filled the sky. Our Wildcats were dogfighting with Japanese Zeroes. Ashore it was relatively quiet, aside from artillery and anti-aircraft fire. However, our naval guns were blasting away and, shortly after midnight, a huge flash lit up the night sky. We imagined that the powder room of a ship had exploded. It seemed that a big naval battle was taking place and that the Japanese were trying to land more reinforcements.

During the morning of 14 November, three companies and Carlson's small headquarters patrolled back to Binu where we drew rations. With security posted, we all went down to the river to wash our clothes and get rid of the stench of the jungle. Under the supervision of Mather, some 200 natives were also drawing rations and being briefed for their next assignment. Two native guides were posted to each raider company while the rest, some armed with Lee Enfield and Japanese rifles, were used to bring up supplies under the watchful eye of Vouza.

Later, we heard that one scout had seen 15 Japanese camped just off the trail that led south from our base, and Carlson ordered Schwerin's F Company to patrol the area. Meanwhile, B Company escorted Carlson to the village of Volimuva, the headquarters of the 7th Marines, to see their commander, Colonel Sims. After a discussion, Carlson was given permission to move back to Asamana and patrol to the south and west of the village, while the 7th Marines covered an area to the east of the Metapona river.

When Schwerin returned to base, he had a remarkable story to tell. His scout had led the company to a natural defile that was guarded by a lone sentry. From a safe point, they had observed the camp until the sentry went for chow, and then slipped in, killing every Japanese in sight. Schwerin's men also picked up some valuable intelligence, including the personal effects of Major-General Kawaguchi, the senior Japanese officer in the area.

On the 17th Carlson led D Company, by this stage under the command of Captain Joe Griffith, into unexplored territory, to a point some 10 miles west of our base. After being ordered to rendezvous with the 1st Marine Division, Carlson and his men double-timed back to our base. Wet with sweat, dirty and exhausted, they refreshed themselves and then started out again, heading for the beach five miles away. There, Carlson was taken to the division's HQ. He returned on the next day with his orders: his mission was to establish a base on the Tenaru river and then patrol around that area and the Lunga river.

We placed two machine guns on a line with the enemy and started firing

On the following day, all the raiders, with the exception of B and F Companies, started out for the upper Tenaru. After spending the night on the trail near the upper Nalimbiu river, the column then moved into the new camp, a few miles south of Henderson airfield. Later, B and F Companies moved up. Between the 20th and 24th, the raiders set up their defences and received the occasional visitor. Lieutenant-Colonel 'Chesty' Puller visited Carlson, and I received a large can of fruit cocktail from Captain Don Peppard – it was delicious beyond words. However, patrols were sent out and on the

26th members of B Company brought in 100 enemy rifles and seven pistols.

On the 28th, after we had moved our base four miles to the west, B and D Companies went out to interdict a Japanese supply route known as the east-west trail. After crossing the upper Tenaru, the columns climbed the steep side of Mombula mountain by a twisting, turning, slippery trail. While B Company established positions across this route, Griffith's men set up positions along the same path but nearer the river, at the base of the mountain. After a quiet night, we started back to base, but we met a friendly scout en route and he guided us to where F Company was fighting a strong enemy force.

One squad, led by Corporal John Yancey, had already advanced through one Japanese position and was tackling another when we finally arrived. Yancey's men accounted for most of the enemy's 75 dead. Later I heard that the company had stumbled into a row of stacked rifles in the dark and killed most of the Japanese as they were running for their weapons. While F Company tidied up, I went over to see the 75mm mountain gun, known as 'Pistol Pete', which had been shooting down our aircraft on Henderson Field. It was still in good shape, as was a 37mm anti-aircraft gun located nearby. The rain poured down during the night, and the mountain air was cold and bitter. After many attempts, we got a fire going to fight off some of the chill.

The next morning, we started patrolling. I led a small patrol team up the Lunga river. At the end of a gorge, we sighted several Japanese sitting in a circle on a sand spit, jabbering away. Without being noticed, we placed two machine guns and several automatic weapons on a line with the enemy and started firing. After a couple of minutes, we moved in

Left: A patrol hacks a path through dense undergrowth on Guadalcanal. Below left: After a vicious exchange of fire, wary raiders enter an abandoned Japanese camp to search for vital intelligence. Below: Marines examine the bodies of enemy troops cut down during an abortive attempt to reinforce the island's beleaguered garrison. Suicidal bravery was no match for US firepower.

and examined the results. The Japanese were a pitiful sight; skinny, pale and sickly. One had a crutch and another had a rough splint on an injured leg. Our return to base was quick and without problems.

After dark, Carlson issued orders for 3 December. Washburn was told to move C, D and E Companies down the Lunga trail into the division's main perimeter. Captain Gary's recently arrived A Company, along with Carlson, B and F Companies, were to patrol Mombula mountain.

About midday, the lead fire team reached the summit of the mountain and deployed to provide security, while the rest of the column climbed the steep slopes to reach their position. A Japanese combat patrol passed the fire team's perimeter and was engaged. Covered by their comrades, Lieutenant Miller and several raiders hurried forward but were caught by Japanese fire. Miller and three of his men were seriously wounded before the enemy troops were eliminated.

Carlson's Raiders had carried out a 150-mile trek and fought over a dozen actions against the Japanese

Bright and early the next morning, B Company led the way back to our main base. The lead fire team had advanced about 100yds beyond our perimeter when it was hit by heavy machine-gun fire. The lead raiders, Privates Farrar and Matelski, were killed instantly. Private Van Buren, trying to take out the enemy guns, jumped off the trail and into a gully. He was also hit. One man, Corporal Croft, had identified the enemy position, and suggested that Sergeant Potter should shake a branch to draw the unfriendly fire. Potter carried out this ploy several times, and each time the enemy fired, he accused Croft of ducking and not being able to spot the machine guns. After another try or two, however, Croft killed the gunner.

Before we moved off, B Company buried the dead, so A and F Companies took the lead. We had not gone far before the battalion surgeon, Dr Charles Robinson, asked to halt the column as Lieutenant Miller was failing fast. A little later, he was dead, and Carlson made his way from the front of the column, pulled a bible and US flag from his pack, and performed a short ceremony.

Slowly, B Company led the rear of the column down the trail and into the low ground near the Matanikau river. We were met by several ambulances on the way in and our stretcher cases were given a ride to the division hospital. We still had a few more miles to hike before reaching our bivouac area. On the morning of 5 December we reached the beach where our transport back to Espiritu Santo was waiting. After a long, tiring month on Guadalcanal, we were pulling out for a well-earned rest. In a period of four weeks, Carlson's Raiders had carried out a 150-mile trek through the jungle and fought over a dozen actions against the Japanese, killing 500 and driving the rest into the interior of the island. Although the battle for Guadalcanal was to last until 9 February 1943, by which stage the Japanese had suffered 25,000 dead, the raiders' operations had undermined the enemy's belief in final victory.

THE AUTHOR Major-General O.F. Peatross served with Carlson's Raiders in World War II, and saw service in Korea and Vietnam. During his long military career he was awarded seven personal decorations including three Legions of Merit.

BORN IN BATTLE

In 1971 the South Vietnamese Marines returned from Operation Lam Son 719 a harder and maturer combat force

TO THE MORE wary, or perhaps the more jaundiced, US advisers in South Vietnam, Operation Lam Son 719 in early 1971 appeared to be a snake-bitten venture from the outset. First, there was a problem of high command. As a test of the Vietnamization programme, the US plan to maximise South Vietnamese involvement in the war, the Lam Son incursion into Laos carried the highest hopes of both Saigon and Washington. But the commander of the operation, Lieutenant-General Hoang Xuan Lam of I Corps, and his staff lacked experience in planning and conducting a mission that involved major units of the Army of the Republic of Vietnam (ARVN) such as the 1st Infantry Division, the 1st Armored Brigade, and a Ranger group augmented by airborne and Marine units from the national reserve; each unit was taking the field at division strength for the first time. Even so, this South Vietnamese task force numbered only 16,000 men – half the size of the combined American-Vietnamese force that had launched a cross-border operation into Cambodia a year earlier.

ARVN MARINES

During its 21-year history, the Thuy Quan Luc Chien (the South Vietnamese Marine Corps) grew from a battalion-sized landing force into the most effective division-strength unit in the ARVN (Army of the Republic of Vietnam). The first battalion was formed on 1 October 1954 from a number of commando and riverine companies that had been operating in North Vietnam before they were moved south under the provisions of the Geneva Accords. The growth and training of the corps was overseen by US advisers, the first being Lieutenant-Colonel Victor Croizat. In 1955, the battalion, by this stage 1000 strong, fought two sharp actions against anti-government forces and bandits.

By 1962, the strength of the Marines had increased five-fold and the unit attained brigade status. Two years later, the corps broke from the navy and began to report directly to the South Vietnamese High Command.

In 1968, after gallant work during the Tet Offensive, the Marines were expanded into a two-brigade division; a third brigade was added in mid-1970 after several successful actions in Cambodia. Part of the division played a key role in Lam Son 719, the incursion into Laos in 1971, and a year later made a major contribution to the defeat of the enemy's Easter Offensive.

After the withdrawal of US ground forces, the Marines functioned as the ARVN's central reserve, for use in specific counter-insurgency operations. The Marines fought against the 1975 invasion from the North but heavy losses around Da Nang effectively removed the division from the ARVN's order of battle. Above: The Marine Brigade's shoulder insignia.

To further complicate matters, there was no love lost between General Lam and the ARVN Marines, who privately referred to him as 'Old Bloody Hands' for the way he would sweep his hands grandly across a battle map while discussing his operational concepts. To the Marines, such bold sweeps would ultimately translate into excessive casualties.

The strategy behind Lam Son 719 called for the creation of a string of helicopter-supported firebases to protect the flanks of a main armoured advance along Route 9 from South Vietnam's Khe Sanh plateau to the principal objective, the village of Tchepone, a point on the Ho Chi Minh Trail lying some 22km inside Laos. Severing the trail would deny the enemy in South Vietnam vital supplies. Such heavy reliance on helicopters, however, was more appropriate to the flatter country of the Mekong delta and Cambodia, as both the terrain and the weather became increasingly less hospitable closer to the rugged de-militarized zone (DMZ) at the 17th Parallel. In such surroundings, the US advisers would have preferred to attack Tchepone with a near-invulnerable foot column of the ARVN divisions, supported by armour, and then swing either north or south as the opportunity arose. They feared that under the existing strategy, the crucial firebases would be subject to defeat in detail.

Opinions also differed as to the strength of the opposition that the North Vietnamese Army (NVA) could muster against the incursion. To some, the intelligence officers' prediction of a sluggish NVA response to Lam Son 719 – one that would be further diluted by a proposed amphibious feint against the North Vietnamese coastal city of Vinh – seemed too optimistic to be taken seriously.

The misgivings of the advisers went unheard during the compartmentalised and tightly guarded planning cycle and, unfortunately, this secrecy did more to isolate the South Vietnamese High Command from reality than to deny essential information to North Vietnamese agents. Thanks to numerous weak spots in South Vietnamese security, the NVA was soon aware of the growing details of the operation on an almost daily basis.

The Marines were designated as the Corps reserve for Lam Son 719, but on D-day, 8 February 1971, none of the division's three brigades had arrived at the Khe Sanh jump-off point. Two were conducting reconnaissance missions in the vicinity of Quang Tri City, also in I Corps, and the third was operating in Cambodia's Neak Louang-Kampong Trabek area. By the end of the month, however, all three brigades were at Khe Sanh and the division's command post had been airlifted from Saigon to assume direct operational control in the field for the first time.

Mastering the mechanics of division-level command and control was only part of the problem that the Marines faced. A psychological barrier still existed. The brigade commanders, acccustomed to the exercise of absolute authority within their own spheres, were reluctant to accept orders, or even advice, from division staff officers who had less seniority. Consequently, a tradition of semi-independent operations persisted, despite a need for more centralised control.

Early in March, Marine Brigades 147 and 258 moved into Laos, and manned firebases Delta and Hotel in order to release troops of the ARVN 1st Division for the final assault on Tchepone. Brigade 369, the only unit remaining in the national reserve, manned the Laotian border.

Page 123: South Vietnamese troops move into Laos at the start of Lam Son 719, the operation to sever the Ho Chi Minh Trail. Far left: The senior commander of the operation, Lieutenant-General Hoang Xuan Lam (right), confers with his field staff. Right: Led by an M113 APC, a South Vietnamese column moves towards the village of Tchepone, the focal point of the attack. Below left: Close artillery support in action. A battery CO plots the co-ordinates of an enemy position. Below: Armed with an M79 grenade launcher, a marine takes cover.

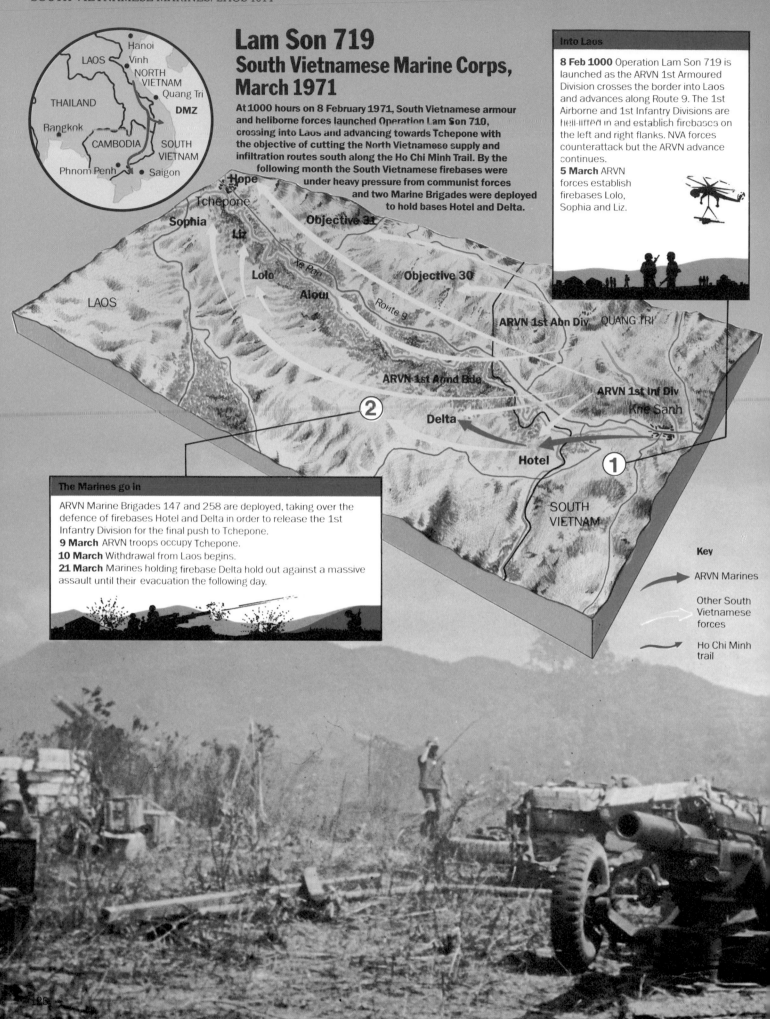

Lam Son 719
South Vietnamese Marine Corps, March 1971

At 1000 hours on 8 February 1971, South Vietnamese armour and heliborne forces launched Operation Lam Son 710, crossing into Laos and advancing towards Tchepone with the objective of cutting the North Vietnamese supply and infiltration routes south along the Ho Chi Minh Trail. By the following month the South Vietnamese firebases were under heavy pressure from communist forces and two Marine Brigades were deployed to hold bases Hotel and Delta.

Into Laos

8 Feb 1000 Operation Lam Son 719 is launched as the ARVN 1st Armoured Division crosses the border into Laos and advances along Route 9. The 1st Airborne and 1st Infantry Divisions are heli-lifted in and establish firebases on the left and right flanks. NVA forces counterattack but the ARVN advance continues.
5 March ARVN forces establish firebases Lolo, Sophia and Liz.

The Marines go in

ARVN Marine Brigades 147 and 258 are deployed, taking over the defence of firebases Hotel and Delta in order to release the 1st Infantry Division for the final push to Tchepone.
9 March ARVN troops occupy Tchepone.
10 March Withdrawal from Laos begins.
21 March Marines holding firebase Delta hold out against a massive assault until their evacuation the following day.

Key
ARVN Marines
Other South Vietnamese forces
Ho Chi Minh trail

Tchepone, by then a deserted, bombed-out village, was occupied briefly by South Vietnamese troops on 9 March. However, earlier plans to sweep southwards had to be abandoned as the NVA was reinforcing its units in the area and was close to achieving a numerical superiority of nearly two-to-one. To make matters worse, even more enemy reinforcements were on the way. The ARVN units, by contrast, were stretched to the limit and additional forces could not be committed to Lam Son 719 without severely weakening their positions in South Vietnam. Furthermore, flying weather was beginning to take a turn for the worse; an ominous portent for the string of firebases still heavily dependent on helicopter support. On 10 March the South Vietnamese forces were ordered to withdraw.

The withdrawal phase of any military operation is inherently the most dangerous, for as fewer and fewer units are left in contact with the enemy, so they must bear proportionately greater burdens in protecting the flanks and rear of the withdrawing force. This axiom was demonstrated once again in Lam Son 719, as the string of firebases fell to NVA attacks. The North Vietnamese tactics were uncomplicated: they would first encircle a base to cut off escape and prevent relief by ground units. Next, the encirclement would be tightened, and anti-aircraft weapons would be brought up to shut off aerial resupply. The NVA would go to almost any lengths to isolate the firebases: American helicopter pilots even saw enemy soldiers lying on their backs beneath the barbed wire that ringed the bases, firing their smallarms straight up into aircraft making their final approaches into landing zones. Then, as helicopter losses mounted and the firebase garrisons grew desperately short of food, water, and ammunition, the attackers would wait for a cloudy day, when close support from fixed-wing aircraft would be impossible. At that point, they could bring up their tanks and overrun the position.

Effective air support was the only means available to the South Vietnamese to counter such tactics. For the Vietnamese Marines, this was usually controlled by a pair of US

VIETNAMIZATION

The communist Tet Offensive of 1968 was the turning point of US involvement in the Vietnam War, and led to the phased withdrawal of US ground troops from South Vietnam. By fuelling domestic disenchantment with the conflict, Tet forced President Lyndon Johnson to introduce sweeping changes in the conduct of the conflict.

The lynch-pin of Johnson's new strategy was the Vietnamization programme. Basically a device to meet the political imperative of reducing US casualties, the so-called 'body count', the programme had three main strands: turning US bases over to the ARVN (Army of the Republic of Vietnam), improving the weapons and training of indigenous forces, and giving them the combat roles previously borne by US forces.

In March 1968, the US administration took the decision to halt the build-up of its forces, and began supplying the ARVN with modern equipment. At the same time, the South Vietnamese introduced a general mobilisation call to all able-bodied males between the ages of 16 and 50, and established the People's Self Defence Force, a militia to protect villages from enemy interference. By the end of the year, the ARVN's strength had risen by nearly 200,000 to 820,000.

When President Richard Nixon took office in early 1969, the programme was intensified; as the ARVN was expanded and re-equipped, US troop levels were reduced. Between 1969 and 1971, the number of US troops in Vietnam fell from 475,000 to 158,000. Despite Vietnamization, the ARVN remained ill-prepared to deal with any major threat from the North. The South Vietnamese forces were relatively untried, and the rate of desertion was alarmingly high. The leadership of the ARVN at all levels was poor and considerably less experienced than the North Vietnamese. In 1975, the final North Vietnamese offensive that led to the fall of Saigon highlighted the shortcomings of Vietnamization.

Left: Building a firebase on the route to Tchepone.

127

Far right: The South Vietnamese offensive soon bogged down into a series of bitter attritional battles focusing on the firebases constructed along the road to Tchepone. Appalling weather hampered air support and the Marines were forced to make a fighting withdrawal. Far right: Hill 30 saw some of the fiercest combat as the North Vietnamese threw the cream of their units against the base's perimeter. Below inset: Lieutenant-General Lam holds a battlefield meeting with one of his American advisers. Political factors prevented US officers from crossing into Laos and made it difficult for them to liaise with the South Vietnamese. Despite these problems, the Marines were able to regroup and defeat the enemy's thrusts towards Khe Sanh. Below: An aerial shot of the route into Laos.

advisers, known as *co-van My*, per battalion, talking to American aircraft overhead. But the Congressional mandate that had brought the advisers out of Cambodia on 30 June 1970 was still in effect, and no *co-van* was permitted to accompany his unit into Laos. Somewhere in the chain of command, one feeble concession to reality had been granted, and a single adviser was permitted to be airborne over the division's sector at any given time. This had more cosmetic than real value as an adviser usually had his hands full while working close support for his own battalion. Meeting the simultaneous requirements of six battalions in contact with the enemy, without a man on the ground to mark targets, and to coach high-performance aircraft onto them, was sometimes more than a single adviser could handle.

The pressure on the outnumbered South Vietnamese units intensified steadily during the withdrawal phase. Some managed to return to their homeland in relatively good order. Others did not, and a notorious news photograph of terrified ARVN soldiers clinging to the skids of an evacuation helicopter became an unfortunate and misleading symbol of Lam Son 719 to newspaper readers around the world.

Towards the end of March, the counter-attacking North Vietnamese forces were able to concentrate upon the two Marine brigades in Laos. Two NVA regiments moved in from South Vietnam's A Shau valley to surround firebase Delta, still defended by Brigade 147. Meanwhile, another North Vietnamese

regiment attacked firebase Hotel, pinning down its defenders from Brigade 258. Following the now-familiar pattern, the NVA units next moved 10 anti-aircraft guns into the hills surrounding Delta, while hammering the firebase with 130mm artillery. The noose was drawing tight.

At first light on 21 March, they attacked. The defenders of Delta combined artillery, close air support and a B-52 bomber strike that landed squarely on a North Vietnamese battalion, killing 400 men, to stall the attack. The respite was shortlived, and the North Vietnamese renewed the assault on the following day from positions within the base's defensive perimeter. Brigade 147's casualties were mounting and their supply of ammunition was becoming dangerously low. Darkness was falling on the second day when the NVA forces launched their final attack. By midnight, they had overrun the firebase. The Marines fell back towards the northeast, trying to break through the encircling forces. By noon of the following day, they had established and secured a helicopter landing zone, to facilitate their evacuation to South Vietnam. Marines who retired from Delta in other directions found themselves having to escape from the enemy by working their way cross-country towards friendly positions.

Back at Khe Sanh, uneasiness grew steadily as hours went by without the base receiving a word from the stragglers. Khe Sanh had other problems as well: the division's command post, dug in and sandbagged after a few carefree days as a tent city, was falling under heavy attack from 122mm and 130mm artillery, adjusted by observers from the massive Co

Roc escarpment that overlooked the Khe Sanh plateau. In a typical bit of graveyard humour, US advisers in the hills surrounding Khe Sanh pretended to adjust the North Vietnamese artillery fire on the *co-van* radio network, for the (presumed) amusement of the division-level advisers located within Khe Sanh.

Clawing their way back into Vietnam, the Marines inflicted as much punishment as they suffered

The advisers in Khe Sanh had their own ways of fighting back. One, a son-in-law of the legendary US Marine general, Lewis 'Chesty' Puller, was a veteran of the 1968 Khe Sanh siege. He had saved his old battle maps. When an incoming artillery round landed near the old landing strip, he pulled out his compass and shot a back azimuth towards the estimated source of fire. Then, he raced to the other end of the old airstrip and shot another back azimuth, that happened to intersect with the first one at the same point on the map where a North Vietnamese artillery position had been plotted back in 1968. The adviser's call for counter-battery fire produced a series of spectacular secondary explosions when a great amount of enemy ammunition went up.

Within two days the Marine stragglers began to return to friendly lines, easing the anxiety at Khe Sanh. By 25 March, after Brigade 258 had conducted an uneventful return by helicopter from firebase Hotel, the casualty figures for the Marine Division were 335 killed in action and 768 wounded, most coming from Brigade 147. On the credit side, the initially high missing-in-action total had shrunk to 37, and the returning Marine riflemen were re-equipping, resolutely re-grouping and moving back into the hills to help defend Khe Sanh.

At first, some of the Marines appeared to be 'whipped' by their searing experience, but it became evident that in clawing their way back into Vietnam, they had inflicted at least as much punishment as they had suffered. An enemy radio broadcast named several regiments that would be returning home for a well-deserved 'rest'. Later, these units quietly disappeared from the North Vietnamese order of battle.

The advisers and the Marine leadership approached their shared re-building tasks with determination. Within a year, these Marines would anchor the defensive line that stopped the North Vietnamese offensive of 1972, and would eventually retake what was left of Quang Tri City.

Accompanying the re-building process was a subtle shift from brigade to division-level thinking. A harbinger of this change appeared shortly after the Marine Division moved from Khe Sanh to the vicinity of Quang Tri. The division's G-3 (operations) officer had flown to one of the brigade command posts, after redrawing boundaries for areas of operation. The brigade commander did not like his new area and, with an almost contemptuous wave of the hand, he told the G-3 to fly back to his HQ and pick out a better area for his brigade.

The G-3 officer was crestfallen, but his US adviser was seething with frustration. Drawing his opposite number aside, the *co-van* spoke with unusual vehemence, 'If you go back to Corps, you will never be a real G-3! You must speak with the authority of the division commander.'

Taken aback by this outburst, the G-3 made two calls, using the field telephone. The first was to the division commander, who confirmed what the adviser had said. Next, the G-3 called the contentious brigade commander. With new authority in his voice, he told the senior officer to carry out his orders, as directed, in his assigned area. He would be a real G-3. The South Vietnamese Marines were coming of age as a fighting division.

THE AUTHOR Colonel John G. Miller, US Marine Corps, (Retired), is the managing editor of the U.S. Naval Institute Proceedings. During his second combat tour in Vietnam, he was an adviser to the Vietnamese Marines at battalion, brigade, and division level. Colonel Miller is the author of the recently published World War II naval history, *The Battle To Save The Houston*, (Naval Institute Press).

On the morning of 6 November 1956, the Royal Marine Commandos stormed ashore at Port Said. Captain Derek Oakley of 42 Commando, who was in the first landing craft to hit the beach, tells the story of that day

IT WAS PROBABLY the slowest Mediterranean convoy since the days of Cleopatra. The vast armada left Malta on 31 October and, taking its speed from the slowest of the amphibious ships, spent the best part of a week sailing east towards Port Said and the entrance to the Suez Canal. Briefings were carried out on board our landing ships during that week, but it was only on the night before the landing that we received new aerial photographs of our initial objec-

Below: Training for the battle of Port Said, Royal Marine Sergeant Yates leads his section in a house-clearing exercise. This type of action was to prove typical of the fighting for the town.

SUEZ COMMANDO

INVASION FORCES

The assault at Suez ultimately involved some 90,000 French and British troops, naval and air personnel, almost equally divided between the two nations. Musketeer, as the operation was codenamed, was structured in three phases. The first stage consisted of an air campaign to secure air superiority over Egypt before any ground forces were committed. Phase two, launched on 5 November, involved an airborne assault by 3 Para at Gamil airfield to the west of Port Said, while a battalion group of French paras from the 10th Colonial Parachute Division landed at the Raswa bridges and to the south of Port Fuad. Phase three of Musketeer consisted of seaborne landings on the morning of 6 November. The British side of this last phase was handled by the men of 3 Commando Brigade with C Squadron of the 6th Royal Tank Regiment and the 3rd Field Squadron of the Royal Engineers. The French contribution consisted of men of the 2nd Colonial Parachute Regiment, three Marine Commandos, and a squadron of AMX tanks. Later in the day, the HQ of 16th Parachute Brigade, together with the 1st and 2nd Battalions, The Parachute Regiment, landed at Port Said harbour, as did A and B Squadrons of the 6th Royal Tank Regiment. Some 14 LSTs (Landing Ship, Tank) had unloaded before night fell on the day of the invasion.

Left: Preparing for the invasion. Royal Marines of 42 Commando prime grenades on board the landing ship *Striker* before embarking in their LVTs. Below left: The officers of B Troop, 42 Commando. On the left is the author, Captain Derek Oakley, with his two subalterns, Lieutenants David Westwood (centre) and Leslie Hudson. Below: An LCA of the second Marine assault wave heads for the beaches.

tives, mostly 'obliques' taken by aircraft of the Fleet Air Arm. To our surprise and consternation we learned that beyond the five rows of wooden huts that stretched along the beach, there were more buildings than we had reckoned on from the out-of-date street maps of Port Said with which we had been issued. The obliques showed quite clearly that our first objectives were far larger than the two-storey buildings we had been led to expect. This new intelligence resulted in a hasty reorganisation of plans and a re-appraisal of operational timings.

After supper on 5 November we had a quiet celebration for the birthday of Lieutenant Jim Burton, our intelligence officer. Perhaps it was an excuse to numb our apprehension for the morrow. Up on deck we could hear in the distance the dull throb of aircraft engines, presumably flying in support of the 3rd Battalion, The Parachute Regiment, who had been dropped on Gamil airfield, some six miles to the west of Port Said, earlier that day. When we had first heard the news of the airdrop, we were a little disappointed that we were not to be the first to land. But our missions were completely different, and we knew we would be the first into Port Said town itself. Bright flashes lit up the evening sky, reminding us that this was Guy Fawkes Night.

It was a restless sleep that most of us went to. I tossed and turned in the stifling heat of my cabin on board HMS *Suvla*, a tank landing ship (LST) which had been brought out of reserve in the Clyde. Like most of the other supporting ships, she had no such modern luxury as air-conditioning. Most of the marines slept with their weapons on the upper deck.

There is a freshness about a Mediterranean dawn that is far from apparent during the later part of the

day. The air is clear and the sun's rays gather strength slowly in the first flushes of the morn. As we clambered up the ladders of *Suvla* into the cool air above, we could see to our starboard a pall of thick smoke lying sluggishly over the sleeping town of Port Said. In the distance, much blacker smoke poured from the oil storage tanks to the south of the town, which had been hit by RAF bombers during the night. My two troop subalterns, Lieutenant Leslie Hudson, who was a regular, and a national serviceman, Lieutenant David Westwood, along with my sergeant major, QMS G.C.N. Casey, inspected the marines, checked their equipment and ammunition, tested their radios and ensured that all was well-prepared for the forthcoming fray. Only a handful had been in action before, either during World War II or in the jungles of Malaya. Of my five fighting sections, one was made up entirely of national servicemen, an educated bunch compared with their more professional, but nonetheless intelligent, regular counterparts. But all were to prove their worth that day.

The order was passed to go down to the tank deck to embark in our tracked amphibious vehicles (LVTs). Each LVT could carry up to 30 men, swim at about five knots in the sea, and then run up the beach on its tracks. At 0410 the bow doors of *Suvla* opened and the vehicles slowly churned their way out, motors thundering in the enclosed space of the tank deck of the mother ship.

With the LVTs circling in our assembly area like a

gaggle of tin boxes wobbling on the broken surface, the marines whispered quietly together. I looked at my watch in the gathering daylight. It was 0425 GMT. Our watches had been set to 'Zulu' time, some three hours ahead of local time, which made the whole operation seem uncannily inaccurate. I glanced at the men crouching or sitting in the well of my LVT, nervously fiddling with the slings of their weapons or

pulling at the straps of their equipment. It was fast approaching the time to start our run-in to the beach. I looked round to see the LVTs of A Troop approaching to join this tight circle, like young ducklings gathering around their mother. The minutes ticked away and the sun's rays gathered strength. Suddenly, with a terrifying roar which rent the stillness, the 4.6in guns of HMS *Decoy*, our own bombardment ship, and her fellow destroyers, opened up as they steamed past, running parallel to

Below: A Royal Marine primes a mortar bomb prior to the amphibious assault. Below left: While a couple of LCAs churn their way towards the smoking town of Port Said, Whirlwind choppers of the heliborne assault wave carry the men of 45 Commando into battle.

MUSKETEER-PHASE ONE

At 1615 hours on 30 October 1956, Britain and France issued an ultimatum to Israel and Egypt to withdraw their forces to a distance of 10 miles from the Suez Canal within the next 12 hours. If they failed to do so, British and French forces would establish themselves in the Canal Zone.

Israeli forces were not within 10 miles of the Canal at that time and the Egyptians, quite predictably, refused to give in to this pressure.

For the paras and Royal Marines to make the airborne and seaborne assaults, it was necessary to achieve air superiority to guard the incoming convoy of ships on its long approach from Malta and to protect the ground forces from Egyptian air attack during the actual invasion. On 31 October Phase One of Operation Musketeer was launched. The air bombardment involved a variety of aircraft including Valiants, Canberras, Venoms, Hunters and Thunderstreaks, operating from bases on Malta and Cyprus. In addition, further attacks were lauched from the carrier force – the British committed five carriers and the French two – involving Sea Hawks, Sea Venoms, Corsairs and Thunderstreaks, flying in from the ships 50 miles off the Egyptian coastline. The first attack to go in was against Almaza airfield, with an RAF Canberra from No.10 Squadron dropping the first bombs. The attack on Almaza was part of a series of raids against 12 Egyptian airfields launched on the first night.

For a week before the landings, Egyptian airfields, military installations and the immediate vicinity of the proposed amphibious landing areas around Port Said and Port Faud were subjected to almost continuous air attack. The campaign succeeded in achieving the air superiorty crucial to the success of the operation as a whole, and a great many Egyptian aircraft were destroyed in the process. With the success of Phase One, the Egyptian capacity to resist the main assault was drastically reduced.

the coast. It was an awe-inspiring sight and one I shall never forget. This was our signal to start the run-in. The adrenalin began to flow, nerves tightened, and a look of qualified anticipation shone on the marines' sunburnt faces. A last-minute decision by the Government in London had limited the size of guns to be used for the bombardment to no larger than 6in. The French battleship *Richelieu* with her 15in guns and the British cruiser HMS *Jamaica* with her 8in armament turned dejectedly away in the distance.

Beneath my feet the LVT engine roared into full power and the Royal Armoured Corps driver turned the unstable craft towards the beach. We were barely a mile offshore, but it would be only minutes before we touched down, not knowing what the enemy had lying in wait for us. We had been assured that there would be no mines in the landing area, but it was not beyond Egyptian ingenuity to give us an unexpected welcome. The next few minutes would decide our fate.

A slight breeze ruffled the waves as we chugged slowly towards the beach. To my left, over in the distance, I could see the long line of Buffaloes carrying the men of 40 Commando, then our own A Troop, commanded by the battle-hardened Captain Hamish Emslie, who had won the Military Cross in Malaya and had also served with the SBS. Little did he know that he was to be Mentioned in Despatches later that day. I turned to my right, and there, speeding across our bows, were our two destroyers, HMS *Decoy* leading HMS *Chaplet*. Their battle ensigns flew taut at the mastheads, almost obliterating their superstructures, while their guns pounded the shoreline to ensure that no enemy were lying in wait for us. I glanced back towards the statue of Ferdinand de Lesseps, proudly guarding the entrance to the Canal, and was horrified to see that the line of LVTs had disappeared and that our lone craft

was now out ahead of them. I poked my head into the cockpit and shouted to my driver to slow down. 'I've got the fastest bloody craft here and we're going to get their first,' came the reply. We did.

With only 400yds to go, I could still see the naval shells bursting on the beach ahead. A couple of Fleet Air Arm Sea Hawks swooped down from the cloudless sky and strafed the beach in front of us. It was exhilarating yet frightening. As we churned relentlessly on, the shells continued to fall and I prayed that the barrage would lift by the time we got there. A glance at my watch told me that we were running about three minutes late, and it was just as well, for yet another pair of fighters attacked the beach huts ahead with all guns firing.

With 100yds still to go to the waterline, I felt the LVT tracks grind against the bar, and as they gripped the sand we slowly and majestically lifted out of the water, increasing our speed as the sea grew shallower. We felt naked and exposed, and took cover against the expected enemy fusilade. But the Royal Navy had done their stuff. The rows of beach huts were mostly ablaze and the smoke obscured our view, acting as a screen before our final approach. There was no resistance here. Above the din of the engine I could hear the occasional sniper shot and ricochet, reminding me that this was no exercise, but any local noise was drowned by the continuing bombardment, which had now lifted to the second block of houses. This was the limit beyond which the Royal Navy would not be allowed to fire for fear of causing civilian casualties. From then on we were on our own.

As we trundled up the beach, Sergeant-Major Casey ordered the rear ramp to be lowered to the horizontal, and the marines prepared themselves physically and mentally for battle. I heard my signalman do his last-minute radio check. Fifty

Suez: assault on Port Said
5-6 Nov 1956

On 26 July 1956, President Nasser of Egypt nationalised the Anglo-French Suez Canal Company, provoking an international crisis that resulted in a joint British and French assault on Port Said. As Britain and France prepared for war, gathering an expeditionary force in the Mediterranean, secret meetings were held with the representatives of the Israeli government. On 29 October, Israel invaded Sinai. An Anglo-French ultimatum to withdraw from the canal zone was rejected by Egypt and the way was open for the RAF to neutralise Egyptian air force bases in the area.

Early on 5 November, 3 Para and 2 RPC made advance airborne landings, and the following morning the main assault went in.

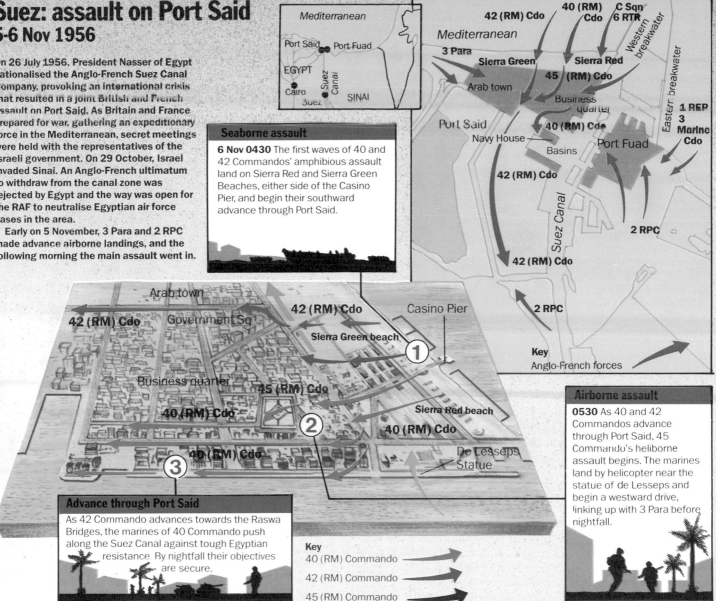

Seaborne assault

6 Nov 0430 The first waves of 40 and 42 Commandos' amphibious assault land on Sierra Red and Sierra Green Beaches, either side of the Casino Pier, and begin their southward advance through Port Said.

Advance through Port Said

As 42 Commando advances towards the Raswa Bridges, the marines of 40 Commando push along the Suez Canal against tough Egyptian resistance. By nightfall their objectives are secure.

Airborne assault

0530 As 40 and 42 Commandos advance through Port Said, 45 Commando's heliborne assault begins. The marines land by helicopter near the statue of de Lesseps and begin a westward drive, linking up with 3 Para before nightfall.

Key
40 (RM) Commando
42 (RM) Commando
45 (RM) Commando

Below: The view from the author's leading LVT as the men of 42 Commando approach Sierra Green Beach at Port Said. When this photograph was taken, the naval and aerial bombardment had not yet lifted. Left: A Sea Hawk is armed up on board the carrier HMS Eagle, prior to a mission against the Egyptian airfields during Phase One of Operation Musketeer.

yards short of the road, the LVTs stopped and the marines felt the first soft touch of sand under their feet as they disembarked and fanned out into defensive positions, prior to attacking the first objectives.

Lieutenant Hudson, an impeccable but very tough Royal Marines officer, who had risen through the ranks, gathered his sections around him. His first objective was a large, oriental building with a huge, solid oak door. It was securely locked. Although there appeared to be no enemy opposition at this stage, he took every possible precaution and called up the Assault Engineers with an explosive 'pole' charge. They lit the fuze and when they had retired to a safe distance, a tremendous explosion rent the air and the massive door disintegrated in a cloud of smoke and dust. I watched this with subdued amusement from across the road. As the smoke died

away, I saw a small dilapidated Egyptian, obviously a caretaker, emerge from a ditch beside the road waving the key!

The commandos stormed the building, some clearing the ground floor, others taking the large main staircase in their stride. Little did the marines know as they cleared this building, consolidated and went on to the next row, that the cellar contained a priceless collection of fine wines. Later we wryly noted that the commanding officer had set up his first headquarters there! Our compatriots in A Troop and the men of 40 Commando were doing a similar job all along the seafront. Aircraft screamed overhead looking for opportunity targets, but the Egyptian Army had withdrawn to the hinterland after the heavy naval bombardment. It subsequently transpired that many had thrown away their

ROYAL MARINES AT SUEZ

In late July 1956, when Egyptian President Gamal Abdel Nasser nationalised the Suez Canal Company, 3 Commando Brigade was stationed in Malta but both 40 and 45 Commandos were fighting in Cyprus, while the operational nucleus of 42 Commando was at Bickleigh in Devon. By the end of August the whole brigade had concentrated in Malta and amphibious assault training exercises were conducted throughout September and October.

At 0430 hours on the morning of 6 November the first assault troops from 40 and 42 Commando hit the beaches. The assault was made in waves, with LVTs landing first, followed by a second wave of LCAs. The men of 40 Commando landed at the base of the western breakwater on Sierra Red Beach, while 42 Commando landed further west on Sierra Green Beach. The two beachheads were clearly separated by the Casino Pier. 42 Commando pushed forward from Sierra Green into the town towards the Raswa bridges, while 40 Commando fought their way along the Canal towards the harbour basins. Egyptian resistance along the Canal was stiff and two officers from 40, Lieutenants McCarthy and Ufton, were killed during the house-clearing operations. As the day closed, 40 Commando took possession of the Canal Company offices and the customs houses, and there was heavy fighting around Navy House. While the Royal Marines of 40 and 42 Commando had made a classic amphibious assault from landing craft,

the men of 45 Commando were deployed in an entirely new way. Embarked on the carriers HMS *Ocean* and HMS *Theseus*, the troops were lifted into battle in the first recorded major helicopter assault in the history of warfare. A joint Army and RAF squadron, flying six Whirlwinds and six Sycamores, was joined by a further eight Whirlwinds of No. 845 FAA Squadron for the operation.

The assault was made in four waves, bringing in the Commando to a landing zone near the statue of de Lesseps an hour or so after the seaborne landings. The choppers brought the marines and their considerable inventory of equipment into the landing zone at three-minute intervals, hovering about a foot from the ground as the marines disembarked. The troops then worked their way westwards, across the town, joining up that evening with the men of 3 Para who had made the drop at Gamil airfield on the 5th. By nightfall, the Brigade HQ was ashore and the three Commandos were deployed at their secured objectives throughout the town. With the declaration of a ceasefire at midnight, the allied forces at Suez were unable to exploit the initial success of the landings and were instructed to hold their fire unless they came under direct attack. Eight days after the landings, the Brigade HQ, along with 40 and 45 Commando had withdrawn to Malta while 42 Commando remained in Egypt until relieved by troops of a United Nations force.

Below, main picture: The Port Said seafront soon after H-hour. In the distance can be seen a thick plume of smoke from one of the victims of the preliminary bombardment. In the foreground is the Casino Pier which marked the boundary between Sierra Green Beach (42 Commando) on the right, and Sierra Red Beach (40 Commando) on the left. Below, inset: Commandant General of the Royal Marines at the time of Suez, Lieutenant-General Campbell Hardy.

Right: Lieutenant Leslie Hudson of B Troop, 42 Commando, in a hurry. Top: On dry land. Having disembarked from their LVTs and LCAs, the Royal Marines move along the seafront. In the background can be seen one of the beach huts, set ablaze during the preliminary barrage.

ern outskirts of the town. It was then that the familiar, comforting face of the Commandant General Royal Marines, Lieutenant-General Campbell Hardy, appeared as he strolled by offering friendly advice and encouragement to all. His visit to the operational area so early after H-hour had been tabooed by the Admiralty, but he had nevertheless landed with 45 Commando by helicopter, and to us he was a most reassuring sight. He spoke to many of the marines, his steely blue eyes shining brightly.

At 0630 we climbed back into our LVTs, this time leaving the rear ramps partly lowered for a quick exit if necessary. The dust which had choked our throats had now been cleared by the refreshing tea, ammunition had been redistributed and we were ready to go. I was well aware that this ride through the town would not be easy, as the Egyptian Army might well have taken up sniping positions on the high, flat-roofed buildings. While I travelled in the cockpit with the driver and his mate, the marines sat in the well of the LVT with their backs to the sides. Lieutenant Westwood and Sergeant-Major Casey, with a Bren gunner, sat in the rear with their feet dangling on the ramp. The plan was that we should move with a Centurion leading, followed by my LVT, another tank, an LVT and so on. A and X Troops followed with the CO's Rover, the Vickers medium machine guns and some Assault Engineers. The land speed of the LVT, about 15mph, governed our rate of progress.

Above the roar of the engines, I suddenly heard a burst of machine-gun fire

Lieutenant Peter Hetherington, a Royal Tank Regiment national service officer, was in the leading tank. We had practised infantry/tank co-operation on numerous exercises in Malta during the autumn, so we understood and trusted one another implicitly. With a roar of engines this long, snake-like column moved off along the seafront, turning inland at the end of the block down one of the widest streets in Port Said, the Rue Mohammed Ali. The time was still only 0645 and, as we rumbled into enemy territory, the adrenalin once again started to flow and nerves became tense. Turning into the wide street, my leading tank seemed to gain on me, making me feel a bit neglected. If felt a tug on my trouser leg and looked down. My driver was trying to say something to me. I cupped my ear and with a remark that relieved all my tensions he asked. 'Sir, do they drive on the right or the left in this country?'

Above the roar of the engines, I suddenly heard a burst of machine-gun fire as we passed one of the many cross-streets. This confirmed that there were enemy about who were not afraid to shoot at us. But there was no time to reply as we pressed on to our objective a mile or so ahead. The tall buildings on either side seemed to engulf us and my eyes were on the roofs, looking for opportunity targets. Another tug at my leg and the wit in the cockpit below said, 'Look sir, the traffic lights are at red...do we stop?' Such is the stuff that fighting men are made of. Another burst of machine-gun fire hit the vehicle, causing it to swerve momentarily. A scream and a moan came from one of the marines sitting in the well. I was sure that the fire had not come in from the top of a building onto their unprotected heads and I could not understand it. Corporal Jim Peerless groaned and said, 'I've been hit,' and as he turned over blood oozed from his buttocks. It was only then that it

uniforms and hidden themselves and their weapons under their long flowing *djellabahs*.

It was now 0535 and we saw with much satisfaction that C Squadron, 6th Royal Tank Regiment, with their Centurions, had now joined us. Our LVTs were being refuelled and mustered in the lee of the seafront houses as C and X Troops passed through us to take blocks of houses further inland. Many of the marines took this opportunity for a quick brew up, as breakfast had been taken so many hours ago. Calling an 'O' Group, I was glad to hear that we had suffered no casualties and that the men were in good heart. But bad news was in store: an uncontrolled air strike mistook some of our supporting anti-tank gunners from the Somerset Light Infantry for enemy and strafed them with disastrous results.

The CO, Lieutenant-Colonel Peter Norcock, called us together and briefed us for the next phase of the battle – a dash through the town in our LVTs, supported by tanks, to secure the Nile Cold Storage Depot and the Port Said power station on the south-

dawned on me what must have happened. When we had left Malta, such was the secrecy surrounding this particular operation, we had thought we were just off on another of the interminable exercises into Malta's Mellieha Bay. Each LVT had the facility for armoured plating to be lowered into the side skins of the craft, but this task took several hours of hard work with a crane and was unpopular with the crew. The awful truth that the sides of the vehicle were not bullet-proof came as a severe shock to morale.

The deserted street looked so peaceful in the morning light, but this was war and danger lurked up every side street. I anxiously peered ahead for our objective, the power station and the area to the south of it where we were to act as stops, when the air was broken by a shout of 'Grenades'. I looked up and caught a glimpse of an Egyptian soldier who had obviously just thrown a grenade from some seven storeys above. His aim was impeccable and he had judged the speed of the vehicle well. But luck was on our side. Instead of exploding in our midst, it landed on the feet of my subaltern, David Westwood, in the rear of the LVT. He twitched as the grenade hit him and it rolled out into the road behind us. When the

Corporal, Royal Marines, Suez invasion 1956

This Royal Marine wears the green beret, topped by World War II vintage gas goggles for protection against sand and dust. Web equipment is '37 pattern, blackened and polished. Armament consists of a 9mm Mk V Sten SMG.

Main picture: The streets of Port Said. After the initial objectives had been taken, the Centurions and LVTs of 42 Commando formed up for the hair-raising dash through the town. All vehicles had an 'H' painted on them for easy identification. The author's LVT is second in line. Bottom left: Marines of Y Troop, 42 Commando, move along the seafront aboard a Centurion of the Royal Tank Regiment. Left: Men of 40 Commando raise a victory Ensign outside Navy House after fighting their way down the west side of the Canal. The battle for Navy House was one of the hardest fought engagements of the day and when the building was taken, 40 Commando netted 20 Egyptian prisoners. Thirty Egyptians were killed during the attack on the building which was supported by the Fleet Air Arm. Bottom right: The author, Captain Derek Oakley of B Troop, 42 Commando.

explosion came, splinters of grenade caught the Sergeant-Major in the head. Our Royal Navy sick berth attendant bandaged him quickly and efficiently, but Casey was not amused that he could no longer wear his green beret because of the dressing.

I could now see the Cold Storage Depot building in the distance, and beyond that our target. As we approached, I warned the marines to be ready to disembark, but to my horror my leading tank had not recognised the buildings. The Centurion rolled relentlessly on. I was in a quandary over what to do: peel off to our stop position without the protection of my tank, or follow him in case he had seen some enemy and was skirting them? I tried in vain to call him up on the radio. In Malta it had worked perfectly, but now we were in action, communications failed. I took the decision to trail him further south and B Troop followed me. A further 150yds down the road, and only just beyond our area, Lieutenant Hetherington's tank calmly turned left through the main gates of an Egyptian Army camp. I shuddered to think what might lie ahead. But to my immense relief the camp was deserted, though signs of recent occupation were all around. My LVT came to a halt and I told the driver to take cover behind a brick hut. The remainder of my troop, with their accompanying tanks, fanned out into defensive positions. Engines were switched off and suddenly there was an uncanny silence. No sound...no movement.

I waited, anxiously assessing the situation and pondering on what to do next, knowing that I had gone a little beyond my objective. My signalman called up Commando headquarters and explained our situation. I was relieved to hear that A and X Troops had taken their objectives against some

spirited resistance, but a few snipers were still causing annoyance. But that was not helping me. Hetherington remained securely locked inside his tank and I waited for him to appear to help sort out the situation. I tried, again in vain, to contact him on the radio. My training had taught me that the second line of communication with a tank was through its telephone encased on the rear of the hull. I tentatively picked it up and whirred the handle. Nothing. I whirred it again. Still nothing. I waited. It was now 10 minutes since our arrival at the camp and a sense of urgency gripped me. I told my signalman that I would try to contact the tank through its turret. I climbed gingerly up onto the hull and, as I was about to knock on the hatch, its main gun fired, throwing me backwards onto the ground in a cloud of dust and sand. I picked myself up and dusted down, more indignant than angry. After a reasonable pause I tried again and this time my knock was answered when Peter Hetherington raised the 'lid' about an inch and a half and said, 'Sorry old boy, I think I've made a mistake.' The understatement of the year! 'I saw something moving in the prison over there and had a pot shot.'

Casey removed his field dressing, put his green beret back on, and refused to go, saying he was alright

A quick conference and 'O' Group were called as I planned to go back to the Cold Storage Depot. Meanwhile, Leslie Hudson had called up rear headquarters for a casevac helicopter for the Sergeant-Major, Corporal Peerless and Marine Chaffey, who had also been wounded. Casey removed his field dressing, put his green beret back on, and refused to go, saying that he was quite alright. It is sad to relate that he was killed in Cyprus six months later.

There had been no enemy to the south and I informed the CO of this. By the time we had withdrawn to the Cold Storage Depot building, our task completed, we heard with some dismay that a temporary cease-fire had been negotiated. We felt, and knew, that we were only half way through our task. Once more a decision taken far away in London had prevailed. We could not even turn a deaf ear and finish the job. There was a distinct feeling of deflation. Leaving A and X Troops in position, I took my troop back down the Rue Mohammed Ali, still being made uncomfortably aware that the snipers had not heard of the cease-fire. We reached the seafront where we fed and watered ourselves in the comfort of some of the buildings which had been our first objective. We were, however, inwardly proud that we had won the day and that our professionalism had been rewarded. It had been a long day since we landed, and as dusk began to fall, our watches told us it was 2230 at night.

This is but the story of one troop, B Troop of 42 Commando, amongst so many others of 40, 42 and 45 Commandos who had fought that day to win the battle of Port Said with ruthless military efficiency, marred only by the ceasefire that had been called by those in London. But at least it saved more lives. The total Royal Marine casualties that day had been 10 killed and 50 wounded.

THE AUTHOR Captain Derek Oakley, MBE, served with the Royal Marine Commandos in Malaya, Hong Kong, the Middle East, Northern Ireland, Brunei and Borneo.

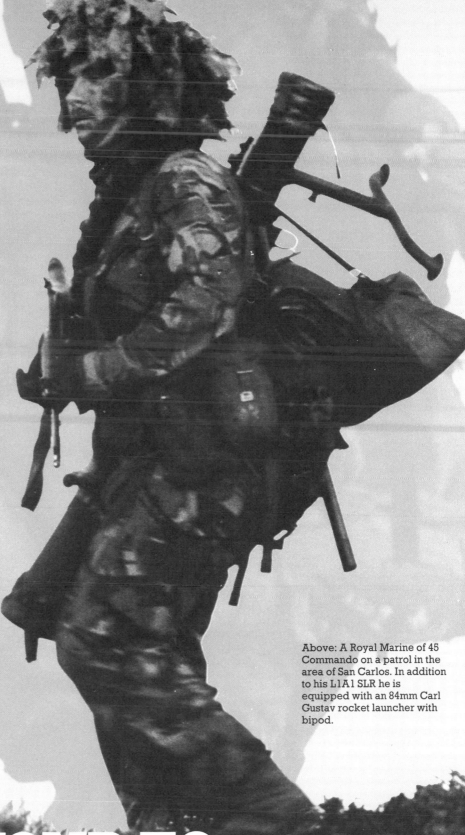

45 Commando marched across East Falkland and then launched a night attack on the Argentinians defending Two Sisters

ON FRIDAY 7 May 1982, the biggest amphibious force put together by Britain since the Suez campaign of 1956 weighed anchor and slipped silently south-wards from Ascension Island towards the Falklands. It was a hot and still night; the ships were fully darkened for war; the atmosphere on board was electric. Three days later, Brigadier Julian Thompson gave his formal orders for the final landing plan onto the San Carlos beach-head. Over 60 men crowded into the wardroom in HMS *Fearless* to listen to their Brigadier. When he was finished, drawing upon the words of the Duke of Wellington, he said: 'Gentlemen, this will be no picnic.' We realised, if we hadn't already, that the affair upon which we had embarked was set on a deadly serious course.

As we continued south, surrounded by sleek destroyer and frigate escorts with the weather growing steadily worse, final preparations for our landing began in earnest. Memories faded of the hilarious line-crossing ceremony in which I, and most of my officers, had been unceremoniously lathered, shaved and dumped in a huge canvas water bath. The sky blackened, the temperature plummeted and the wind howled, giving us useful protection against Argentinian aerial surveillance, which, as we grew closer to our target, was an ever-increasing threat. Final adjustments to the tactical loading were carried out at sea and Zulu Company moved across to HMS *Intrepid*.

The masters and crews of the Royal Fleet Auxilliaries which took us south bent over backwards to cope with their tasks in overloaded amphibious attack transport ships. To a man they were flexible, energetic, helpful and good-humoured. Over the weeks since we had first embarked we became good friends with these admirable men.

On 20 May came the order for which we had been waiting, giving D-day as 21 May, H-hour as 0630 hours (GMT) and authorising the breakdown and issue of first-line ammunition. My regimental sergeant major, always a step ahead of the crowd, was already preparing to issue the 34kg of ammunition that each man would carry. I turned to one of my company commanders, a Scot, like many in 45 Commando Group, and just said: 'We're off.' He nodded and went away to tell his company. I walked below to find my operations officer. As the word spread through the ship, excitement mounted.

We were to land at Ajax Bay, on the south side of the beach-head, at 0945 hours GMT, that is, 0545 hours local time. (The Task Force operated on GMT,

Above: A Royal Marine of 45 Commando on a patrol in the area of San Carlos. In addition to his L1A1 SLR he is equipped with an 84mm Carl Gustav rocket launcher with bipod.

YOMP TO
VICTORY

COLONEL ANDREW WHITEHEAD

Colonel Whitehead joined the Royal Marines as a second lieutenant in 1958. After serving with 42 Commando in the Far East he joined 40 Commando in Malta, participating in operations in Brunei and Borneo. After two years with 43 Commando, he commanded the Royal Marines Detachment aboard HMS *Zest* (1966-67). Two years followed as an officer instructor at Lympstone. In 1971, after staff training in Canada, he was appointed Staff Officer, Joint Exercise Division, HQ, Allied Forces Northern Europe at Oslo. He went on to command K Company, 42 Commando, in Northern Ireland, the Caribbean and Canada, and then joined the Directorate of Naval Plans at the MOD in London.
From March 1978 to May 1080 he served as brigade major (chief of staff) of 3 Commando Brigade, Royal Marines. Promoted to

lieutenant-colonel, he was selected for command of 45 Commando Group in April 1981. The Commando served an operational tour in Northern Ireland, during which Colonel Whitehead received a Mention in Dispatches. After 45 Commando's return from the Falklands Colonel Whitehead was awarded the DSO.
He relinquished command in April 1983 on appointment to the British Defence Staff, Washington, as Chief of Staff, Joint Warfare Representative and Assistant Defence Attaché.

not local time.) That would give 45 Commando one-and-a-quarter precious hours of darkness in which to secure its objectives, the old mutton factory and the ridge of hills 1000m beyond it. We were to land in four LCUs, the large landing craft crewed by Royal Marines based in *Fearless* and *Intrepid* and were to be the second unit ashore. However, the unit ahead of us was delayed for over an hour in getting ashore, and communications with Brigade Headquarters chose that precise moment to break down, as did one of the landing craft. So we endured an agonising wait, standing on the deck of *Stromness* listening to the steady crump of naval gunfire falling upon the hills around us and the distant crackle of rifle fire as the SBS dealt with a small pocket of resistance on Fanning Head in the northern sector of the beach-head. It was light enough to see when I finally crammed 45 into the three remaining landing craft and we began our run up San Carlos Water towards the beach at Ajax Bay.

It was now extremely quiet. I felt very naked and exposed as I travelled in one of the landing craft with X-Ray and Yankee Companies. This was the most vulnerable period of the amphibious operation, the time when the first marines had to jump onto hostile soil and begin to move inland to their objectives.

The ramps went down and the leading sections of X-Ray and Yankee moved up the shallow beach. It was deserted, and in a matter of only a few minutes X-Ray Company had passed through the mutton factory, reported it clear, and started up the steep rocky slope in a southwesterly direction towards Mount Campito, the highest point of our objective. Yankee was also pouring ashore, spreading out and moving westwards up the hill. Some 15 minutes later came Zulu, completing the clearance of the beach area and swinging south to prepare for the arrival of our gunner support later in the morning. It had been

Left: While Britain's attempt to negotiate a peaceful solution to the Falklands conflict went through its final stages, 45 Commando limbered up at Ascension Island for the coming fray. Below: Recognising the imminent danger of air attacks, the men of 45 Commando were quick to dig in at San Carlos. It was not to be long before their expectations were confirmed. Below right: Lieutenant-Colonel Whitehead insisted that the men of his command should write home regularly to ease the anxiety of their wives and families.

an uneventful landing, and by noon 45 Commando had 'disappeared' like chameleons into the hillside, the marines quickly digging themselves in to the soft peaty soil or building sangars of rock where the ground was too hard for a shovel to penetrate.

Across the water I could see the marines of 40 Commando preparing their positions and below me a battery of artillery was being flown in. Rapier air defence missiles were being positioned by helicopter on the hills around the beach-head and even a few vehicles, groaning with radio sets and ammunition, were struggling across the difficult terrain from the beach.

It was not until well into the afternoon of D-day that the relative quiet of this scene was shattered by the arrival of the Argentinian Air Force. Flying at mast-head height, weaving and twisting among the mountains which surrounded the beach-head, the Argentinian Skyhawk pilots displayed incredible skill and courage. Their targets were the ships unloading in San Carlos Water and we watched – in helpless fascination – the extraordinary spectacle being played out below us, as the Royal Navy flung everything it had into the sky against the aerial invaders. The Argentinian Air Force paid a terrible price for each assault, and by the end of D-day something like 16 aircraft had been shot down, either by the navy's Harriers, ship-borne air defence, or our own Rapier

THE JOURNEY SOUTH

The CO of 45 Commando describes how he and his men prepared for war: 'The journey south can be characterised by two words: training and planning. In the limited space available to us aboard our ships we kept ourselves fit, practised and re-practised the skills of our profession, particularly weapon handling, first-aid and radio procedures, and pored over the slowly increasing amount of intelligence material which became available to us. Twice a day we gathered around the ship's radio to listen to the BBC World Service as the diplomatic crisis in the South Atlantic unfolded. No-one seriously believed, as the days went by, that the Falkland Islands would be restored to their occupants except by means of a military operation. Furthermore, no-one in 3 Commando Brigade had any serious doubts that such an operation would ultimately be successful.

'We spent nearly three weeks anchored off Ascension Island while the search for a political solution went on. It was a welcome period, allowing us to get ashore to take some exercise, test fire our weapons and to carry out rehearsal helicopter and landing craft assaults.

'As intelligence about the Falkland Islands and their occupying force began to improve and the options available to the Brigade Commander, Julian Thompson, began to narrow, so a plan for an amphibious assault on East Falkland emerged. I had been briefed on several alternatives, but eventually a final plan came through: a landing on the western coast of East Falkland in the San Carlos/Ajax Bay area. Reconnaissance had revealed that the Argentinians were either not occupying that area at all or, at least, were there only in small numbers.'

45 COMMANDO GROUP

45 Commando, Royal Marines, along with its direct-support battery (7 Sphinx Commando Battery, Royal Artillery) and its field engineer troop (Condor Troop Royal Engineers) make up 45 Commando Group. Although the Group is very much a part of 3 Commando Brigade, because it is based in Arbroath in Scotland, there is a certain independence about the unit, a feeling of extra comradeship which comes from working, living and playing together over many years. From duty in Northern Ireland, through mountain and arctic training in the Cairngorms and Norway, to operations in the South Atlantic, 45 Commando developed that team spirit which was to stand it in good stead in combat.

Like every other unit in 3 Commando Brigade, 45 is at seven days notice to move, although it was widely dispersed when the call came through on 2 April 1982. Yankee Company was in Brunei, in the act of returning through Hong Kong from a month's jungle training; Zulu Company was scattered throughout the United Kingdom, engaged in various adventure training activities; while the third rifle company – X-Ray – and the remainder of the unit were within hours of going on Easter leave. The CO was in Germany and on his return that evening he and his staff quickly brought the Commando to a state of operational readiness. By noon on 3 April, 45 Commando Group was ready to go anywhere.

and Blowpipe missiles ashore. Smallarms were effective too, if only in spoiling the pilot's aim, and there was hardly a marine in 45 who did not, with a twinkle in his eye, claim personally to have shot down his own Skyhawk with his rifle.

We spent five days on the beach-head while the build-up of supplies ashore continued with painful slowness. We later learned the reason: *Atlantic Conveyor*, with much of our heavy-lift helicopter support on board, had been sunk. Furthermore, due to the immense vulnerability of the ships in the bay in daylight, unloading was to be continued only at night. What became known as 'the Ajax Bay Air Show' among the marines continued unabated below us, with some of the more enthusiastic shots from the navy's air-defence gunners landing uncomfortably close to our own positions, just to make sure – as one of the officers put it – that we felt wanted.

Finally, on the evening of Wednesday 26 May, I was summoned across to San Carlos for fresh orders from Brigadier Thompson. His orders were simple: we were to break out of the beach-head at dawn the following morning and, taking everything we owned on our backs, were to move first by landing craft across the water to Port San Carlos and then on foot to Douglas Settlement, some 35km to the northeast.

Dawn on 27 May found the Commando packed and waiting on the beach for the landing craft that were to take us across the water to Port San Carlos. Each man in fighting order carried 55kg of kit; some of the mortar men and radio operators were humping considerably more. But we had all we needed and thus equipped could go anywhere and do anything (though it was to be one hell of a yomp!).

We disembarked at Port San Carlos and moved slowly up the hill through 42 Commando's positions.

Left: Burdened by up to 55kg of kit and weaponry, men of 45 Commando leave San Carlos to begin their epic yomp across East Falkland. Right: The Westland Sea King, a vital tool of the Task Force. Below: 45 Commando's seven Volvo Bv202 tracked over-snow vehicles were used mainly to carry heavy equipment. Below right: Lieutenant-Colonel Whitehead (on left) and his Orders Group, well camouflaged in the bracken of Ajax Bay.

Their commanding officer, Lieutenant-Colonel Nick Vaux, appeared, offered me coffee and, together with one of his officers who had served in the Falklands before, briefed me on the terrain ahead. We moved off in high spirits with my Surveillance Troop protecting the flanks.

We marched throughout that day, pausing before nightfall to cook a hot meal and then continuing until the following morning. It rained most of the time and the wind was around 25 to 30 knots. The ground was rough: wet, spongy peat with hummocks of tundra-like tussock grass combined with our heavy loads to make walking an ankle-wrenching business. Our boots, which were an excellent make of civilian mountain boot, became sodden, as did our clothing. 45 Commando, with its reconnaissance teams in front and to the flanks, was spread out by companies over a distance of nearly 3km. Pausing at New House at 0200 hours on 28 May, we slept until dawn before dumping our packs and continuing in tactical formation to secure Douglas Settlement by 1600 hours on the same day. As we came down off the high ground overlooking the tiny collection of houses at Douglas, I was able to watch my two leading rifle companies advancing spread out towards the settlement. I felt very proud of my lads: we were wet, we were tired but we had covered the distance in much less than the time predicted for us, and we were ready to fight.

The Argentinians had pulled out of Douglas before we got there. The locals were, quite naturally, pleased to see us and we accepted gratefully their offers of farm buildings and outhouses in which to shelter. Over half of my men were able to get under some form of cover, while with the remainder I sited defensive trenches and put out patrols and OPs around the area. That night the news of our first fatal casualties came in. Back at Ajax Bay, five NCOs and marines had been the victims of a night-time bombing raid, with several more seriously injured. It was a bitter blow: the first of several. A brief vision of our Chief Wren and her team, supported by our wives, coping with our first group of widows passed across my mind. Not a happy thought.

We set off at dawn on Sunday 30 May and began marching again, splashing across rivers and inlets and arriving finally at the settlement at Teal Inlet shortly after midnight. We dug in, patrolled forward, rested and waited for helicopters to lift us up to our next objective, Mount Kent. Bad weather and the increasing demands being made upon our small fleet of helicopters meant that, by Thursday 3 June, we were off again at first light, on foot. As my indomitable provost sergeant, a cheerful Yorkshireman, said, 'We've come all this way on foot, we might as well walk to Stanley.' He was right.

By 1700 hours the Commando arrived, wet and weary, on the western slopes of Mount Kent. 42 Commando had secured the mountain, having been lifted in by helicopter, and had spent over a week with very little equipment in the ferocious weather conditions that existed around the summit of this inhospitable mountain. Our task, along with the rest of 3 Commando Brigade, was really just beginning: to prepare ourselves using patrols, OPs and any other intelligence-gathering techniques available to us, for an assault on the mountains dominating the approaches to Stanley. Our objective was Two Sisters.

During each of the next four nights the patrols of 45 Commando went out towards the twin peaks of Two Sisters and gradually my intelligence officer was able to piece together a picture of what was facing us. The young lieutenant commanding the Reconnaissance Troop led a spectacularly successful patrol, catching the Argentinians by surprise and causing them a number of casualties before fighting his way off the position in broad daylight. A troop commander in X-Ray Company – with his entire troop – performed a similar feat, harassing the enemy, increasing their uncertainty about where or when we would strike and bringing back priceless information about their strength and dispositions.

Below: Captain Ballantyne leading his support group. Directly behind him a marine is carrying an L2A3 9mm Sterling Mk 4 sub-machine gun. Above right: Sergeant Dickinson (on left) the lead driver of 45 Commando's Bv202s, with Captain Irwin.

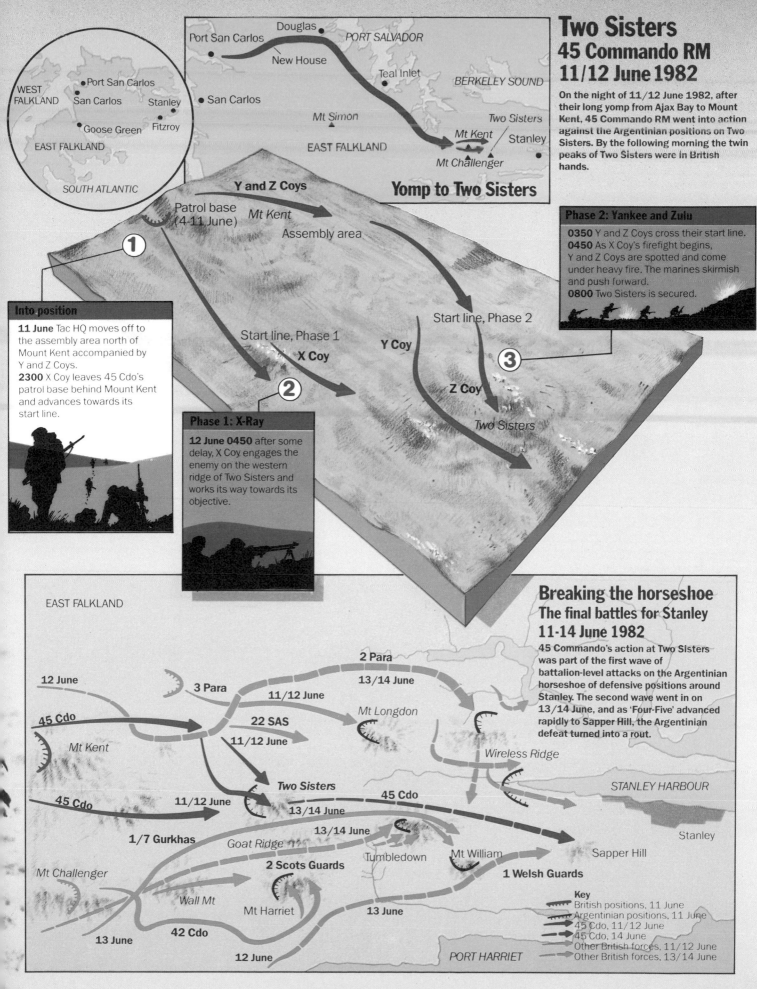

Two Sisters
45 Commando RM
11/12 June 1982

On the night of 11/12 June 1982, after their long yomp from Ajax Bay to Mount Kent, 45 Commando RM went into action against the Argentinian positions on Two Sisters. By the following morning the twin peaks of Two Sisters were in British hands.

Yomp to Two Sisters

- Douglas
- Port San Carlos
- New House
- PORT SALVADOR
- Teal Inlet
- BERKELEY SOUND
- San Carlos
- Mt Simon
- Two Sisters
- Mt Kent
- Stanley
- EAST FALKLAND
- Mt Challenger

WEST FALKLAND / EAST FALKLAND (inset)
- Port San Carlos
- San Carlos
- Stanley
- Goose Green
- Fitzroy
- SOUTH ATLANTIC

Y and Z Coys

Patrol base (4-11 June)
Mt Kent
Assembly area

(1) Into position

11 June Tac HQ moves off to the assembly area north of Mount Kent accompanied by Y and Z Coys.
2300 X Coy leaves 45 Cdo's patrol base behind Mount Kent and advances towards its start line.

Start line, Phase 1
X Coy

Start line, Phase 2
Y Coy
Z Coy
Two Sisters

(2) Phase 1: X-Ray

12 June 0450 after some delay, X Coy engages the enemy on the western ridge of Two Sisters and works its way towards its objective.

(3) Phase 2: Yankee and Zulu

0350 Y and Z Coys cross their start line.
0450 As X Coy's firefight begins, Y and Z Coys are spotted and come under heavy fire. The marines skirmish and push forward.
0800 Two Sisters is secured.

Breaking the horseshoe
The final battles for Stanley
11-14 June 1982

45 Commando's action at Two Sisters was part of the first wave of battalion-level attacks on the Argentinian horseshoe of defensive positions around Stanley. The second wave went in on 13/14 June, and as 'Four-Five' advanced rapidly to Sapper Hill, the Argentinian defeat turned into a rout.

EAST FALKLAND

- 12 June
- 45 Cdo
- 3 Para
- 2 Para
- 13/14 June
- 11/12 June
- Mt Kent
- 22 SAS
- 11/12 June
- Mt Longdon
- Wireless Ridge
- STANLEY HARBOUR
- Two Sisters
- 45 Cdo
- 45 Cdo
- 11/12 June
- 13/14 June
- Stanley
- 1/7 Gurkhas
- Goat Ridge
- 13/14 June
- Mt William
- Sapper Hill
- Mt Challenger
- 2 Scots Guards
- Tumbledown
- 1 Welsh Guards
- Wall Mt
- Mt Harriet
- 13 June
- 42 Cdo
- 13 June
- 12 June
- PORT HARRIET

Key
British positions, 11 June
Argentinian positions, 11 June
45 Cdo, 11/12 June
45 Cdo, 14 June
Other British forces, 11/12 June
Other British forces, 13/14 June

The Commando's preparations for battle proceeded smoothly. My artillery battery commander carefully constructed his fire plan; the mortars had been moved into position earlier to bring them within range and their troop commander had predumped a large amount of ammunition in preparation for the assault. Engineer reconnaissance parties had accompanied every patrol to search for mines. Orders were flowing down from the Commando Headquarters through the companies to the marine riflemen upon whose shoulders the ultimate responsibility for the assault would lie. The team of 45 Commando Group was working well.

The attack would be silent, with guns and mortars only being used if and when surprise was lost

The plan of attack was simple: X-Ray would attack the western 'Sister' at 0100 hours from the west followed two hours later by Yankee and Zulu from the northwest onto the eastern Sister. The attack would be silent, with guns and mortars only being used if and when surprise was lost. Casualty collecting parties were detailed-off, and radios and weapons were checked for the hundredth time. Radio silence was imposed. Around the Commando, as we made our final preparations to move to our start-line from the assembly area, a curious tension was evident. Officers, NCOs, and marines stood in small groups talking quietly. As it grew dark we began to form up. Reconnaissance Troop in the lead, followed by Yankee, Tac HQ and Zulu. We were 5km from the enemy.

We moved off at 2300 hours, picking our way cautiously and carefully over the rocky terrain towards the forming-up position secured by my recon-

By Thursday 10 June we had received our orders from Brigade and my own plan was complete. I gave my orders on the morning of 11 June and by late afternoon my own small tactical headquarters, plus Yankee and Zulu Companies were moving around the north side of Mount Kent to an assembly area from which we would launch our two-phase attack that night. X-Ray Company remained where it was since it was to undertake the first phase, attacking due east onto the nearer of the two peaks.

Above and below: 45 Commando on the long forced march to Stanley. The endless tussocks of the marshy moorland caused many twisted ankles, and trench foot from waterlogged boots became a persistent problem. Even a few yards aboard a Bv202 (right) came as a relief from the ordeal.

FALKLANDS STRATEGY

Given the size of the Falklands and the poor quality of his men, the Argentinian commander, General Menendez, opted to concentrate his forces in the ring of hills to the west of Port Stanley and leave small garrisons at possible landing sites around the islands. In doing so, he unwittingly allowed the British to come ashore at San Carlos relatively unhindered and, once Goose Green had been recaptured, move on the capital from the north and south.

The loss of Goose Green had even wider repercussions as the Argentinians had reinforced the garrison with troops from Mount Kent and Mount Challenger, leaving the two key elements of the outer defensive ring undermanned. On 31 May, Menendez paid for this mistake when Royal Marines took Mount Kent. After this move, the enemy garrisoning Fitzroy and Bluff Cove had to fall back to avoid being outflanked from the north. British strategy at this stage was to pin the enemy to their positions and weaken their will to resist with a combination of artillery fire and aggressive patrolling.

Although a number of choices were available for the final offensive, it was decided to attack simultaneously on a broad front and pierce the enemy's hill-top positions at a number of points. Co-ordinated assaults, backed by heavy artillery fire and follow-on attacks, would prevent the enemy from reforming to defend the capital.

In the event, the plans came to fruition perfectly: the enemy crumbled under a series of body blows and the road to Stanley opened.

naissance troop an hour or so before. It was very dark, but with a dangerously clear sky and a sharp frost. A full moon was due to rise later that night, exposing us to Argentinian observation, although it would also silhouette the enemy.

As we arrived at our start-line at 0255 hours I was in an agony of uncertainty about the progress of X-Ray's attack. I did not want to run out of darkness for the second and bigger phase of the assault, but I had to be certain that X-Ray was secure before I launched Yankee and Zulu. Fortunately for me, the X-Ray company commander disobeyed the rules on radio silence to inform me that he had been badly delayed negotiating the rocky terrain towards his objective, through carrying the heavy Milan anti-tank missiles which were to support his attack. Down in our position, 2km away, I allowed the time for H-Hour Phase 2 to come and go, knowing that I must wait until I was sure that X-Ray was well on the way to capturing its objective. As we waited, lying among the rocks, an Argentinian artillery bombardment came down about 100m ahead of us. Had we started our attack on time we would have been right in the middle of it.

By 0350 hours I could wait no longer and passed the word for our assault to begin. Marines rose silently from their positions and moved forward in extended formation towards our objective, clearly visible under a rising moon. To my amazement we were able to get within 450m of the enemy without being spotted. At this point two things happened simultaneously. X-Ray, moving up the spine of rocks to its objective, became engaged in a sharp fire-fight with the enemy, while at the same time, the Argentinians on the eastern Sister realised that Yankee and Zulu were on their doorstep. The battle now began.

Argentinian fire from mortars, 0.5in machine guns and smallarms poured down onto our position. In return our own artillery and mortars responded quickly to calls for fire. The full weight of the fire power of two Commando rifle companies was brought to bear on the objective. For 15 to 20 minutes it was a ding-dong fire-fight until the progress of the marines of Zulu Company began to gather momentum as, screaming their war cry of 'Zulu Zulu,' they

Royal Marine Commando, Falklands, 1982

This Royal Marine, a corporal of the Milan troop of 40 Commando, was attached to 45 Commando's Milan troop after the latter suffered casualties in an Argentinian bomb attack. He is wearing the standard green beret and DPM jacket and trousers of the Royal Marines with woollen puttees and ammunition boots. His weapons are the L1A1 SLR, and a fighting/survival knife. A field dressing is taped to the knife's sheath. He carries '58 pattern webbing equipment and a foam-rubber kipmat. His radio is the PRC 350, often used by section and platoon commanders. In the British Army each level of command uses a separate radio frequency.

Above left: The Argentinians laid a complex system of mines along the approaches to Stanley. This road is officially cleared but 45 Commando was taking no chances. Above: Argentinian prisoners await repatriation in Stanley. The sunshine belies the bitterly cold winds which were sweeping up from the Antarctic. Above right: HQ Group 45 Commando on the summit of Sapper Hill the morning after Argentina's surrender.

skirmished their way forward. Yankee on my right came driving in, swinging east and moving to the extreme end of the feature, clearing the enemy from the rocks as they went. X-Ray, supported by Milan missiles, reached the summit of their objective, finishing off an Argentinian machine-gun post which had proved particularly troublesome.

This was the time when the junior leaders, the corporals and second-lieutenants, came into their own. Guided by their company commanders, they were the men who, with their young marines, sustained the aggression of the attack and allowed us to secure the position. By first light the feature was ours. Prisoners were being rounded-up, ammunition redistributed and reports were coming in to me, telling me of the cost of the night's work: four dead and 10 wounded. It could have been much worse. As I looked back down over the direction from which we had assaulted, the enormity of our success came home to me, for the position was theoretically impregnable. As one of my company commanders said: 'With 120 marines, I could have died of old age up here.'

Our chaplain, a tough little Welshman who pursued God's work in his own particularly aggressive way, had accompanied X-Ray during the assault, because, as he admitted privately later, he expected them to take the most casualties. Returning across the 600m of open ground which separated the two peaks to rejoin X-Ray after briefly coming over to check on the spiritual welfare of his commanding officer, he realised that in the rocks above him were 120 marines, their adrenalin pumping, their fingers on the trigger. Out of the lightening dawn came a high-pitched Welsh cry: 'X-Company, X-Company, don't shoot, it's the chaplain, and I've forgotten the bloody password.'

The remainder of the story is, by comparison, of little consequence. We buried the enemy dead and I discussed with our brigadier, and later with my operations officer and battery commander, plans for the final phase of the assault on Stanley, for which our objective was to be Sapper Hill. During this time we were subjected to continuous, though ineffective,

Argentinian artillery fire. It did us no harm but made us the more determined to get on and finish the business. As I was making my final preparations on the morning of Monday 14 June, it became apparent from reports on the radio that the Argentinians were giving up. At the same time I received orders to get my Commando on to Sapper Hill by the shortest route as fast as possible. Dumping our rucksacks we hurled ourselves in an easterly direction, arriving on Sapper Hill at about 1600 hours on the same day, in time to capture one solitary Argentinian marine, who seemed to have missed the news that his companions had left. It was over.

45 Commando spent two more days on Sapper Hill before moving, still on foot, into Stanley to take part in the clear-up of the extraordinary debris left there by a retreating Argentinian army. We spent a week in the town before re-embarking to a joyful reunion in *Stromness* and *Canberra* for our return to the UK. The welcome we received from the people of Scotland when we got back is something that will remain in my memory for a very long time.

There are two groups of people, aside from my own officers, NCOs and marines, to whom I would pay tribute. Firstly, our wives and families. Often suffering the anxieties of inaccurate or incomplete information, coping bravely with the tragedies of the death and injury of their loved ones, they never gave up. They never abandoned the collective spirit that makes 45 Commando Group something special. The other group cannot speak for themselves. They are the thirteen who did not come back. They died bravely; they did not die in vain. Their names, carved in stone at the entrance to 45 Commando Group's camp in Scotland, are also engraved in our hearts. They had been part of a team which had yomped to victory.

THE AUTHOR Lieutenant-Colonel Andrew Whitehead, DSO, was commander of 45 Commando, Royal Marines in the Falklands campaign. He is currently Chief of Staff, Joint Warfare Representative and Assistant Defence Attaché in the British Defence Staff at Washington.

Striking from the sea without warning, or preparing ambushes in the mountains, the British Commandos were a constant threat to the Germans during the Italian campaign of World War II.

A HEAVY SEA was running on a black night as the crews of No.40 (Royal Marine) Commando's assault craft searched for San Venere harbour. Its quay was indistinguishable from the hills looming behind the coastline, and the craft ran parallel to the beach for over an hour, sorely trying the patience of Lieutenant-Colonel 'Pops' Manners, CO of the Commando. His men should have landed at 0300 hours that Wednesday, 8 September 1943, with No.3 Commando coming ashore on an adjacent beach, to seize San Venere, 160km south of Naples on the west coast of Italy. The commandos had been making reconnaissance raids throughout the previous fortnight, seeking out intelligence of the positions of German forces likely to oppose the Eighth Army when it crossed from Sicily to the mainland.

As time was passing and the Commando would have so little time ashore before full daylight, Manners asked the landing craft officers to put three of his five Troops ashore, regardless of their position in relation to the little harbour. In the event they beached 800m west of their intended landing point at about 0430. No.3 Commando, who had been delayed in the rough water while transferring from their ship to their assault craft, landed in the correct spot but were also late. The rest of No.40(RM) then came ashore from their landing-craft, which had run in alongside the San Venere quay. With commendable speed the two Troops cleared the town of resistance. By then the other Troops had driven the Germans from their beach defences, and together Nos.3 and 40(RM) set up a series of defended areas around the beach-head. Although the Germans were shelling the quays the first infantry battalions were able to get

Right: A member of No.9 Commando in Italy. The commando force deployed in the Mediterranean included both British Army and Royal Marine Commandos. By 1943 the commandos were a proven elite force, among the best soldiers in the world.

MEDITERRANEAN
RAIDERS

The successful raids carried out by the Commandos of Combined Operations Command (whose badge is shown above) during the final two years of the war in Italy and the Adriatic were the culmination of the activities of various specialist raiding forces created by the British in the Mediterranean theatre. In June 1940 the Long Range Desert Group (LRDG) was formed to carry out sabotage and reconnaissance work deep behind enemy lines. Then in March 1941, 'Layforce', comprising Nos. 7, 8 and 11 Commandos, later joined by Nos. 50 and 52 (Middle East) Commandos, arrived in Egypt. After several raids 'Layforce' was disbanded, but by that time Second-Lieutenant David Stirling had formed 'L' Detachment, which in October 1942 was renamed the 1st Special Air Service Regiment (1 SAS). Also, No. 8 Commando's Special Boat Section was expanded into Lord Jellicoe's Special Boat Squadron (SBS) in the summer of 1942. Operating over vast distances, these Special Forces mounted some spectacular raids on enemy airfields and ports. During 1942 and 1943 the Royal Marines reorganised their battalions into Commandos. In July 1943 Nos. 2 and 3 Commando, Nos. 40 and 41 (RM) Commando, and Bill Darby's US Rangers formed the spearhead of the invasion of Sicily by the British Eighth Army and the American Seventh Army. Then, in late August, reconnaissance began for the invasion of mainland Italy.

ashore with little difficulty.

At 0815 came the first serious counter-attack, from a parachute battalion supported by elements of the 26th Panzer Division, and there were 40 commando casualties in the next hour or so from shelling by an 88mm anti-tank gun, until this was stalked and its crew captured by B Troop of No.40(RM). The Commando's A Troop eventually located a second 88mm and destroyed it, and by mid-morning the whole German Kampfgruppe (battle group) was embroiled in fluid battle with the commandos and those infantry battalions of the Devonshire and Dorset Regiments that had been landed. The beach-head was held and within 72 hours 20th Beach Group was operating in the harbour, using it as a forward supply base.

Meanwhile, Nos. 2 and 41(RM) Commando were moving that day to Salerno on the west coast, where they would form the flank guard for the Fifth Army's main landings in the bay. Their objectives were near the main beaches, and included a coast battery, the village of Vietri, and a narrow valley leading inland from the flank of the Allied assault. This defile was dominated by hills that ran southeast to overlook the length of the bay. The hills were covered with patches of dense scrub and slashed by deep ravines, giving the Germans natural lines of cover through to the landing area defences.

Deadly splinters sprayed out from mortar bombs bursting on the sun-baked ground

Having found the coast battery unmanned, the commandos, under the leadership of Brigadier Bob Laycock, pressed on to Vietri, clearing the Germans from the area. In Vietri all was quiet. The leading sections of No.41(RM) passed on up the valley at a steady noiseless trot, surprising the sleeping crew of a Panzer Mk IV tank who were stretched out in its lee. The tankmen were all killed or wounded by a burst of fire, and a fragmentation grenade lobbed into the open turret immobilised the tank. The force pushed on and by daylight that Thursday held positions on both sides of the defile near La Molina.

In the next few days they and No.2 Commando had to hold on without reinforcements or relief while the main landings met fierce resistance in Salerno and from four panzer battle groups in the hills. The German patrols greatly outnumbered the 700 or so commandos ashore (both No.2 and No.41(RM) were under strength) and Germans infiltrated up the

gulleys between some of the commando defence positions. Part of No.41(RM) was overrun and No.2 had to counter-attack to restore the position. Then, just before dark, men of No.2 Commando scaled the steep-sided Dragone hill, driving out German machine-gunners who overlooked No.41(RM)'s positions. This enabled the commandos to hold on through Saturday, but their casualties mounted and, with over 100 men killed or wounded, they were withdrawn. Their respite was a short one and next morning they were back in their hill positions, although now these were at 100m intervals. It became a soldiers' battle. When their neighbours fell silent in the small trenches around them, solitary men had to keep an iron nerve and not abandon their tiny defence area, even though they were frequently attacked on all sides. Intense mortar and artillery fire added to the danger as deadly splinters sprayed out from mortar bombs bursting on the sun-baked ground. During the Sunday morning the Germans again got machine guns onto Dragone hill and the commandos only regained it after a bloody fight in which they lost another 100 men. But this final defeat sent the Germans eastward and the commandos were moved to the opposite flank to clear a series of valleys. After these actions they were withdrawn to rebuild their strength from volunteers, including ships' marines who were allowed to transfer to Nos.40 and 41(RM). Reinforcements arrived as No.9 and No.43(RM) Commandos landed in Italy.

Nos.3 and 40(RM), with elements of the Special Raiding Force of the SAS, landed at Termoli on the east coast in early October. After heavy fighting they secured the Eighth Army's crossing of the Bifurno river. In late December No.9 made a diversionary landing in the estuary of the Garigliano river 55km north of Naples, enabling the Guards Brigade to disengage the enemy and move inland, and another, three weeks later at Anzio.

Having crossed the Garigliano river, the Allied Fifth Army was faced by a series of well-defended mountain passes in the central Appennines. On Mount Faito and Mount Ornito German battalions dominated the country to the south and west, their positions on Mount Ornito overlooking the forward troops of the British 46th Infantry Division who were just south of the crest of Mount Tuga. Nos.9 and 43(RM) Commando were given the task of infiltrating the German forward defences and seizing the peak of Mount Faito. This would then form a springboard from which the Allies could exploit their recent crossing of the Garigliano.

Speed and surprise were the keys to the success of the British Special Forces' raiding operations. The sea-borne raids that devastated German strongholds along the Adriatic coast made extensive use of fast motor torpedo boats (Left: Commandos board an MTB before the raid on Cherso island in August 1944.) On the Italian mainland, the commandos used Jeeps to make a quick getaway after pushing deep behind German lines. (Below: Commandos return to base with German prisoners.)

Moving forward from the river on the night of 31 January 1944, the commandos were slowed by the mules carrying their combat stores. These delays, and the lack of sleep that resulted for his men, led Brigadier Tom Churchill to postpone the proposed assault for 24 hours.

On Friday 1 February, when the brigadier had hoped that his officers would be able to view the ground over which they would move that night, a heavy mist obscured the snowy mountain valleys for most of the day. But studies of maps and aerial photographs were some help, and the plans for fire support were worked out in detail. A field regiment of 25-pounders and heavier artillery of 46th Division were on call to forward observation officers with each Commando, and their own machine guns were to lay cones of fire to protect the west flank of the assault. Then the original operational plan had to be modified after the brigadier learnt that two enemy platoons held a feature known as Hill 711 in the valley between Tuga and Ornito. In the final plan, therefore, the commandos avoided Hill 711 by infiltrating from the east side of Tuga. The leading Troop of No.43(RM), with orders not to tangle with enemy patrols, would loop northeast and, followed by the other Troops of No.43(RM), capture Mount Ornito and then exploit to the southwest and take Hill 711. No.9 Commando, setting out an hour after No.43(RM), would use Ornito as its starting-point to move northwest and take Hill 803, and then move on to capture the summit of Mount Faito an important feature in the German defences.

D Troop of No.43(RM) Commando led off at 1830 hours on a dark night, while British infantry patrols screened their movement for 500m in front of Tuga on the commandos' west flank. Spasmodic enemy shelling continued to fall on the British trenches and emplacements to the rear, shelling which caused 25 commando casualties even before the operation began. D Troop avoided contact, and slipped quietly across the valley. However, it may have been impossible to move without catching the enemy's attention, and when C Troop followed, prepared to meet any threats to the exposed east flank of the infiltration, German machine-gunners opened fire. Several spirited section attacks were needed to chase these gunners northward and clear the threat to the rest of the force following up. By this time D Troop had reached the top of Ornito and after the rest of No.43(RM) had secured the mountain top, 60 marines moved off and took Hill 711 without difficulty.

No.9 Commando reached the northern side of Ornito without incident and began the second phase of its operation by moving to the northwest. But part of the cover for the infiltration had been a feint attack to the west earlier that night, and among other actions this had alerted the Germans. Their illuminating shells, flares and Very lights lit up the night with a brilliance that clearly showed the lines of commandos crossing the bare mountainsides. German machine-gunners on a hillock 500m short of Hill 803 took a particularly heavy toll until the post was knocked out by 1 Troop. No.9 continued advancing, but over a crest 200m further along the mountainside they encountered another German strongpoint, an isolated house.

The attack went in that afternoon and in places came within grenade-throwing range of the commandos

Small-arms fire from the house was well aimed and the German artillery and mortar fire was also becoming more accurate. (Later it was discovered that the Germans who were directing artillery and mortar fire were using this building as their observation post.) Lieutenant-Colonel Ronnie Tod, commander of No.9, was wounded going forward to organise an attack on the house. In the face of such accurate and heavy fire there was no way in which his Commando could scale Faito, and he therefore withdrew the troops. The brigadier came to evaluate their positions about 1030 the next morning.

Brigadier Churchill had to order Tod to go back for medical attention. The medical officer came back from the forward areas below Faito, satisfied that all the wounded had been evacuated. With great courage he had stayed on the mountainside even though it was inevitable that the enemy would counter-attack. The attack went in that afternoon and in places came within grenade-throwing range of No.43(RM), but artillery fire and commando tenacity prevented the Germans from recapturing Ornito, and the attack faded out before nightfall. After a sally was made against Hill 759, only to find it undefended, the commandos prepared to be relieved. They marched out of the mountains that night and down to the Garigliano river where they were bussed out to X Corps' rear area.

Lieutenant Barton, posing as a shepherd, broke into the German headquarters building and killed the commander

Action for the majority of the commandos then moved to the Adriatic, where No.2 Commando had been based on the rocky island of Vis, off the coast of Yugoslavia, since 16 January 1944 as part of the 1000-strong Force 133 (later Force 266). Their role was to reinforce the garrison of local partisans and to mount raids to distract the Germans from their operations against Marshal Tito's forces in the mountains. Nevertheless, the relationship between the two forces was politically delicate, and the CO of No.2 Commando, Colonel Jack Churchill, brother of Tom, the brigadier, could not begin his raids on the Dalmatian Islands without first securing the partisans' agreement.

At first the raids were small-scale. Lieutenant Barton, for example, posing as a shepherd with two

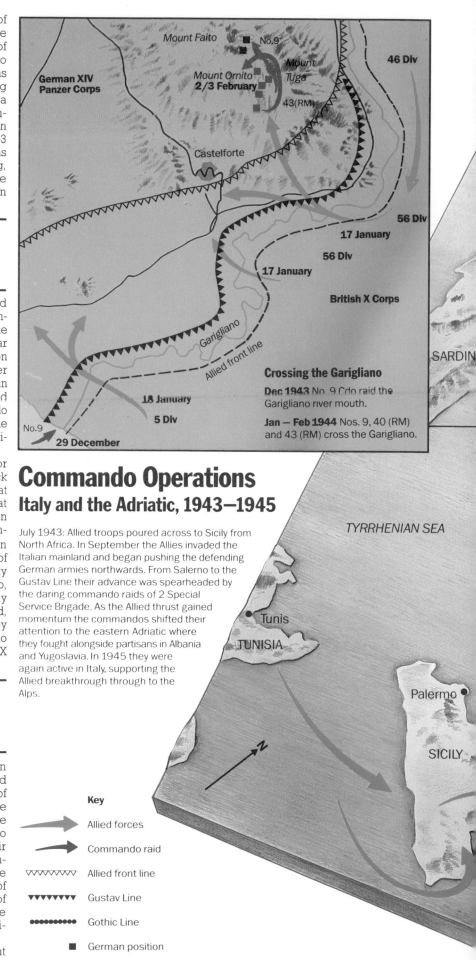

Commando Operations
Italy and the Adriatic, 1943–1945

July 1943: Allied troops poured across to Sicily from North Africa. In September the Allies invaded the Italian mainland and began pushing the defending German armies northwards. From Salerno to the Gustav Line their advance was spearheaded by the daring commando raids of 2 Special Service Brigade. As the Allied thrust gained momentum the commandos shifted their attention to the eastern Adriatic where they fought alongside partisans in Albania and Yugoslavia. In 1945 they were again active in Italy, supporting the Allied breakthrough through to the Alps.

Crossing the Garigliano

Dec 1943 No.9 Cdo raid the Garigliano river mouth.

Jan – Feb 1944 Nos. 9, 40 (RM) and 43 (RM) cross the Garigliano.

Key

→ Allied forces
→ Commando raid
ⱽⱽⱽⱽⱽⱽⱽ Allied front line
▼▼▼▼▼▼▼ Gustav Line
●●●●●●●● Gothic Line
■ German position
■ British position

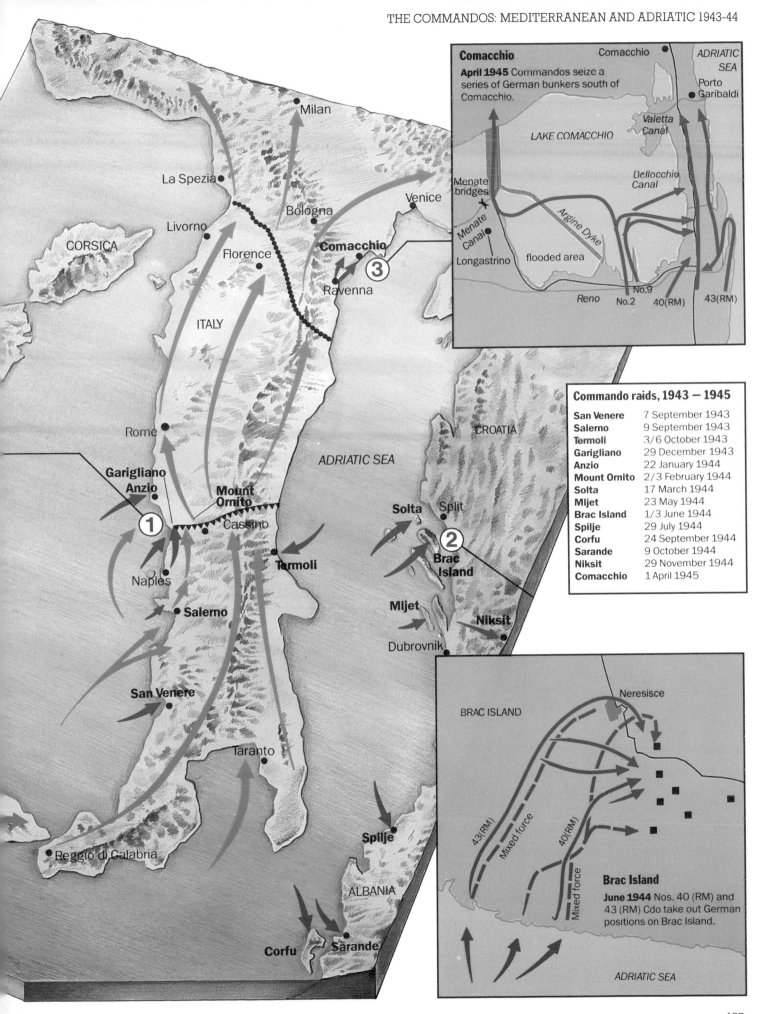

Comacchio

April 1945 Commandos seize a series of German bunkers south of Comacchio.

ADRIATIC SEA

Comacchio

Porto Garibaldi

LAKE COMACCHIO

Valetta Canal

Dellocchio Canal

Menate bridges

Menate Canal

Argine Dyke

Longastrino

flooded area

Reno   No.2   No.9   40(RM)   43(RM)

Milan

La Spezia

Bologna

Livorno

Venice

CORSICA

Florence

Comacchio

ITALY

Ravenna

Rome

CROATIA

ADRIATIC SEA

Garigliano Anzio

Mount Ornito

Cassino

Solta

Split

Brac Island

Naples

Termoli

Salerno

Mljet

Niksit

Dubrovnik

San Venere

Taranto

Commando raids, 1943 — 1945

San Venere	7 September 1943
Salerno	9 September 1943
Termoli	3/6 October 1943
Garigliano	29 December 1943
Anzio	22 January 1944
Mount Ornito	2/3 February 1944
Solta	17 March 1944
Mljet	23 May 1944
Brac Island	1/3 June 1944
Spilje	29 July 1944
Corfu	24 September 1944
Sarande	9 October 1944
Niksit	29 November 1944
Comacchio	1 April 1945

Spilje

Reggio di Calabria

ALBANIA

Corfu   **Sarande**

BRAC ISLAND

Neresisce

43(RM)

Mixed force

40(RM)

Mixed force

Mixed force

Brac Island

June 1944 Nos. 40 (RM) and 43 (RM) Cdo take out German positions on Brac Island.

ADRIATIC SEA

partisans, broke into the German headquarters building on Brac and killed the garrison commander. Then 500 men, including 100 Americans of the SOE's Special Operations Groups, made a successful landing on Solta and cornered its garrison after a difficult approach through the vineyards on a steep hillside. Not all the raids were so successful: the garrison on Mljet dodged the commando search-parties.

The German garrisons were then withdrawn from the smaller islands, but on Brac 1200 men remained to hold positions including a series of strongpoints along a ridge that protected the coast battery. These had been blasted from the living rock, and were reinforced concrete bunkers topped by great boulders. All the ground for 500m or more around them had been cleared of scrub, and minefields laid to protect the barbed-wire entanglements around each post. These formidable defences were attacked on two nights in early June by men of Nos. 40 and 43(RM) Commando, supported by some 500 partisans. On 4 June three Troops of No.40(RM) managed with great difficulty to seize the key strongpoint, which had been held briefly by No.43(RM) a few

hours earlier. The Germans again counter-attacked and 'Pops' Manners was mortally wounded. Jack Churchill was wounded and captured. He had been playing his bagpipes to rally men to his point on the ridge when he was hit by grenade or mortar bomb fragments.

Later that summer the commandos' operations moved to the Albanian coast, where on 29 July Lieutenant-Colonel F.W. Fynn, MC, took No.2 Commando ashore 6km south of Spilje. The village was to be captured and handed over to the Albanian partisans as a base through which the Allies could supply them.

They landed just after midnight and were met by SOE agents and a patrol of the redeployed Long Range Desert Group (LRDG). At 0300 hours the force was at its forming-up positions. Those on the east flank had objectives on a hill and a spur where the defenders were dug in against possible attacks from partisans, while on the beach the targets were a fortified house and other defences that had been set up to prevent landings from the sea. All these positions were bombarded from 0500 by naval des-

troyers, yet after sustaining 800 rounds of explosive shells the strongpoints were less damaged than was expected. More successful was a strafe by Spitfires at 0615, just before the main assault went in.

The troops on the east flank then went straight into the attack, without any pause on their intended start-line as this was being shelled. They came across newly dug slit trenches, met sustained machine-gun fire, and might well have been stalled in the attack were it not for their speed and skill in using the minimal cover. In 40 minutes the defences were cleared.

After shelling from the destroyers the house was taken, but then the men came under fire from machine-guns in caves on a hill

The fortified house proved a difficult strongpoint to take. Its approaches had been cleared of cover and some of the other defence positions were giving it strong fire-support. After a shelling from the destroyers the house was taken, but then the men came under fire from machine guns in caves on a hill overlooking the house. Other groups in the force were coming against fierce resistance from fanatical Nazi supporters among the villagers who feared reprisals if captured. At 1030 Fynn ordered the commandos to withdraw.

The raid had not completely overcome the defences, but the commandos had driven many Germans into the hills. The pro-Nazi civilians apparently fled as soon as the commandos withdrew, and only 30 weary Germans were left holding the beach defences.

The commandos landed 10 weeks later to seize Sarande further north on the Albanian coast. There, on 9 October, Nos. 2 and 40(RM) with 500 partisans broke into the town despite stubborn resistance. The Germans held out around their town-centre headquarters, but after six hours of street fighting the CO of No.40(RM), Lieutenant-Colonel Bob Sankey, led a decisive assault on the building and the garrison surrendered.

No.2 Commando Brigade spent the next few months in Italy, although units were detached for periods of service in the Yugoslav mountains and on Corfu. On 2 and 3 April 1945 the brigade attacked a series of heavily defended bunkers on a spit of land between the sea and the lagoon of Comacchio. Despite the difficulties in taking the men by landing craft and assault boat across the water to breach these defences from the inland side, the positions were cleared, and in 48 hours Nos. 2 and 9 Commando, and No.43(RM) Commando with elements of No.40(RM), had advanced 12km to the Valetta canal.

The commando actions on the coastal stretch of the battle line led the Germans to believe that this was the point where the British would attack their last line of defence in Italy. It was exactly what the Allied planners had hoped the Germans would believe, and after the Germans had moved troops to the eastern part of their line the Allies finally punched through at Argenta, over 30km from the coast to begin the final fight for victory.

Far left: Sergeant Stanley Stevenson of No.2 Commando, armed with an automatic pistol, photographed in the process of stalking a sniper. Top: A team of gunners manhandle a 75mm pack howitzer up a pebble beach in Albania. Above: German prisoners, taken on the Albanian coast near Spilje, carry medical supplies to LCIs (Landing Craft Infantry) waiting to take out the raiding force. Left: A sapper prepares the demolition of a bridge at Niskit in Yugoslavia. A total of 4000lb of explosives was used to blow the bridge. Above left: Commandos unload their assault boat under heavy mortar fire on the muddy shore of Lake Comacchio on the east coast of Italy. This raid diverted German troops away from the point where the Allies later broke through further to the west. Two commandos, Corporal Tom Hunter and Major Anders Lassen, were awarded posthumous VCs for their actions at Comacchio.

THE AUTHOR James D Ladd is one of Britain's acknowledged experts on the British Commandos. His previous works include *Inside the Commandos, Commandos and Rangers of World War II* and his account of assault ships and landing craft in World War II, *Assault from the Sea 1939-45*.

EXTENDED TRAINING

The extended training offered by the Royal Marines to newly accepted recruits leads to four categories of qualifications. Specialist qualifications (SQs), the first category, are those which are required by General Duties branch to meet fundamental operational and training needs. A marine may qualify as aircrewman, assault engineer, drill instructor, driver, mountain leader, marine provost, helicopter pilot, signaller or swimmer canoeist, or in such subjects as heavy weapons (air defence, anti-tank or mortar), landing craft, physical training or platoon weapons.

The second category, technical qualifications (TQs), is administered by Technical branch and includes armourer, vehicle artificer, bugler, carpenter, clerk, cook, illustrator, metalsmith, musician, printer, stores accountant, telecommunications technician and vehicle mechanic.

Within the third category of extended training open to Royal Marines are command courses, whose function is to prepare the candidate for promotion. In practice, it is often the case that in addition to passing a command course an SQ or TQ is required before promotion can be considered.

Finally, Royal Marines may be required to gain additional qualifications (adquals). These are qualifications beyond those specified for a particular rank or SQ/TQ, but which are needed in order to perform a particular job. For example, para training is regarded as being an adqual, but no marine could qualify as a mountain leader without it. Similarly, officers or men wanting to serve with a recce troop are well advised to gain para training.

When recruits of the Royal Marines have completed their basic training at the Commando Training Centre at Lympstone in Devon, they are offered a wide choice of skills in which to gain qualifications

THE TRADITION of self-sufficiency that has evolved during the 300-year history of the Royal Marines owes much to the Corps' original function, that of providing complements of fighting men to sail aboard British warships. Nowadays, the Royal

Advanced training in the Royal Marines encompasses an enormous range of skills. Mountain leaders must learn to command teams in ice-climbing (left) and rock-scaling (below). Marines may qualify as helicopter pilots (below right), signallers (top right) or vehicle mechanics (bottom, far right). For many marines training specifically for combat roles, an additional qualification (adqual) in parachuting (inset bottom right) must be gained before they fully qualify in their chosen field.

BEYOND LYMPSTONE

Marines are no longer divided into numerous isolated ship-board units, or at least nowhere near the extent they were in the last century and beyond, yet the esprit de corps and principle of self-sufficiency are still vigorously maintained. Though now developed into a modern 'go anywhere, do anything' force, the Corps still demands that every member is fully integrated and that standards are continually improved.

True, there is a role within 3 Commando Brigade for attached British Army or Navy personnel fulfilling certain highly specialised functions, but all these personnel must undergo commando training. While there is no shortage of volunteers from the Royal Artillery and the Royal Engineers for these duties, there is an understandable reluctance on the part of other army corps personnel to serve with 3 Commando Brigade. After all, if a clerk from the Royal Army Ordnance Corps had been that interested in serving with the Royal Marines, he probably would have joined them in the first place. Nevertheless, the Royal Marines are expected to provide such specialised personnel as mountain leaders, landing craft coxswains and swimmer canoeists, and with so many unique job functions, the practice is to raise the specialised personnel as much as possible from within the Corps.

When a Royal Marine has finished his basic training at Lympstone and has earned his green beret and commando flash, he is encouraged to progress in his career by gaining one or several of the Royal Marines' specialist qualifications (SQs) or technical qualifications (TQs). Altogether there are 28 SQs and TQs. There is not enough space to describe them all in detail, and indeed many are self-explanatory. It is probably better, therefore, to cover just three SQs, the three that will, hopefully, best illustrate the unique nature of the Royal Marines and their present role. The SQs chosen are drill leader, swimmer canoeist (Special Boat Squadron (SBS)), and assault engineer. Undoubtedly there will be one or two

complaints about this, probably from Royal Marines with other SQs or TQs. Just put it down to yet another example of a pongo not understanding the pussers' Corps!

One officer of the Royal Marines remembers:

'The first Royal Marine I met when I arrived at Lympstone was our drill leader – a sergeant who seemed to be about seven feet tall, was immaculately dressed in lovat green, scared the hell out of me and altogether was one of the most impressive men I've ever met. By the time we passed out, there wasn't a single young officer who wouldn't have cheerfully followed that man anywhere. Looking back on it, he taught us more about self-discipline than we realised at the time.'

For most soldiers, military life begins and ends with drill, with ceremony and parades. Often reviled by those obliged to take part, always a source of embarrassing moments, drill is thought by many to have less and less value in modern warfare. As far as drill for drill's sake goes, the Royal Marines would not disagree. But then, their drill leaders are far more than loud, well-creased voices that squawk, scream and squeak their way into a soldier's memories.

To begin with, since both young officers and recruits train at Lympstone, often alongside each other, the 'family' atmosphere that pervades the Corps begins to develop very early on. It is one of the functions of the drill leader to foster this family feeling. Drill leaders in the Royal Marines see themselves very much as being the guardians of Corps history, standards and traditions, and they are determined that no-one will let the traditions down.

Secondly, they firmly believe in the role of drill. One instructor has stated:

'Drill is the cold face of discipline. In the Corps we pride ourselves on self-discipline, but before a man can learn self-discipline we must impose discipline. Not in an attempt to break his spirit, but in order to instil into him those standards that he will have to apply to his own conduct in future.'

These standards include not only being able to obey an order instantly but also willingness to maintain a high standard of dress and cleanliness, and readiness to perform to the top of personal ability under the worst possible circumstances.

Drill leaders are very much born, not made. A large part of their job entails 'mothering' new recruits (and potential officers) through the first confusing months of training. A drill leader is someone with a natural parental instinct – and someone who is able to command by force of personality and personal example alone. Drill leaders do not shout and scream on parade – well, not very often, and certainly not as often as many of their army colleagues.

When he has passed the command course that makes him a corporal, the Royal Marine may, if he wishes, apply for the Drill Leader Two (DL2) course.

Below: Parade-ground discipline lies at the heart of Royal Marines training. The drill leader (far right) must himself be exemplary if traditional standards are to be maintained.

Long before that, he will have to have shown an interest in and a knowledge of Corps history and tradition, a high competence on the parade-ground, and high standards of dress and deportment.

If he is accepted, the DL 2 course will last six weeks. Should he pass, he is judged competent to instruct at recruit level, and he may be posted at this point to Lympstone. It is equally likely that he will return to a fighting company (for whatever SQ or TQ a man may obtain, he remains first and foremost a fighting marine). He is then expected to start continuation training, and a minimum of one day a week is spent in brushing up his knowledge and adding to it, always maintaining the high standards he has set himself. If he does well, he will go on to become a Drill Leader One after he has passed his command

As Royal Marines gain advanced qualifications they are issued with cuff badges. Those who achieve Class I qualifications are entitled to instruct in their speciality. The Class I badges shown (from left to right) denote Signals, Platoon Weapons/Drill Leader, Physical Training, Assault Engineer, Heavy Weapons, Swimmer Canoeist and Landing Craft. They are worn with No.2 lovat uniform.

As the amphibious specialists of the British armed forces, the Royal Marines have a wide range of water craft at their disposal. Canoes (above) are used by the SBS for covert reconnaissance, while rigid raiding craft (below) and Gemini inflatable assault craft (right) carry small raiding parties. Larger operations are mounted from landing craft (below right).

course for sergeant.

From the moment that he passes his DL 2 course, the drill leader becomes the authority on drill and ceremonial wherever he is posted to in the Corps. And all the time he is being watched, not so much by his commanding officer as by other drill leaders, to make sure that he does not let the DL branch down. As upholder of traditions and standards, the DL branch is probably one of the most fiercely self-critical branches of the Royal Marines. It has to be. There is no-one to watch over the drill leaders, to make sure that they have got the ceremonial right, or that they are handling a particular, awkward recruit in the way calculated to bring the best out in him.

Ultimately, does this have any bearing on the job that the Royal Marines have to do? At the retreat from the Chosin reservoir, during the Korean War, when No. 41 (Independent) Commando escorted United States Marine Corps units to safety, the USMC was frankly astounded at the way the Royal Marines marched, paraded, and generally deported themselves. A rout was turned into a disciplined retreat, and far fewer casualties were sustained as a result. Again, the long march or 'yomp' that the Royal Marines successfully completed in the Falklands would not have been possible without the rigorous discipline that had been instilled on the parade-ground in the early stages of the marines' careers.

The specialist qualification of swimmer canoeist in the SBS calls for different personal qualities. Imagine yourself in the thick of preliminary training. You have been without sleep now for the best part of seven days. During that time you have run faster and further than you ever thought possible, usually carrying a particularly awkward and heavy pack. You have been without food for long periods, and when it did eventually arrive it was mostly inedible. Which was just as well, because you were not given that much time to eat before being sent out on yet another gruelling task. When you were allowed to get your head down, you were invariably woken up after an hour or so and sent out on a 30-mile forced march. The last time this happened, you were promised a square meal at the end of it. The square meal turned out to be an Oxo cube.

And now you are sitting in a classroom, with the heat turned up abnormally high, with very little ventilation, watching an incredibly boring film about men loading petrol drums onto a lorry. The drums are different colours, yet are being loaded in a totally haphazard manner. Some of the drums are taken off again. The film lasts for over an hour. At the end of that time, you will be woken up (because you are bound to have fallen asleep at your desk) and given a written test on how many drums of what colour were loaded onto the lorry and in what sequence. You had better be able to get at least a few of the questions correct, otherwise you will be Returned to Unit, or 'binned'. Either way, those opening remarks made by the CO when you and a few other hopefuls first arrived have begun to make sense: 'This is called the Special Boat Squadron. But it's the men who are special, not the bloody boats!'

At some point in his career, nearly every Royal Marine toys with the idea of becoming a swimmer canoeist and joining the SBS. This usually happens when he is a recruit; as he progresses through training and learns a little more about the SBS, he is likely to think twice. Aside from anything else, he has to be an excellent swimmer, with a natural affinity for the water. That, plus the fact that it is very hard for a recruit to discover what it is that the SBS actually

does, often means that he develops other career goals. In any event, there is no way that he would be considered for the SBS before he had completed his first tour of duty with a fighting company. By that time, he will have discovered that whatever the SBS does, it is very special and unless he is absolutely positive that he has what it takes – whatever that is – he should not waste either his or the branch's time.

Unlike the Special Air Service (SAS), the SBS remains almost totally shrouded in mystery. In recruiting pamphlets it is described as being the branch that specialises in clandestine operations. In practice this translates into the SBS belief that if anyone – enemy, potential enemy or neutral observer – is aware that the unit is operating in the vicinity, then the SBS has failed. The SBS does not like to advertise its presence. This is due, not so much to a natural and becoming modesty, but to the fact that one of the squadron's most important roles is reconnaissance, particularly in preparation for beach landings. An enemy who learnt that an SBS team was mapping a potential landing zone could make the assumption, which would probably be correct, that a commando force would shortly arrive there. Secrecy thus becomes second nature to the SBS operative, as it has become to the SBS branch as a whole.

Throughout the pre-selection course, volunteers are successively 'binned', quietly and without any fuss

The SBS is far smaller than the SAS. While official manning levels are highly classified, it can be said that there are less than 300 SBS trained Royal Marines active at any one time, while the SAS always has close to 1000 men on active regimental duty. However, the SAS role often demands an overt fighting capability, which sometimes necessitates an increase of the basic four-man patrol to platoon or company strength. Within the Royal Marines this overt function would probably be performed by a reconnaissance troop from one of the fighting companies. At the same time, the SBS is so specialised that it would be difficult to increase the strength even if it were considered necessary. Again, while in the SAS the volunteer is able to choose between several jobs, according to his character and ability, the SBS offers only one job. If he cannot do that one, he fails the course.

It is generally accepted that the SBS pre-selection course is physically more rigorous than that of the SAS. It lasts for two weeks and is designed to strip all illusion from the would-be candidate. It is during this phase that the man goes without sleep for long periods of time and is placed under the most extreme mental and physical pressure. In this way, the training staff can discover which men really have an aptitude for the work. Throughout the pre-selection course, volunteers are successively 'binned', quietly and without any fuss. One candidate described the process:

'Usually, the first time you realise that someone's been binned is when you notice that his locker's empty. The training staff are very good at picking them up during a forced march or whatever, when no-one else is looking. Or just having a quiet word, so there's no drama about it. All the same, it does have an effect on you when you see more and more empty lockers, and begin to wonder how soon it will be before someone discreetly taps you on the shoulder and tells you that you've failed. Twenty-five of us started out in my pre-selection course. There were six of us left at the end of it.' And of those six, at least two are likely to fail at some time during the year-long branch training that takes place after those first two weeks. A year in which they will learn to swim, dive, canoe, parachute, water parachute (to a rendezvous with a submerged submarine), and blow up a variety of buildings from a bridge to a railway station. They use a selection of cameras barely heard about by the average professional photographer, let alone seen by him. They become expert in morse and cryptography. They learn to live off the land, in Europe, in the jungles of the Far East and in the deserts of the Middle East – indeed, one of the continuing arguments between the SAS and the SBS is about the best way to prepare and eat worms.

Obviously, all this equips a man to do quite a lot more than simply recce a beach landing site. Probably the best way of describing the role of the SBS is to say that it is responsible for all those covert operations that precede the successful completion of any operation with which a larger Royal Marines formation has been tasked. However, the Permanent Cadre of the Mountain and Arctic Warfare (M&AW) branch does have its own responsibility in the role of long-range covert reconnaissance. In fact, some SBS personnel have been heard to complain that since the M&AW Cadre has gained its increased recognition there are fewer volunteers of a sufficiently high standard coming forward to the SBS.

The equipment of the AEs is mostly man-portable to enable them to work closely with the fighting companies

While both drill leaders and SBS operatives have their army equivalents, there is one SQ branch that is totally unique – the assault engineers (AEs). Although there is a permanent unit of commando-trained Royal Engineers, 59 Squadron, RE, attached to 3 Commando Brigade, the Royal Marines have found it necessary to maintain their own integrated engineer capability. Whereas 59 Squadron operates with heavy plant equipment, the equipment of the AEs is mostly man-portable to enable them to work closely with the fighting companies, providing immediate technical expertise and experience when the companies are in combat.

The Assault Engineer branch, unlike the SBS but similar to the Drill Leader branch, is staffed exclusively by NCOs. There is a practical reason for this. Although AEs do take various courses, the vast bulk of their training has to be in the field, taking the form of continual day-in, day-out learning over a period of many years. An officer, in contrast, simply does not have enough time to learn how to become an assault engineer if he is going to develop his own officer skills.

The type of man sought by the Royal Marines as a potential AE has a practical bent and enjoys getting his hands dirty. The AEs' warrant officer commanding has said:

'Ideally, we'd like a marine who had spent time in one of the building or allied trades before joining the Corps – a carpenter, electrician or simply a builder's labourer. Again, the man must have a basic aptitude for the job, must be inherently practical. If he is that, plus being a good marine, over the years we'll teach him all he needs to know.'

There are three grades within the Assault Engineer branch – AE One, Two and Three. A Royal Marine can take his AE Three course as soon as he has finished commando training. It lasts for six weeks, as does the AE Two course which he would take in order to be promoted to corporal. The AE One course, for promotion to sergeant, lasts 10 weeks and concentrates as much on academic aspects as it does on practical training.

As an assault engineer, a man is expected to know about a wide variety of subjects, from establishing and maintaining a clean, fresh water supply to sowing or clearing a minefield; from building or blowing up a bridge, to overseeing the digging of trenches strong enough to withstand an artillery bombardment with shells landing every five square metres; from setting booby traps to teaching others how to avoid and even disarm them. Furthermore, every AE is a trained coxswain, since the Assault Engineer branch is also responsible for the river crossings.

There are only between 50 and 60 assault engineers at any one time within 3 Commando Brigade, and these are distributed throughout the fighting companies, where they will be tasked by the Commando CO, company OC and the recce commander. They are regarded as the experts and it is assumed that they can turn their hands to anything. During the Falklands War, one AE colour sergeant found himself helping his colleagues in the Royal Engineers to defuse unexploded Argentinian shells. He had not been trained for it, but there were more than enough shells to go round and it was fairly important that they should be made safe as quickly as possible. So, after a brief on-the-job training lesson, he started work and won the BEM as a result. The other Royal Marines were naturally pleased that he had been decorated, but no-one was really surprised that he had managed to avoid blowing himself up. After all, as an AE One he was an expert – and could naturally turn his hand to anything.

The Royal Marines have an attitude towards those of their number who are SQ or TQ qualified that may be expressed as, 'Well, you're the expert, you're the man who wanted to do the job, so get on with it.' And they do, without any fuss and with as little drama as possible. Which again is one of the reasons that Royal Marines drill leaders do not scream on the parade-ground.

THE AUTHOR Nigel Foster served in the British Army's Intelligence Corps. Following training at Lympstone, he was attached to 3 Commando Brigade.

Traditionally a fighting force that relied as little as possible on support from other units, the Royal Marines now use a wide range of weapons in the field. Men qualified to instruct in platoon weapons will take squads into the field for group training with the new SA80 rifle (bottom left). Heavy weapons personnel will specialise either in air-

defence weapons such as the
man-portable Blowpipe anti-
aircraft missile system
(bottom right), or mortars
(below). Anti-tank armament
offers a third category in
which heavy weapons men
may qualify.

BOOBY TRAP

Within the Royal Marines,
the assault engineers are
trained to carry out a
bewildering variety of tasks.
In the sequence of
photographs (left) an AE is
preparing a special form of
booby trap designed to be
set up by feel alone in
complete darkness. It
incorporates an F1A1 firing
device which can be set to
detonate plastic explosive
either by an increase or
decrease of pressure, or by
a pull or tension release
when attached to a trip-
wire. Here, it is being set up
for detonation by a pull on a
trip-wire.
Top: The firing device is
secured firmly to a tree. In
order to demonstrate how
the trap works, the coupling
base on the firing device is
shown pointing upward.
Normally it would be
secured the other way
round to make it as easy as
possible to conceal the fuze.
Then the trip-wire is
attached and a pivot pin is
removed (above centre) to
allow free movement of the
firing mechanism. The fuze
is then screwed into the
coupling base (centre). A
dummy charge is then
shown being connected to
the fuze (below centre) –
normally the fuze would
be of a much greater
length. Finally (bottom)
the safety pin is pulled
out. The charge may
now be detonated by
a pull on the trip-
wire.

BOOBY TRAP

In December 1942, a small detachment of Royal Marines launched a daring canoe-borne raid up the Gironde and Garonne rivers to attack shipping in the port of Bordeaux

THE SUBMARINE HMS *Tuna* lay silent on the glassy swell. 'Beastly clear night,' said her commander as the last of the canoes came through the forward hatch. Gently, each canoe was hoisted out, its two-man crew already inside it. A German patrol boat prowled nearby, but such was its position that it could not see the submarine. It was then that the first disaster of the night struck. As the canoe *Cachalot* came through the hatch, its canvas split right along one side. The two disappointed crewmen had no choice but to remain behind as the other five boats began to pull away. At 2022 hours *Tuna's* commander gave the order to dive and the submarine submerged as silently as she had surfaced.

So began, on the evening of 7 December 1942, one of the most daring and audacious commando raids of World War II. Given the codename Operation Frankton, the group's mission was to paddle up the Gironde and Garonne rivers to the inland port of Bordeaux. Situated on the Atlantic seaboard of Occupied France, Bordeaux had become the main haven for merchant ships running the Allied blockade from the Far East, and each cargo that was brought in, of such vital goods as tin, tungsten and fuel oil, served to strengthen the Axis war effort. It was the intention of the small sabotage group to cripple as many as possible of the blockade-runners in Bordeaux.

The planning of the raid had commenced in July 1942 and it coincided with the formation of the Royal Marine Boom Patrol Detachment, comprising 34 men of all ranks under Major H.G. 'Blondie' Hasler. On 30 October, No. 1 Section, consisting of 12 marines and six canoes, travelled to Scotland for training exercises. On the morning of 30 November, Hasler and his section embarked in *Tuna*, commanded by Lieutenant-Commander R.P. Raikes, DSO, RN. Only when the hatches were secured did Hasler reveal to his men that they were about to carry out a real operation. At this point he offered each one the chance to withdraw, but not one man stood down.

The force was to be organised into two divisions,

COCKLESHELL HEROES

Left: Members of the Royal Marine Boom Patrol Detachment (RMBPD) during training. Seven of the nine men (far side – Sheard, Sparks, Ewart and Laver, near side – Wallace on left and Conway on right, and coxswain Mackinnon) were selected for Operation Frankton, led by Major H.G. Hasler (inset bottom). Training included insertion by canoe (below), launching from dry land (below right) and the operation of electrically-driven submersible canoes (bottom).

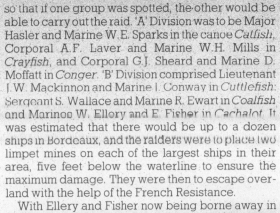

so that if one group was spotted, the other would be able to carry out the raid. 'A' Division was to be Major Hasler and Marine W.E. Sparks in the canoe *Catfish*, Corporal A.F. Laver and Marine W.H. Mills in *Crayfish*, and Corporal G.J. Sheard and Marine D. Moffatt in *Conger*. 'B' Division comprised Lieutenant J.W. Mackinnon and Marine I. Conway in *Cuttlefish*; Sergeant S. Wallace and Marine R. Ewart in *Coalfish* and Marines W. Ellery and E. Fisher in *Cachalot*. It was estimated that there would be up to a dozen ships in Bordeaux, and the raiders were to place two limpet mines on each of the largest ships in their area, five feet below the waterline to ensure the maximum damage. They were then to escape overland with the help of the French Resistance.

With Ellery and Fisher now being borne away in *Tuna* with their damaged canoe, the five remaining boats rode easily on the light swell. It was extremely cold, but the paddling soon warmed the 10 marines. After some three hours, Hasler and Sparks in the leading canoe heard the unmistakable sound of a tide-race (rough water caused by opposing tides) ahead. Through this unexpected hazard four canoes came safely, but as they waited in the calmer waters beyond, *Coalfish*, with Sergeant Wallace and Marine Ewart, failed to appear. In accordance with their orders, the others pressed on, the current now running strongly against them. The outline of the

OPERATION FRANKTON

Though long considered a prime target by the Allied planners, the ships and dockyard facilities at Bordeaux were virtually invulnerable to conventional attack. A large concentration of French civilians in the area made bombing impossible, and heavy defences along the 60-mile Gironde river ruled out a large-scale amphibious assault. However, in July 1942, Combined Operations began to consider a small commando raid, using a canoe force inserted by submarine. The idea was codenamed Operation Frankton.

The Royal Marine Boom Patrol Detachment, an offshoot of Captain T.A. Hussey's Combined Operations Development Centre at Portsmouth, seemed the ideal unit for the raid. Formed on 6 July 1942, it trained hard in swimming, endurance, deployment from submarines, and physical fitness. On 21 September its commander, Major H.G. 'Blondie' Hasler, was summoned to Combined Operations HQ in London to study the problems involved in the operation. Hasler was fired with enthusiasm and immediately proposed to lead the raid himself: the time was fixed for early December.

Since the mouth of the Gironde was monitored by German radar and patrol boats, the submarine insertion had to be smooth and brief. Accordingly, a boom was fixed to the submarine's gun, enabling each laden canoe and its two-man crew to be swung out and lowered into the water. In the event, although the entire process took only 31 minutes, the German radar station was able to pinpoint the vessel and alert the gun-crews along the Gironde.

lighthouse at the Pointe de Grave was seen and they welcomed it as an identifiable landmark. But at this very moment they heard with anxiety a second tide-race ahead. They braced themselves, but it was worse than before. The waves, five feet high, threw them about like matches. A sudden cry heralded more trouble: *Conger* had capsized, throwing Corporal Sheard and Marine Moffatt into the icy waters. Hasler made the difficult but brave decision to scuttle her, and the two unlucky marines, clinging to the sterns of other canoes, were towed as near inshore as possible in order to give them a chance to get ashore and make good their escape.

By 0300 hours on 8 December the main party had rounded the headland opposite Pointe de Grave, under the very eyes of the enemy in the village of Le Verdon, and were in the quieter waters of the Gironde. Although Hasler had hoped to lie up for the first day on the east bank, this was found to be impracticable. Traversing the end of a jetty in single file, they waited once again for the others to follow, but *Cuttlefish*, with Mackinnon and Conway, did not appear. At 0630, just as the four remaining marines pulled their canoes ashore, the first glimmer of daylight was appearing. Shaken and tired, the exasperated men camouflaged themselves and tried to settle down to eat and sleep.

The rest of that December day was extremely cold, and the marines spent a cheerless time waiting for nightfall. When it came, Hasler set off at a furious pace that warmed the marines' frozen limbs and gave them a renewed sense of urgency. It has to be very cold to freeze sea water, but that night the spray breaking over them froze on the covers. Most of them took a benzedrine tablet to keep awake. As the dawn of 9 December approached, Hasler, whose night vision was exceptionally keen, found a particularly good hiding place. Although they were not far from a French farmhouse, they brewed up some tea before settling down to yet another fitful sleep.

The plan for the following night, 9/10 December, was complicated by the fact that the crews would have only three hours of flood tide, then six hours whilst it ebbed, to give them a further three hours paddling before dawn. After the first three hours, Hasler decided to lie up on an outcrop known to them as 'Desert Island', which was covered with thick reeds and had very muddy banks. At 2145, therefore, they secured their canoes for a few hours' rest, aiming to set off again at 0300. Their route lay

between some islands where the passage was very narrow. They allowed themselves only single paddles, and kept their profile as low as possible in the water, gliding on the swift stream to their resting place at the southern end of the Ile de Cazeau. They had made only 15 miles that night, compared to over 20 on each of the previous nights. It left Hasler with a problem. He had hoped to carry out the attack on the next night, 10/11 December, but they had only just entered the Garonne river and his targets lay some 10 miles ahead at Bordeaux. Although they might reach them, they would have little chance of withdrawing on the ebb tide after laying their charges.

As they launched their canoes down the steep and slippery banks at 0300, they were unaware that Mackinnon and Conway had also spent that night on another part of the same island. Setting off, *Catfish* and *Crayfish* kept to the centre of the stream for the first two miles, then moved to the reed-lined western bank. As they rounded a bend in the Garonne, they suddenly saw two ships and a small jetty. Here at last were the first of the targets they had been seeking. Their hearts beat faster and they even began to sweat, despite the icy conditions. Just beyond the jetty they found an ideal lying-up place in a small stream hidden by high reeds. There for the rest of the night and the whole of the next day they remained almost motionless in their canoes. During 10 December Hasler made his plans. He calculated that they had to reach the target area about an hour before high water, so they could drift through the docks on the last of the flood tide, then turn on the ebb and lay their mines as they moved silently downstream.

After about 90 minutes they rounded a bend and saw their prey, securely stretched out before them

As darkness fell, the two canoes were stowed, excess equipment was ditched, and the marines gingerly fuzed their limpet mines. . . for real this time. So many times in rehearsal they had dreamt of this moment, and as they looked at their small, coloured-glass time capsules, Hasler murmured that they would use the orange ones, giving a nominal nine hours' delay. In this bitterly cold weather they would probably run much longer.

Right: The development of the Cockle MK II that was used on Operation Frankton was preceded by experimentation with many different types of canoe. Above right: Marines carefully pass a canoe down the forward torpedo hatch of a submarine.

Far right: 'Feathered' paddles (the blades were set at right angles to each other) were employed to minimise wind resistance and reduce the silhouette of the canoe team.

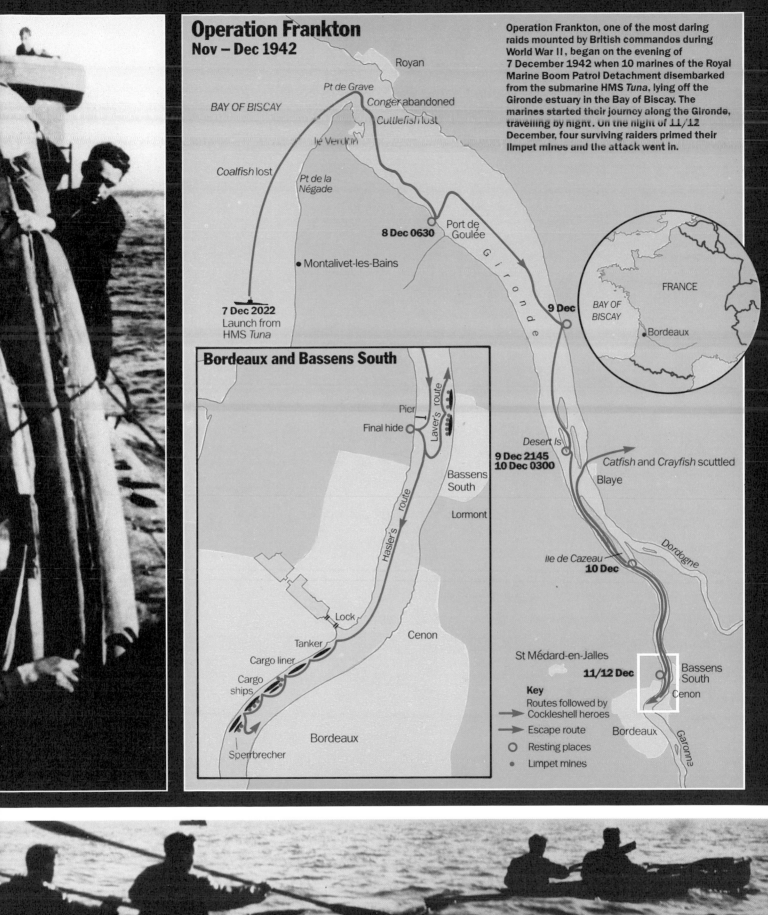

Operation Frankton
Nov – Dec 1942

Operation Frankton, one of the most daring raids mounted by British commandos during World War II, began on the evening of 7 December 1942 when 10 marines of the Royal Marine Boom Patrol Detachment disembarked from the submarine HMS *Tuna*, lying off the Gironde estuary in the Bay of Biscay. The marines started their journey along the Gironde, travelling by night. On the night of 11/12 December, four surviving raiders primed their limpet mines and the attack went in.

Royan

BAY OF BISCAY

Pt de Grave

Conger abandoned

Cuttlefish lost

Île Verdon

Coalfish lost

Pt de la Négade

8 Dec 0630

Port de Goulée

● Montalivet-les-Bains

7 Dec 2022
Launch from
HMS *Tuna*

Gironde

9 Dec

FRANCE

BAY OF BISCAY

● Bordeaux

Bordeaux and Bassens South

Pier

Laver's route

Final hide

Bassens South

Lormont

Hasler's route

Desert Is

9 Dec 2145
10 Dec 0300

Catfish and *Crayfish* scuttled

Blaye

Dordogne

Île de Cazeau

10 Dec

Lock

Tanker

Cargo liner

Cargo ships

Cenon

Bordeaux

Sperrbrecher

St Médard-en-Jalles

11/12 Dec

Bassens South

Cenon

Bordeaux

Garonne

Key
→ Routes followed by Cockleshell heroes
→ Escape route
○ Resting places
● Limpet mines

LIMPET MINES

Specifically designed to be attached to the side of a steel ship, the limpet mine consisted of a canister of high explosive mounted on a frame, to which were fitted six 'horseshoe' magnets. At one end was a fuze cavity into which was inserted a sealed glass bulb containing acid. To prime the mine, a thumbscrew was turned that broke the glass, releasing the acid onto a washer holding back a striking pin. When the washer dissolved the pin sprang forward and fired the detonator. Clamped to the other end was a sympathetic fuze, consisting of a percussion cap designed to be set off by vibration. Active only after a period underwater, this fuze ensured that, rather than allowing the limpet to be shaken off by the explosion of another mine, the charge would simultaneously explode. Though weighing only 10lb, the limpet could blow a hole three feet in diameter in a ship's side, causing an uncontrollable rush of water into the vessel. However, it needed to be placed five feet below the surface. To achieve this, one canoeist would steady the boat against the ship, using a magnetic hold-fast, while his companion used a jointed, steel placing rod with a hook at the far end to lower the mine into position. Both the hold-fast and the mine had to be applied very carefully if the team was to avoid betrayal by a loud clang as the magnets slammed against the steel.

As the hour for leaving approached, Hasler was distressed to see that the sky was clear for he knew that the young moon would not set until 2130 hours. Accordingly, he held back their start for an hour, which did nothing to relieve the tension. The delay would give them less time to drift down to the end of the line of targets. The river was flat calm as they stole out from their canopy of leaves, their limpets already fizzing away quietly. Now that they had only two canoes, the modified plan was for Laver and Mills in *Crayfish* to lay their limpets on the eastern bank at Bassens South, while Hasler and Sparks in *Catfish* dealt with ships on the Bordeaux side. They wished each other good luck and the two canoes parted.

Hasler was disconcerted to find that, unlike at British ports, there was no black-out and lights shone brightly upon the river. He therefore had to keep near the mid-stream. After about 90 minutes they rounded a bend and saw their prey, securely stretched out before them. The ships were illuminated brightly with clusters of lamps, so *Catfish* crept alongside their hulls to avoid being spotted. But time was not on their side, and they could feel the tide was already beginning to turn. They had nearly reached the end of the line of vessels, so Hasler decided to lay his first two limpets on a nearby cargo ship. Holding on to its side, he allowed Sparks to use his placing rod to lower the first charge about five feet below the waterline. This was a thrilling moment. After a short paddle they reached the top of the line and found that the last ship was a 'Sperrbrechter', a German naval frigate. Sparks placed two more mines on this, but now the tide was pulling them downstream.

Hasler had seen a particularly tempting prize further down, and as they drifted towards it he could hear the rumble of her engines and knew exactly where he should place his charges. As the two men were intent on their purpose, a torchlight suddenly shone on them from above. They froze, waiting for the inevitable bullet that would follow from the sentry they could see outlined above. However, the sentry seemed satisfied that all he had seen was a log floating past.

They laid their remaining limpets on a tanker and cargo ship lying alongside each other. They were aware that tankers had watertight compartments and that their mines would cause limited damage,

but time was passing quickly and they had to escape as far as possible before the time fuzes ran out. At that moment, Hasler said later, he felt like Atlas holding up the world. He turned with a grin and shook Sparks firmly by the hand. On the far bank, Corporal Laver and Marine Mills were in great spirits as they laid their eight limpets on two large merchant ships.

Both crews paddled as fast as they could with the tide and it was about 45 minutes later, during a pause in their efforts, that Hasler heard the unmistakable sounds of his fellow raiders. They closed together, shook hands all round and Hasler did a quick debrief of Laver and Mills. They would now paddle on and drift past the village of Blaye on the east bank and then go their separate ways. It was a little past 0600 hours on 11 December when Hasler gave the final order to 'raft up' and the two canoes came together. 'Well, Corporal,' said Hasler, 'This is where we have to part. Go straight ashore here and carry out your escape instructions.' 'Very good, sir,' retorted Laver, adding, 'Best of luck to you.'

Five ships were severely damaged by the limpets they had laid, two of which subsequently sank

As the men began their long overland journey, they were too far away to hear the explosions that resounded around Bordeaux. Five ships were severely damaged by the limpets they had laid, two of which subsequently sank. But euphoria at their success would have been tempered had they known the fate of the others in the party. Within hours of them laying their charges, two of their number, Sergeant Wallace and Marine Ewart, who had been captured on 8 December after capsizing near the Pointe de Grave lighthouse, were being executed in Bordeaux, despite their wearing Royal Marine shoulder flashes and badges of rank. The fate of the others in the party was not known until after the war.

Marine Moffatt's body was washed ashore on 7 December, but of Corporal Sheard nothing was ever

heard. Lieutenant Mackinnon and Marine Conway, although separated from the force while they were off Le Verdon, carried on with their mission for three lonely days. After laying up on the Ile de Cazeau on 10 December, they hit a submerged obstruction and *Cuttlefish* was wrecked. A few days before Christmas, having made contact with the French, they caught a train south, but on reaching Le Reole they were betrayed, and seized by the Germans. Corporal Laver and Marine Mills, who had scuttled *Crayfish* just north of Blaye, managed to make good progress for two days, but they were unable to find any civilian clothes, were picked up by the French police and subsequently handed over to the German Security Police in Bordeaux. For several weeks the four Royal Marines were tortured and interrogated, some of their inquisition taking place in Paris. But then, probably on 23 March 1943, in accordance with Hitler's orders concerning commandos, the four were taken out at dead of night and shot. Not one betrayed his comrades or his mission.

Major Hasler and Marine Sparks, maybe because of the officer's knowledge of French, perhaps because luck was on their side, soon found plain clothes, shelter, and finally the French Resistance. In mid-January they made contact with the legendary 'Marie-Claire', an Englishwoman who had lived most of her life in France, who bravely put them on the freedom trail through Vichy France, across the Pyrenees and into Spain. They reached Gibraltar on 1 April 1943 after 1400 miles of adventures. Subsequently, Major 'Blondie' Hasler was awarded the DSO, and Marine Bill Sparks the DSM. Corporal A.F. Laver and Marine W.H. Mills were Mentioned in Despatches, which, other than the VC, was the only award possible at that time for those killed in action.

THE AUTHOR Captain Derek Oakley, MBE, served with the Royal Marines Commandos in Malaya, Hong Kong, the Middle East, Northern Ireland, Brunei and Borneo. He is now the editor of *The Globe and Laurel*, the journal of the Royal Marines.

Far left: A RMBPD team practises naval sabotage with limpet mines. Note the canoeist's 'feathered' double paddle and the 'half' paddle on the side of the canoe. Top and above left: Lying on a camouflage net are some of the items used by the raiders at Bordeaux: a magnetic hold-fast, a Fairburn Sykes commando knife, a silenced pistol, camouflage cream, self-heating soup, and a 'bird-call' whistle (which gave the cry of a seagull) for communication between boats. Left: Major Hasler and Marine Sparks at the unveiling of the Operation Frankton memorial at Poole in Dorset on 11 December 1983. When Marine Sparks was awarded the DSM in 1943 he received the letter of congratulation from Lord Louis Mountbatten shown alongside.

SURVIVAL

Food, water and warmth: these three essentials constitute the basic elements for survival in the field. If you should find yourself isolated from your unit and short of supplies, therefore, here are some basic rules to follow.

In many areas, the most readily accessible source of food is meat. The secret of successful hunting is to see your quarry before it sees you. Early morning and dusk are the best times to concentrate your efforts. Tracks, trails, trampled undergrowth and droppings are good indications that animals pass that way and, having chosen your killing ground, apply the military principles of movement and concealment.

Stand downwind from your quarry so that it does not detect your scent, and freeze if it should look your way. Take careful aim – chest, head or neck shots are best in the case of large animals – then whistle sharply to encourage the quarry to stop. Bleed the animal immediately by cutting its throat and hanging it downwards, but wait for the body temperature to cool before you clean the skin and carcass – fleas and parasites will leave their host soon after death.

For capturing smaller animals, the most basic snare is one that is set at a perpendicular to a hole or trail and attached to a heavy branch or stone. As the quarry moves into the snare opening, the slip knot you have fastened secures the loop around its neck and chest. As the animal struggles to free itself, the loop will tighten. One simple variation on this technique is the baited spring snare. Fasten a slip noose to the end of a bent sapling, making sure that the opening is wide enough to fit over the animal's head, but not wide enough for its body to slip through. Finally, secure a trigger mechanism to the sapling – a slight jerk of the noose will then trap the quarry.

If there are fish in the vicinity, improvise hooks and weights from insignia, pins, bone, coins or wood, and concentrate your efforts along the banks of the water using any bait that comes to hand – worms, for example. Alternatively, try your hand at shooting the fish. Take the distortion of parallax in account, and aim slightly under the fish in water less than three feet. (However, do not fire your weapon with the barrel underwater. The water will seal the weapon, resulting in a potentially lethal backward blast.) If you spot a school of fish, explode a hand grenade in the centre of them – this method should provide food for days.

There are over 300,000 different kinds of wild plants in the world, and a large number of these – wild onion, certain parts of bracken, dandelions and blackberries, for example – are edible. Roots, tubers, shoots and stems, leaves, nuts, seeds, fruit and bark are all potential sources of food. Plants can also provide water, but never drink milky or coloured sap unless it is from a cactus or coconut. Become thoroughly acquainted with the plant life of the area in which you are operating, it could save you life. If you are in doubt over which plants to eat, however, observe the eating habits of the animals around you – this should provide an indication of which plants are safe to consume. Another useful tip – cook all plant

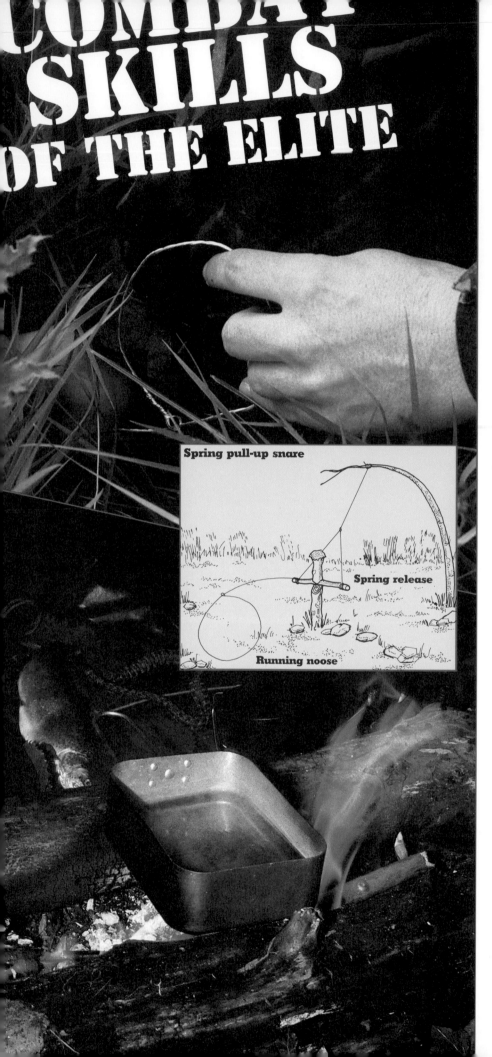

Spring pull-up snare

Spring release

Running noose

Top left: A simple snare, consisting of a free-running noose of non-ferrous wire, is set in an animal run. Bottom left: Slow-burning hardwood logs shield the kindling and focus the heat of a fire.

food that you are unsure about: most food poisons are removed by cooking.

The second prerequisite for survival is water. Assuming no physical activity, a man can last without drinking water for up to 109 days in temperatures of 50 degrees Fahrenheit, seven days at 90 degrees, and two days at 120 degrees. Beyond these limits, your body becomes incapacitated by dehydration – death would become inevitable. However, there is one crucial point to remember – your degree of thirst is not always an accurate indication of your need for water; if you are involved in strenuous activity in a cold climate, a lack of thirst may wrongly lead you to believe that you are in no danger of becoming dehydrated.

On no account should you drink water that has not been treated against disease or hostile organisms. Either boil your supply of drinking water for at least one minute, or use water treatment tablets if they are available. If you suspect dysentery, try drinking the juice of boiled bark to clear your system.

If necessity forces you to drink water from a muddy or stagnant pool, pour a small quantity into a cloth that has been filled with sand or fine gravel. Boil the residue and add charcoal from the fire to remove the pungent odour. Then leave the water to stand for 45 minutes before you drink it.

If no surface water is available, you will have to tap into the area's water table. Look at the contour of the land. If you are in mountainous terrain, try digging in dry stream beds. The presence of rocky soil should tell you that there are springs or seepages in the

If it is impossible to boil or sterilise drinking water, the safest natural source is a clear, running stream (below). The green vegetation nearby is a sign that there is no chemical pollution close to the ground surface. If possible, the stream should be examined for at least 50yds upstream from where the water is to be taken, in order to ensure that it contains no dead animals or other obvious sources of pollution. Pure drinking water can be collected in a solar still (inset). A container is placed at the centre of a pit which is covered by a plastic sheet weighted at its centre. The sun's heat raises the air temperature in the pit, causing water to condense on the underside of the sheet. Droplets of water trickle down the inside of the sheet and are collected in the container.

area. Alternatively, look for water along valley floors. Locate a relatively green area under a steep slope and dig down to a depth of approximately two feet – the water table should be close to the surface, and very little digging usually yields a good supply. Along the seashore, look in hollows between sand dunes for visible signs of water, and dig if the sand is moist. Never drink seawater, however, as its salt concentration is so high that your kidneys will eventually stop functioning.

Look for places where animals have recently scratched the soil, or where flies hover. These signs indicate recent surface water. Collect dew on heavy nights by sponging it up with a cloth – you should be able to collect about a pint an hour in a heavy dew.

The third basic element for survival is that of fire. This you will need for warmth, keeping dry, signalling, cooking and purifying your water supply. If you have no matches, all is not lost. One of the surest methods of starting a fire without matches is to use the powder from several of your cartridges. Place a small mound of powder underneath a sheltered pile of kindling and wood. Take two rocks and sprinkle a little more powder on one of them. Then grind the two rocks together immediately above the powder at the base of the pile. If you have no cartridges, try using the convex lens from a binocular or telescopic sight to focus the sun's rays.

Scavenge around for dry, dead branches for fuel, and bank the fire with green logs to ensure that it burns slowly. In an arctic environment, use blubber or other animal fat as a source of fuel.

COMBAT SKILLS OF THE ELITE

Solar still

Approx. 3 feet

Weights

Plastic sheet

Drinking tube